W9-ATH-152

When Pain Strikes

Edited by

Sandra Buckley

Michael Hardt

Brian Massumi

THEORY OUT OF BOUNDS

When Pain Strikes

Bill Burns

Cathy Busby

Kim Sawchuk, *editors*

Theory out of Bounds   *Volume 14*

University of Minnesota Press

Minneapolis • London

This work is a collaboration between the Walter Phillips Gallery of the Banff Centre for the Arts
and the University of Minnesota Press.

Published by the University of Minnesota Press
111 Third Avenue South, Suite 290
Minneapolis, MN 55401-2520
http://www.upress.umn.edu

Printed in the United States of America on acid-free paper

LIBRARY OF CONGRESS CATALOGING-IN-PUBLICATION DATA
When Pain Strikes / Bill Burns, Cathy Busby, and Kim Sawchuk, editors.
p.   cm.— (Theory out of bounds ; v. 14)
Includes bibliographical references and index.
ISBN 0-8166-2948-X (hc : alk. paper), — ISBN 0-8166-2949-8 (pbk. : alk. paper)
1. Pain—Psychological aspects. I. Burns, Bill, 1956-   .
II. Busby, Cathy, 1958-   . III. Sawchuk, Kim. IV. Series.
BF515.W45   1998
152. 1'824—dc21
98-26535

10 09 08 07 06 05 04 03 02 01 99   10 9 8 7 6 5 4 3 2 1

Contents

3. Cut It Open

4. Take a Pill

5. Intensify It

Acknowledgments

WE ARE CATCHING our breath. It seems that our lungs, brains, backs, and hearts have gone into *When Pain Strikes* for a number of years. So many wonderful people and institutions have played roles in realizing this anthology. First, we appreciate the direction and support of Sandra Buckley, Brian Massumi, and Michael Hardt, the series editors of *Theory out of Bounds*. Exceptional design work by Associés libres, in collaboration with the University of Minnesota Press, has brought coherence to this diversity of material. We appreciate their flexibility in accommodating our production schedule. Thanks to Lisa Wood, Darcelle Hall, Katarina Soukup, and Emily Moody for providing research and administrative skills. Special appreciation to Sheri Zernentsch, who managed the project day-to-day with care and élan, particularly in compiling the manuscript and managing its immense paper trail. We pooled ideas from many sources beyond what appears in *When Pain Strikes* and are grateful to those individuals who contributed time and effort, yet whose work ultimately did not fit. We acknowledge the contributors—artists and writers—for their commitment and hard work in developing pieces for the volume. We particularly wish to thank D. L. Pughe, Stephen Busby, and Bob Flanagan for their exceptional perseverance in reflecting on pain through periods of illness.

We have had generous and ongoing financial support from the Canada Council for the Arts. Without this assistance, *When Pain Strikes* would not have been possible. We are grateful to the Banff Centre for the Arts and the Walter Phillips Gallery for their belief in our pioneering approach to bringing artists, academics, and activists together in the same collection, and for their long-term support of the project; we thank Daina Augaitis, Sylvie Gilbert, Mary Anne Moser, Lorne Falk, Catherine Crowston, Jon Tupper, Lori Burwash, and Sara Diamond. Further institutional support came from Concordia University, Department of Communication Studies, and the Dean of Arts and Sciences; the Canadian Department of Foreign Affairs provided research funding for the anthology. A variety of galleries have kindly lent images, including Metro Pictures, Galerie Rochefort, Galerie Rene Blouin, Andrea Rosen Gallery, the Vancouver Art Gallery, and the German Apothecary Museum.

    Finally, we would like to thank our families and friends for their support, particularly Krys Verral, Louise Burns-Murray, Mike Burns, Norah Busby, Miriam Busby, Elizabeth Anderson, Jules Pidduck, Todd and Shirley Sawchuk, and Robert Prenovault.

Introduction

When Pain Strikes, do you . . .

__ A. Measure it
__ B. Scream and yell
__ C. Cut it open
__ D. Take a pill
__ E. Intensify it
__ F. All or some of the above
__ G. None of the above

"The joy (and pain) of getting there"
Globe and Mail
September 15, 1992

"Of politics and pain for South Koreans"
New York Times
June 14, 1996

"Slay 'em again, Sam: Blood, sweat, and coke blur the lines between pleasure and pain in new biography of director Sam Peckinpah"
Mirabella
Fall 1991

SUDDEN, DISORIENTING, jolting, alarming. *When Pain Strikes* conjures up tabloid headlines alerting the reader to yet another frightening event or disaster. It waves a red flag. Stop. Be alert. Danger is around the corner. When pain invades the sanctity of our corporeal walls, we may look to both immediate and distant occurrences to try and derive the cause, in the hope that this will lead to a remedy.

You wake up nauseated, a discomfort in your stomach. Could it be something you ate? Words that provide a feasible explanation rush toward you. A virus? Bacteria? Nerves? A joint aches relentlessly as you sit at your desk. Is it an old or recent injury? Your posture? Or is it a sign of your desire to make a career shift? You develop a headache. Is it your job, your family, or a distant memory that refuses to be identified yet leaves in its wake a physical manifestation? Is the headache caused by tension or a sinus condition exacerbated by the building you work in? Locating origins becomes increasingly difficult as you run down the list of probabilities that led to the event that is your pain.

When we ask why, we are left with a litany of conjectures and possibilities: "It may be. . . ." You fill in the blank. Identifying pain in biomedical terms seems to confirm the reality of the sensation for oneself and for others. The desire for certainty is a potent operative when the body is in pain: knowing may bring a remedy, and the remedy, relief. But naming can be comforting or discomforting, dependent as it is on the current social status of the disease, the stigmas attached to it, and the prognosis for wellness or rehabilitation.

Doctors have tried to codify the language of pain to delineate its contours, but pain is ubiquitous and resistant to our feeble attempts to circumscribe it clearly and precisely. Much of our cultural thinking on pain assumes that there is a direct relation between cause and sensation. This is a relatively recent phenomenon that gained support with Louis Pasteur and Robert Koch's discovery of bacteria. David Bakan identifies this as the doctrine of "specific etiology," "the notion that for every disease there is a specific cause."[1] While disease is not our terrain, for this would confine pain to physical hurt, this doctrine does intersect with the discourse on disease, which in turn makes its way into our contemporary painscape.

The explanations promoted in the practice of Western biomedicine are often inadequate to the experience of pain, which is multilayered, diffuse, and unnameable. Pain seems to unfold in endless layers, eluding our attempts to put it into language or images.

"Bridging the Apple-IBM
divide: Switching between
two formats doesn't have to
be a pain when you know how
to swap"
Financial Times of Canada
June 24, 1994

"Croatian war-shrine plan
revives pain"
New York Times
May 19, 1996

"Can teddy bears ease Gaza's
economic pains?"
Montreal Gazette
May 15, 1993

"Pains in the neck: Motorists
block highway to gawk at
bungee-jumpers"
Montreal Gazette
August 1, 1992

"Germans, Jews and blame:
New book, new pain"
New York Times
April 25, 1996

"TV Violence desensitizing
kids to pain, as promised 36th
Legislature opening"
Vancouver Sun
September 27, 1995

"Israel's artillery. Lebanon's
pain. Syria's victory"
New York Times
April 21, 1996

"Strangers in Pain: He—Pain
that she will never know: Blue
balls, swift kick in the groin.
She—Pain that he will never
know: Cold speculum, men-
strual cramps, childbirth,
bikini wax"
Glamour
March 1992

Elaine Scarry aptly describes the chasm in her classic *The Body in Pain: The Making and Unmaking of the World*: for the person who is in pain there is certainty, while for the person who watches, sees, or communicates with the person in pain there is uncertainty.[2] Despite the feeling that intense pain can be, as Scarry says, world destroying, it is only through the use of images, metaphors, and analogies that medicine can comprehend this sensation and capture the contours of a lived phenomenon, a phenomenon that is nonlinear and amorphous through and through: it may be burning, throbbing, intense, and subdued all at once. Open, visible injuries to the body may function as signs confirming that the sensation is real. When the pain is internal, invisible, emotional, it is often taken as unreal or less legitimate—even by the person who is experiencing it.[3]

Three Prescriptions

Pain is not without its practices, institutions, and experts. The body of work in pain studies, like the body in pain, has been the subject of intense scrutiny and vivisection. In our culture this has taken the form of three competing, but not necessarily mutually exclusive, prescriptions to manage pain: Christianity, secular humanism, and medical science. Each charts the pain corpus with precision within its own worldview. The Judeo-Christian vivisectionist demarcates the soul. The humanist vivisectionist speaks to the psychic location, imagined as "in the head." And the medical vivisectionist cuts into the somatic location.

soul

Many of our conceptions of pain, suffering, and disease—the holy trinity of pain studies—are rooted in the Bible. In Christian theology pain reminds us of our inherent evil and sinfulness. To be human and close to God is to suffer, and this suffering is born of sin. Two Old Testament stories directly relate to *When Pain Strikes*: the story of Job, who lost his children and property and was afflicted with boils; and that of Eve and the expulsion of humankind from the Garden of Eden. In the story of Job, the disintegration and decay of the flesh signify moral weakness. Contemporary images display the monstrous or diseased body to invoke pity and fear for purposes of charity, reinforcing the division between the normal and the abnormal.

Femininity is central to the second biblical tale. In this doctrine, Eve initiates suffering and pain because she took the apple from the Tree of Knowledge. Pain in childbirth reminds us of original sin and eternally punishes the "daughters of Eve." These attitudes seep into many contemporary childbirth rituals.[4] In the Christian worldview pain can never be eliminated, only minimized through the act of confession in Catholicism, or the doing of good works in Protestantism. Acts of atonement redeem the sufferer and baptism may prevent one from suffering eternally in a fiery hell, but original sin stays with humankind.

Recently, Christianity has been resurrected for more heretical purposes. The sixteenth- and seventeenth-century paintings of saints left a veritable archive of ritualistic pain—images of martyrdom, the piercing of the flesh, and the acting out of the Passion of Christ. This ecstatic experience has modern referents in the practices of tattooing and body piercing, which do not obliterate pain but elaborate it through a rich iconography. Do these practices provide new ways to feel in an alienated social environment or do they allegorically resist official emotional denial and repression? The answer to both questions is probably yes. These neoprimitivist urban rituals merge with a distinctively North American desire to return to preindustrialized worlds romanticized as the last bastion of corporeal authenticity, affect, intensity, and emotion—sensations that are

"Easing the pain: Black teacher returns to school that symbolized racial inequality in Nova Scotia"
Montreal Gazette
September 4, 1993

"As U.S. payments lag, U.N. agencies feel pain"
New York Times
March 25, 1996

"Balladur prepare la douloureuse"
Libération
April 22, 1993

"Cycle of pain: Children follow ancestors in refugee exodus from Sarajevo"
Montreal Gazette
August 13, 1992

"Is it possible to rub away the pain of arthritis?"
Montreal Gazette
November 20, 1994

"O Richler! The debate is all about pain"
Globe and Mail
April 4, 1992

"Downsizing statistics don't show the pain"
New York Times
February 27, 1996

"Putting titanium in our backbones: A Canadian surgeon has invented an artificial spinal disc to ease the pain of an aching back"
Globe and Mail
August 1, 1992

"Marijuana club helps those in pain"
New York Times
February 25, 1996

understood to be absent from an increasingly cybernetic culture where the body is losing material ground, at least rhetorically.

psyche

The Christian inheritance abounds in many manifestations of secular humanism, among them the recovery from emotional trauma. In the late 1940s Alcoholics Anonymous founded the twelve-step program, which supplies the format for much contemporary self-help literature. Gregory Bateson has charted the correspondence between secular humanism, Christianity, and cybernetic theory, while the confessional nature of these therapeutic discourses has been investigated by Michel Foucault in his first volume of *The History of Sexuality*.[5] The practices of storytelling and talk, which give voice to one's deepest, internal, repressed pain and lead to catharsis, connect this second prescription to Christianity.

Self-help literature fills the shelves of North American book vendors, offering advice on every possible pain imaginable. This is politically contentious terrain, particularly for contemporary feminism: witness the debates in the popular press over whether incest survivors are victims of false memory syndrome or actual sexual abuse.[6] A therapy backlash suggests that only whiners seek therapy or counseling and that all therapists are charlatans, prepared to implant memories of abuse in order to drum up business. Feminist critics are cognizant of the dilemma facing the survivor of childhood sexual abuse: speaking may bolster the position of psychiatric experts and institutions rather than empower the subjects who speak.[7] Focus on the individual in this form of treatment may neglect the larger social context that fuels individual pathology.

Critics also recognize the historical connection of some social services to colonialism.

"Spot of pain: Peter Van
Vossen's penalty kick beats
Chris Woods"
Daily Mail
April 29, 1993

"Winners dealing with pain in
the Australian Open"
New York Times
January 20, 1996

"Health-care tiff a pain for
Albertans"
Toronto Star
January 4, 1996

"Pain of October Crisis
lingers: Kidnapping, arrests of
25 years ago still color the
feelings of Quebec nationalists: Where are they now?"
Toronto Star
October 5, 1995

"On strike: Public servants
promise Tories as much pain
as possible"
Toronto Star
February 26, 1996

"Pain the way to glory"
Toronto Star
June 19, 1995

"PM relieves national
migraine: Five long years of
negotiations were considered
an unnecessary headache by
many Canadians"
Globe and Mail
1992

"Sharp pain of interest rate
increases will be felt throughout economy"
Montreal Gazette
April 21, 1994

Under the guise of one of the tenets of modernity—enlightenment and progress through education—this secular humanist discourse has informed assimilationist policies in Canada, such as those leading to the formation of residential schools. These practices of removing children from their communities for the sake of education have led to unimaginable upheaval and have left their scars on generations within communities of indigenous peoples.

The talking cure is never a simple matter, and therapy should not be eliminated *tout court*. It may help to dispel pain, particularly in light of considerable pain research on the connection between psyche and soma.[8] Questioning therapeutic techniques implies attending to how subjects tell stories about their pain and thus locate themselves inside these dominant cultural narratives. What narrative structures are appropriate? Confessions? Testimonials? Interviews? The multiplicity of voices used to tell these stories subverts the assumption that there is a unitary subject, with a single story to tell, who speaks a unified, coherent narrative.[9]

Likewise, therapeutic processes are not abstract or disembodied. Talk may not always come from the mouth. It may come from the body—a back, for instance, that is so big, especially for our expectations of a woman, that it seems hard to contain, a back that has the strength to turn away from its audience. Talk takes place in definite social spaces: on TV shows, in homes, in doctors' offices, and rarely alone. Narratives can be constructed communally, built from diverse tales around a shared physical experience in pain centers that accept a variety of treatments and methods. Pain is located in contradictory spaces, such as those of the family, at once a zone of conflict and brutality, the target of cultural genocide, and a place of refuge and comfort. Perhaps this is why many artists and writers in this volume invoke architectural metaphors for the

"Spreading the pain was key strategy in budget: Martin"
Montreal Gazette
March 1, 1995

"Do women cope with pain better than men?"
Montreal Gazette
August 2, 1992

"December 6 survivor recalls the pain of the Montreal Massacre"
Montreal Gazette
December 10, 1994

"Short-term pain seen in Tory cuts"
Toronto Star
April 12, 1996

"Nobel winners talk of fragility of peace: Arafat, Rabin and Peres acknowledge pain enemies have suffered"
Vancouver Sun
December 12, 1994

"No escape from pain of war in Bosnia: Wounds treated without anesthetic in besieged city"
Montreal Gazette
August 18, 1992

"At the pumps high-octane pain: rising fuel prices leave drivers looking to place the blame"
New York Times
May 3, 1996

"Mercy or Murder: Sometimes the pain is so great, death is a merciful release"
Montreal Gazette
November 24, 1994

body, speak allegorically of a "house in pain," or are concerned with how the design of space was connected to body awareness during the pop cultural movements of the 1960s.

Unfolding the layers of victim/survivor identity, survivor culture, and the recovery or self-help industry is crucial. As it is used in this book, storytelling interrogates victimology and pain in the first person, questioning the language of winners and losers, sufferers and redeemers.

soma

Although medical practice indeed offers something to those with bruised bodies, and biomedical research into pain is varied, the cultural authority of medical discourse cannot be overstated. Our understanding of this terrain is indebted to the pioneering efforts of Ronald Melzack and Patrick Wall, whose pain research and subsequent questionnaire attempted to chart a shared, common language for pain that could be used by clinicians.[10] The sensorial descriptors supplied by the questionnaire are ticked off by the patient and then mapped onto an image meant to represent the human body. This information assists the clinical diagnosis that will lead to treatment. But such a schematic rendering of the body contains significant bias. The questionnaire presents the body in empty space, devoid of an environment or social context. It is a standardized, androgenous, corporeal form that must fit everyone and hence fits no one.[11] This image recurs in different manifestations throughout this anthology.

Biomedicine works with at least two conceptions of the body that are relevant to the study and treatment of pain. They are distinct, but they are not incompatible. One part of the biomedical paradigm perceives the body as a mechanical device. Pain signals a malfunction caused by injury to a specific part that can be repaired: a prosthesis can be added or, conversely, an undesirable part can be cut out. This is the old story in which the broken body meets Doctor Fix-It. The doctor mends the body, but this repaired body returns to the same job, the same living conditions, and the same food, drugs, and television. From the second perspective, biomedicine views the body as an electrical system: pain is a neurochemical short circuit, a fuse box on the fritz. A physician prescribes a drug that stops the sensation of pain or a neurointerlocutor, like Prozac, to alter our perception. In both conceptions, surgical or chemical means knock out the pain.

Many of our authors question the efficacy of these prescriptions. A magic bullet that wipes out pain without side effects does not exist. In fact, these militaristic metaphors may hinder relief. In childbirth, for example, viewing pain as the enemy tightens up the body, which in turn exacerbates the discomfort, while the newer "routine" practices of obstetrics and gynecology often result in unnecessary, expensive, and dangerous interventions. The geopolitical terrain of industrialized medicine needs to be mined in the context of our globalized economies, shrinking job prospects, corporate mergers, and contemporary marketing strategies. Side effects on the social, political, economic, as well as physiological levels have been evident from the early days of the fight between surgeons in the United States to patent inhalation anesthesia.[12] Who profits from our pain? These technologies, aimed at the body in pain, ask us to speak on its behalf in survey after survey. What big stakes! What a healthy business it is! What a job it is presenting an ecologically safe, caring, benevolent corporate future world where drugs will surgically strike targeted areas without residual consequences!

In the words of Jean Jackson, the physical and psychological recovery industry is built on long and complicated pain careers, which, except for

"Eastern bloc humor reflects
the pain of transition to
capitalism"
Montreal Gazette
July 19, 1992

"Provinces to feel the pain as
Ottawa cuts"
Financial Post
February 26, 1994

"The pain of change:
Economic woes shorten life
expectancy of Russian men"
Montreal Gazette
February 3, 1994

"Cape Breton suffers pain of
future foreclosed"
Toronto Star
August 15, 1992

"In Cuba, music eases the
pain: A have-not society finds
its music in the streets and on
outdoor stages"
New York Times
March 31, 1996

"Three companies introduce
electronic systems that could
take the pain out of filing
expenses"
New York Times
April 17, 1996

"Pain caused by Christian
Brothers won't go away"
Toronto Star
February 13, 1994

"Peace with Syria might
require 'painful price,' Rabin
says"
Montreal Gazette
January 19, 1994

"Time pops poison pill;
Seagram gets headache"
Globe and Mail
January 23, 1994

those in graveyards, are perhaps the most striking example of the failures of Western medicine.[13] Many of the patients in chronic pain clinics are there because previous surgery has left irreparable scar tissue. Because the practices of science and medicine, and the goals of the pharmaceutical industry are interconnected, we must carefully untangle their distinct histories. Existing biomedical remedies cannot be dismissed; when one has an infection, a pill may take care of it. But that same pill may also cause a host of other problems that often are not discussed or explained to the patient before he or she leaves the doctor's office. Doctors may not even be cognizant of potentially harmful side effects, even though the same companies that market the pills may be conducting clinical trials on that drug.

Such examples highlight acknowledged paradoxes in the medical domain. While medicine in the institutionalized doctor-patient relationship must offer certainty in order to be prescriptive, scientific research in the field of pain acknowledges uncertainty. Pain can be a trickster: the place where the pain is felt may not be the place where the trauma is located. Psychoanalytic discourse knows this as displacement, while doctors call the somatic variation of this "referred pain."[14] Phenomena like a phantom limb are not well understood. These phenomena, in fact, query the idea of interior spatial limits to the body and bodily sensation. Supermicroscopes, microcameras, CAT scans, X rays, and ultrasound all unveil the inner space of the body; medicine instigates a confession of the flesh.[15] But do present methods of describing and picturing allow us to grasp the accumulation of maladies suffered in and on the body? As Katherine Foley, director of pain services at Memorial Hospital, New York, states, "We have people with very bad scans who are in no discomfort, and people with clear scans who are in agony."[16] Pain remains an elusive horizon, even within the discourse of biomedicine.

"Plenty of pain, little gain for Haiti"
Globe and Mail
January 22, 1994

"Budget pain goes from bad to worse"
Toronto Star
October 19, 1994

"At trial, Kevorkian asserts 'duty as a doctor': 'My intent was to relieve pain and suffering' "
New York Times
May 4, 1996

"Northern Ireland problem complex, painful"
Globe and Mail
December 8, 1993

"Putting off the pain. Did business, labor and government act in harmony at the economic summit or was it simply procrastination?"
Montreal Gazette
March 23, 1996

"Short-term gain, long-term pain: A contrarian forecasts a brief spike in an otherwise bear market"
Financial Times of Canada
October 22, 1994

"Yeltsin platform pledges to treat 'pain' of Russians"
New York Times
June 1, 1996

"Polish voters want less pain"
Montreal Gazette
September 21, 1993

"Unsightly nail syndrome's pain gets stomped by new drug"
Financial Post
September 20, 1993

Imaging Pain

These issues foreground the social and political force of representation. Neither medicine nor science has ever been independent of visual representation or language in the diagnosis of injury and disease. As Barbara Maria Stafford explains, "The investigations conducted by eighteenth-century students of visual and medical arts were mutually interdependent."[17] Clinical discourse integrates images into its repertoire of diagnostic tools. Three interwoven images recur in medical discourse: the walled body, the scale, and the pain center. These representational systems isolate pain within the body as an experience that can be located, analyzed, and measured.

The first image places the skin as a barrier between the interiority of the subject and the exteriority of the social world. Pain figures as a force invading the fortress body, smashing against its walls like the hammer that hits the head in a classic Bufferin advertisement from the midseventies. The skin is presented as a thick black line with a definite interior and exterior, rather than a permeable border that continually opens out and into the world. Accompanying this body is our second image, the scale, which demands that we grade the intensity of the experience—from no pain to as bad as it could be.[18] The scale confines pain to the fortified body in order to reconfigure pain as a definable experience that can be quantified on a scale of one to ten. While a useful diagnostic tool, this reduction of language to numbers divorces pain from a network of social relations.[19] The third image of a pain center in the body informs most medical texts on pain and most images of headaches in popular culture. This portrait comes to us from René Descartes. Here, pain is depicted moving through the body from outside to inside, from the point of contact to an actual location in the brain that is the final reception point of sensation.

The power of these metaphors, whether in our speech acts or in our pictures, is inextricably attached to what we think of as common sense. Is it happenstance that our most abiding viral, religious, artistic, electronic, and legal metaphors refer to gates and gatekeepers, ports and harbors, thresholds and new frontiers? Blockades are deployed to keep pain at bay and to reestablish symbolically the solid black line, that generic picture, of the walled body. Pain in this schema must not only be minimized for the subject but it must also be prevented from escaping one body and moving on to another. The old body imagined with a skin, a wall, or a thick black line may have been compelling at other historical moments, but it is now economically, socially, chemically, and electronically blurred.

These dominant metaphors and images provide a fecund point of investigation for all the contributors to this collection. In *When Pain Strikes* a variety of images and writings are used as investigative tools. All of our contributors appropriate the lexicon and vocabulary of these three prescriptions, asking what difference other representations and stories would make to the understanding, diagnosis, and treatment of various kinds of pain. Is there another way of retelling, reorganizing this sequential narrative of sensation, identification, origin, and treatment that might lead to more effective responses to pain? New fictions are needed to parallel these dominant therapeutic narratives.

Ordinary Pain and Everyday Wounds

Pain meets medicine at a terminal where disappointed citizens are disembarking to rewrite and relive the stories of their lives. Simultaneously momentous, cataclysmic, banal, and quotidian, pain creeps up slowly, not because of anything immediate but through a collection of habits and encounters that leave their traces. At the same time as we are told that our bodies are socially,

"A pain in the ear"
Toronto Star
May 4, 1993

"Grappling with growing
pains in Europe"
Globe and Mail
July 28, 1992

"White House budgets for
recovery"
Guardian
April 9, 1993

"Smiling through pain: Many
people suffer needlessly from
undiagnosed jaw disorders"
Toronto Star
March 4, 1993

"Patients turn to chiropractors
for both pain and financial
relief"
New York Times
May 25, 1996

"For Joe Gibbs, greatest pain
is in leaving the Redskins"
New York Times
March 6, 1993

"For Mexicans, pain relief is
both a medical and a political
problem"
New York Times
June 19, 1996

"Air conditioning expensive
pain for auto industry"
Globe and Mail
March 2, 1993

"Treating the symptoms in
Bosnia"
Montreal Gazette
August 13, 1992

"Official sees pain in a health
policy"
New York Times
March 3, 1993

technologically, and biologically obsolete, chronic pain has become rampant within an increasingly insecure and competitive postindustrial economic environment.[20] Our bodies hurt as much as ever. Indeed, in a world that is more and more silicon based, pain may function as the ultimate sign and inevitable test of "humanness" because it is believed to be predicated on consciousness. But not just human bodies suffer. Entire nations experience pain; economies feel pressure and likewise cause pain. Airlines suffer from self-inflicted injuries. Headaches afflict corporations, and they in turn swallow poison pills. These metaphors are endlessly transportable. Our cities, our jobs, our economies, and our anomie are written on and outside our bodies. As our collection of newspaper and magazine headlines presented here indicates, a variety of pains circulate discursively in our daily lives.

Locating pain as a provisional thematic center opens a theater of wounds. It provides a locus to identify and combat a neoconservative agenda that tells us not to feel bad but to get on with life, be productive—"I haven't got time for the pain"—cajoling us to be happy. Asserting that one is in pain is not a declaration of victimhood or self-pity, or "the new narcissism,"[21] but an acknowledgment that we are not independent agents in absolute control. We inhabit pain-filled environments.

Coda

When Pain Strikes intentionally covers a wide—although not exhaustive—spectrum of intellectual and political positions on what Ronald Melzack has deemed "the puzzle of pain."[22] This project is not an attempt to definitively circumscribe or provide a coherent mapping of the discursive deployment of the term *pain*. We have not touched on areas, such as war and torture, that have been included in other accounts.[23] Similarly, while instances of cross-cultural comparison occur in many of

"Threshold of pain"
[commentary on state of
the world]
New York Times
March 3, 1993

"Guide may ease pain of
travel insurance"
Globe and Mail
February 3, 1993

"Law called bitter pill to
swallow"
Globe and Mail
January 19, 1993

"Execution of murderer eased
pain, victims' parents say"
Montreal Gazette
January 9, 1993

"Native probe looks past the
pain"
Toronto Star
January 23, 1993

"Chronic pain fells many yet
lacks clear cause"
New York Times
December 29, 1992

"Recession recovery 'slow,
painful and mean,' CMA
says"
Globe and Mail
December 23, 1992

"For Jenkins, great pain
follows the fame"
Globe and Mail
December 18, 1992

"A Molson executive predicts
'painful' competition when
U.S. beer starts flowing freely
in Canada"
Montreal Gazette
December 17, 1992

the texts, we focus on the Canadian and American contexts. Nevertheless, the intellectual and experiential bases of the contributing writers and artists traverse the boundaries of art criticism, literature, visual arts, community activism, the sciences, history, political economy, sociology, practicing midwifery, marketing, and architecture.

While all touch on some aspect of pain, the perspectives of the contributors and editors cannot be collapsed into a single thesis on pain. As TV watchers, self-described recreational drug users, caregivers or recipients of medical attention, chronic aspirin takers, or HIV-positive, we are not external to medical practice, the experience of pain, or the marketing of pain relief. Rather than challenging the dominant prescriptions from a position of absolute alterity, the contributors and editors of *When Pain Strikes* offer a model of strategic insertion, lancing the poisonous assumption that the only possible response to pain is its elimination through drugs, surgery, or therapy. *When Pain Strikes* does not propose an easy remedy for the erasure of pain—indeed, achieving a zero on the pain-measurement scale may not even be desirable. Just as we question the nature of trauma, we ask whether there is a single way to measure pain, or any guarantee that we can ever reach its threshold. Like Gregory Whitehead's vulnerologist, we believe that one must interpret our contemporary woundscape before treating the damage.

We do not want to replace the stories of commerce and medicine with those of art and culture. *When Pain Strikes* imagines sites and vectors that differ from those acknowledged by science and business. We want to see what stories can be written over the texts of pain and its relief from a location that is both inside and outside of medicine, popular culture, commerce, the leisure industry, the recovery movement and industry, and pharmacology. We have divided the

"Drugs focus on relief of pain"
Globe and Mail
November 10, 1992

"Last labor pains in 1990:
Either side can reopen con-
tract this year" [baseball]
Montreal Gazette
October 28, 1992

"Plenty of economic pain, but
very little gain"
Globe and Mail
October 17, 1992

"Public hearing, public pain
probes Thomas-Hill morality
play"
Montreal Gazette
October 13, 1992

"Pain makes depressed
teenager feel better"
[Ann Landers]
Montreal Gazette
October 6, 1992

"Gretzky paying painful price
for simply being too good"
Montreal Gazette
September 24, 1992

"Hypnosis gains credence as
influence on the body: It helps
control pain, fear and habits"
New York Times
February 24, 1996

"Struggle for redress exorcises
community's pain"
[Japanese internment]
Montreal Gazette

"Dollar's gains mean more
pain for Ontario"
Financial Times of Canada
August 31, 1992

book into five sections that suggest possible ways to respond to pain. In doing so, we have tried to move beyond the usual divisions for describing pain: emotional/physical, real/unreal, temporary/chronic. The sections do not seek to contain the essays in neat categories—there are too many overlaps between contributors for this to be successful. Instead, we invite our readers to insert themselves into the sentence as predicate and subject of pain. You may fill out our opening questionnaire and imagine other ways to complete the sentence . . .

Kim Sawchuk, Cathy Busby, Bill Burns

February 1998

Notes

1. David Bakan, *Disease, Pain and Sacrifice: Towards a Psychology of Suffering* (Boston and Chicago: Beacon Press and University of Chicago, 1968), 11.

2. Elaine Scarry, *The Body in Pain: The Making and Unmaking of the World* (New York: Oxford University Press, 1985).

3. Jean Jackson, " 'After a While No One Believes You': Real and Unreal Pain," in *Pain and Human Experience: Anthropological Perspectives on the Lived Worlds of Chronic Pain Patients in North America*, ed. M. J. Good, P. Brodwin, A. Kleinman, and B. Good (Berkeley and Los Angeles: University of California Press, 1992).

4. Emily Martin, *The Woman in the Body: A Cultural Analysis of Reproduction* (Boston: Beacon Press, 1987); Isabelle Brabant, *Une Naissance heureuse* (Montreal: Editions Saint-Martin, 1991).

5. Gregory Bateson, "Cybernetics of 'Self': A Theory of Alcoholism," in *Steps Towards an Ecology of Mind* (New York: Ballantine Books, 1972); Michel Foucault, *The History of Sexuality: Volume One, An Introduction* (New York: Pantheon Press, 1978).

6. Journalist Barbara Amiel and cultural observer Wendy Kaminer have vociferously criticized our therapeutic culture recently. See Barbara Amiel, "The Noise of Women's Turmoil," *Maclean's* (October 28, 1991): 13; Wendy Kaminer, *I'm Dysfunctional, You're Dysfunctional: The Recovery Movement and Other Self-Help Fashions* (Reading, Mass.: Addison-Wesley, 1992). For an earlier critique from the perspective of critical theory, see Philip Rieff, *The Triumph of the Therapeutic* (New York: Harper and Row, 1966).

7. Linda Alcoff and Laura Gray, "Survivor Discourse: Transgression or Recuperation?" *Signs: Journal of Women in Culture and Society*, vol. 18, no. 2 (winter 1993): 260–90.

8. Arthur Kleinman, *The Illness Narrative: Suffering, Healing and the Human Condition* (New York: Basic Books, 1988).

"The next wave: Famous guru Alvin Toffler sees decades of great danger and pain ahead due to changes in technology, The Third Wave"
Toronto Star
January 28, 1996

"How to escape the crush of high mortgage rates"
Montreal Gazette
August 17, 1992

"Trying to take the pain out of memory management"
[personal computing]
Montreal Gazette
September 5, 1992

9. Jean Jackson, "The Rashomon Approach to Chronic Pain," unpublished paper, 1991.

10. Ronald Melzack and Patrick Wall, *The Challenge of Pain* (New York: Basic Books, 1983); Ronald Melzack, *The Puzzle of Pain* (London: Penguin, 1973); Ronald Melzack, "The Tragedy of Needless Pain," *Scientific American*, vol. 262, no. 2 (February, 1990): 27–33.

11. The McGill Pain Questionnaire comes in two forms, one long and another short, to allow for a speedy diagnosis.

12. Nancy Knight, *Pain and Its Relief* (Washington, D.C.: Smithsonian Institute, 1983), 37–39; Charles C. Mann and Mark L. Plummer, *The Aspirin Wars: Money, Medicine and 100 Years of Rampant Competition* (New York: Knopf, 1991).

13. Jean Jackson, interview, Cambridge, Mass., August 20, 1992.

14. Melzack and Wall, *Challenge of Pain*, 124–27.

15. Barbara Maria Stafford explores this desire to see into the flesh in *Body Criticism: Imaging the Unseen in Enlightenment Art and Medicine* (Cambridge, Mass.: MIT Press, 1991).

16. Cited in Elisabeth Rosenthal, "Chronic Pain Fells Many Yet Lacks Clear Cause," *New York Times* (December 29, 1992): C1.

17. Stafford, *Body Criticism*, 2.

18. These scales are the historical progeny of tests that measured pain by attaching a nut grater to a blood pressure gauge. Knight, *Pain and Its Relief*, 8.

19. Kleinman, *The Illness Narrative*.

20. Rosenthal, "Chronic Pain Fells Many."

21. Christopher Lasch, *The Culture of Narcissism: American Life in the Age of Diminishing Expectations* (New York: W. W. Norton, 1978).

22. See note 10.

23. Scarry, *The Body in Pain*.

Pain

as bad as it could be

10
9
8
7
6
5
4
3
2
1
0

no pain

Measure It

Measure It

D. L. Pughe

Letter from the Far Territories

For Kathleen Doerr

THINGS ARE getting better after a summer of uncertainty. When I awoke from abdominal surgery in July, I knew the pain would be fierce, but was so relieved I wasn't facing a fatal corridor. Then it felt like a bullet had lodged in my neck, and I've been unable to move and use my left arm, apparently an allergic reaction to the anesthesia and possible spinal damage when they pulled back my head to put a tube down my throat. In between visits to various neurosurgeons and neurologists I have been in traction and physical therapy for two months with some improvement. The neurosurgeons have cheerfully suggested another operation to fix me right up, including slitting my throat and fusing my neck vertebrae. Now there's a temptation! I have resisted their eager offers to cut me open again and am trying to gain a little perspective. To date, my physical therapist has been the only person imagining hope on my horizon.

Being injured or ill embarrasses me more than anything I know. Unable to participate in things I enjoy, I feel grounded by some ugly parent of fate. What did I do wrong? Then, when I discuss the symptoms, I bore myself more profoundly than I thought possible. The words hunch over into lame sheep lying in the road. If there is an incentive to get well, it is first to rid myself of these snarling ropes of *invalid*ity and move again with music in my step.

Or to swim again in the ocean, the thing I miss now the most! It is the only way of moving that helps me feel whole.

Lately, I have been given strength by a recurring dream of swimming the Bering Strait, heading out from Alaska to the Russian shore. Pushing chunks of ice out of the way with the arm that doesn't work now, stroking masterfully with the other. Kicking up a lather of waves behind with my fins. Since I have just had to lay off over half of my twenty-one employees due to the economic plight of the museums, I've added a large inflatable raft pulled by a rope in my teeth, with all the folks on board laughing and calling to the seals.

When I reach the Russian side, perhaps a photograph to send to the neurosurgeons would be appropriate, with a short note:

"Apparently I did not need surgery after all!"

In waking life, the dream is helping me progress. I can lift a can of baked beans and was able to float in Lake Anza on Sunday. I am not able to wave gaily yet, but I am determined to overcome the odds and swim, if not the Bering Strait, at least across Lake Louise. I'll even be reasonable and try it in the summer.

Of the few interesting things I have discovered during this test, one is that neurosurgery is thought an art not a science. Neurosurgeons are pianists looking for a piano to play. I have chosen not to become their clavichord. In diagnostic sessions they also speak of my "pictures," those shadowy films of my interior, as damaged paintings they can restore. They base their success on subtle changes in dark and light zones in the "after" images, impressing colleagues with their accurate cuts. But these monochrome X rays leave no record of the pigment of pain before and after. The tangle of nerves is invisible, the clotted scars are not recorded. Both are what compel and determine your suffering, your sense of being alive, and your capacity for hope. Your biological machine may be restored to normal "looking" black and white cogs but has no relation to how you feel.

You are forced instead to find your place and define yourself in the spectrum of malady. Noting you're worse off than a colleague with a nosebleed, you are facing nothing when compared with that friend receiving drips of morphine every fifteen seconds, dying of AIDS. While offering slim consolation, it gives you back a relationship to a social world, one that has been stolen from you for too long. Shakespeare suggests "Pain pays the means of each precious thing"; "That which does not kill us makes us stronger," Nietzsche claims. We wander furtively avoiding personal suffering and then ache to dignify it when it appears as an act enlarging our soul. Instead, we find an abyss without meaning, without purpose, and most certainly without conscience.

Injury means everything in your life is given a new range of value. Pain becomes relative; in therapy you must report each week where it lies between the poles of painlessness and the most painful thing you have ever known. But you cannot remember what it was like to be without pain, nor are you inclined to recall pain of the past. Your memory thankfully sets aside only a crawl space for agony.

Unconsciously you compare your current pain to when it is worse or better than its own bad self. And you find you silently define the numbers you are asked to give:

> 1 is a tweak or pull, unpretentious and fleeting. It nearly always goes unremarked.

> A 2 twists into a pinch. You absently touch it throughout the day. You are surprised when it lies down with you at night, uninvited.

> In 3 it spreads to a pang, it provokes a lament. You shift your step and lower your head in an attempt to dodge it. You're able to sleep but find knife-wielding thugs catapulting toward you in dreams.

> At 4 you testify to an incendiary pierce or barb that scuttles off quickly after an attack. You forget it on occasion, but in an unguarded moment it causes you to swear. As you toss and turn, it wraps tighter around you.

> In 5 it becomes more persistent, adding a steady whine of ache and burn to the sorties. It wakes you once or twice in the night with a short cry, and when you can sleep, you whimper.

> A 6 extends your night with large chunks of free time to consider parts that are wringing and throbbing and others waiting in line. Daytime finds you eyeing each person warily in case they bump against you, and you scan every room for a place to fling yourself down.

At 7 you are certain the grating and grinding are loud enough to trouble the neighbors; you pace in the dark. Still able to move, you try to fool it by remembering something more horrible, by hurting something else. Then you curl into a helpless ball and it smiles inside, cradled and chewing.

In 8 the gnaw leaves you bulging and wide-eyed, relieved only by the shift from tearing to burning, stabbing to wringing, shooting to screaming. Minutes become hours, hours smear together, a single second sometimes lasts a day. You have no clue how often your face is wet with tears.

At 9 you're knocked down, pinned flat, unable to wriggle, assaulted from all sides. You beg for mercy and are kicked in the teeth. Every remaining muscle, nerve, voice, organ turns against you, and your rage of betrayal tries to suffocate you in its own bitter foam.

In 10, with nothing left to muster, you pray for someone to shoot you. Defenseless, in a purgatory of time, your last hope: if it wins, it will leave you alone. You play dead, but it sees through you. A dark menacing laughter intent on entirely robbing you of your soul chatters louder and louder in your bones. Unrecognizable screams force their way out of your throat and begin to circle in the air above you.

Then someone shines a light into your pitch-black corner. A beautiful woman with sparkling eyes and a warm smile leads your smoldering battlefield of pain toward a cool calm pool. She explains things along the way. Instead of swinging information over your head like a guillotine as the surgeons do, she makes it palpable and presses it into your hands. You're astonished to find someone addressing you as a breathing person capable of change. She slowly raises you from the hierarchical pit of pain into a new scale, one of strength. She tells you what can be done. At each turn she gives you the power to continue on without her. When the surgeons score every improvement against you and insist only *they* can fix what's wrong, she restores your dignity. When you return to her all humped over and desperate, she helps you face the depths of nothingness and begin again:

At zero level of strength you find that someone, in a cruel joke, has substituted another person's limb for your own. You look at the numb foreign thing dangling there and, out of politeness, refrain from commenting on its appearance. Who knows whose it could be . . . You wonder when yours will make a prodigal return.

You reach 1 only as you are being lifted and realize a faint part of you is invisibly clinging back.

In 2 you manage to use this alien body to wobble toward a common tool, a pencil or a spoon, and are terrified its weight will crush you. You imagine with pleasure a time when you will finally be able to detect an itch, and look on enviously as someone scratches theirs, wondering how it's done.

In 3 you fight to raise a tin can to your heart and are overjoyed when you bring a cup of tea as far as your lips without spilling more than half. When a curtain flaps against you, you masterfully push it away. In sunlight you feel a desire rising deep from within you to punch the sky.

At 4 you can move without hunching or jerking and suddenly recognize certain muscles as former friends. They complain loudly at each new weight you shoulder and kick and lob, but then smile happily and beg for more. They find most of the tests of the surgeons entirely resistible.

In 5, miraculously, your whole vocabulary is restored. You can not only walk but amble, not only sprint but run in a carefree trajectory. Though your energy is impressive, it proves not nearly so great as the act of threading a needle.

Beyond 5 I have no idea—is there a limit to the possibilities? The spirit cavorting with its corporeal self in a way I can now only dream of:

Rowing a handsome blue boat down a lush tree-lined stream that winds for miles and straightens out into the sea. An island far in the distance has a small steep peak, and I easily swim through the white caps to its nearest shore with a bow and quiver in my teeth. In the forest I find a course of targets, each down a corridor of grass tucked into the trees, each with a mysterious and provocative painting that begs for an arrow of sight. They lead in a spiral to the mountaintop where I fling myself down, able to feel every tired muscle and limb and the sun. Then, remembering nothing of surgeons and pain, I recall the warm encouragement of *her* smile. My secular bones agree to avert their eyes for a moment to acknowledge an angel. And give thanks and thanks and thanks.

Patrick D. Wall

Some Notes on the Future of Pain

Intractable Pain

THERE ARE those who have led the hugely successful fight against tractable pains with the remarkably effective use of narcotics in the control of the majority of cancer pains. Their success not only over the pains but over the resistance of their colleagues naturally encourages them to continue the same logical strategy. For them, there are no intractable pains, only intractable doctors. Good luck to them. In a sense they are correct since it is certainly possible to hold a patient in a continuous state that approaches general anesthesia. However, there is also a group of highly skilled physicians and surgeons who are deeply distressed by their inability to control some types of pain in certain patients, short of demolition.

By far the most common group of these patients have suffered peripheral or central nerve damage. Amputees, nerve injury cases, and those afflicted with the various neuropathies make up the largest numbers. Talking to such chronic cases, one learns a lot about their disease and about their doctors. They move like draught horses, uncomplaining, heads down in continuous driving snow. Not only have their multiple treatments failed but they have suffered the indignity of being told that their pain will go away and/or that it is all in their head. They have learned that to continue to complain is to alienate and to isolate. These stoical characters plod on, often counted as cured because they no longer go to the doctors or take their ineffective medicine.

Fortunately, there is a real future hope for these unfortunates. Now that most scientists have abandoned the idea of a line-labeled, pain-dedicated hard-wire nervous system, we are moving into a period of acceptance of plasticity and control. Mechanisms are being discovered by which nerve impulses drive the nervous system into a continuous state of pain production. More relevant to these deafferentation states is a quite different mechanism. The nervous system is the master of homeostasis. When central nerve cells discover that they are isolated from their normal source of afferent input, they react by increasing their excitability in an attempt to compensate for the decreased input. The mechanisms by which these cells achieve their exalted states of excitability are being unraveled and clearly offer the possibility of new radical therapy. A quite different approach centers on the question of how deafferented cells "know" that they have lost their input. The answers appear to relate to substances that are transported or fail to be transported. This has led to intense studies on growth factors produced by tissue and distributed by the transport mechanism within nerve fibers. These studies offer considerable hope for the future elimination of intractable pains, but single "magic bullets" are highly unlikely since there are multiple mechanisms by which nerve cells maintain their stable state even when that state is pathological.

Chronic Pain

I have always been puzzled by the meaning of the phrase *chronic pain*, as distinct from *intractable pain*. Does it mean that there is a group of patients with tractable pain who never had access to a competent doctor? Does it mean that some patients progress through a treatable stage that is neglected and then later evolve into a perpetual intractable state? Or does it mean that the prolonged experience of pain can itself induce a separate and independent irreversible psychopathological state? As an outsider, someone who is not a clinician, I read allusions to these questions but find mixed, confusing answers.

One aspect of the phrase is clear. There are many conditions that are treatable but only up to a point. Arthritis is the most common example. Even in studies when hip replacement is followed by pain relief in two-thirds of the patients, the rationale for treating pain is a complete mystery. Medicinal treatments ameliorate the pain in most patients, but there are few who can tolerate the long-term side effects of the full doses that completely relieve the minority. For this reason one particularly welcomes the intense revival of interest in the nature of inflammation as described here. The subject lay fallow for almost a century after Rudolf Virchow. The discovery of prostaglandins opened the door to the full power of modern molecular biology. It now becomes apparent that a huge orchestrated cascade of changes form up under the single umbrella word *inflammation*. Each change offers a future of therapeutic interest, but it is highly unlikely that silencing one member of the orchestra will silence the entire cacophonous symphony.

Euthanasia

In early 1993, the Dutch Parliament was the first in the world to free doctors from prosecution if they deliberately ended a patient's life under precisely defined conditions. These conditions include the formal request of the alert patient, the agreement of two independent doctors, and the presence of intolerable pain. I include this matter here not because of the philosophical, practical, ethical, and religious issues but because it forewarns doctors concerned with pain that they will find themselves in particular cases in a position where they are required to make legal public pronouncements on the existence of intractable pain. In 1992, a British rheumatologist was found guilty and given a suspended sentence for injecting a patient with a lethal dose of potassium chloride. The seventy-one-year-old patient had been in the rheumatologist's care for many years with rheumatic heart disease, widespread progressive rheumatoid arthritis, and, eventually, collapsed vertebrae and infection. She legally requested a withdrawal of all therapy except for pain control. Within a few days, she was rapidly deteriorating and would clearly die soon, but intravenous narcotics were failing to control her pain. On the urging of the patient and her two sons, the doctor terminated this shambles. After his conviction, the doctor's case was naturally referred to the General Medical Council, which is responsible for the licenses permitting medical practice. It was decided that the doctor should not be suspended, but a condition was attached that the doctor must take a training course in established pain management clinics. I describe this case because it is clear that doctors concerned with pain will have to become quite clear about their responsibility to individual patients and also their responsibility in training their fellow physicians.

Epidemiology and Women

The aim of most general surveys is to establish the prevalence of pain. They stress the huge economic loss and the lack of available medical care for social and financial reasons. They should also discuss the social reputation of doctors and their treatments and the reasons for the growing popularity of alternative medicine. In a recent anonymous survey of an entire class of clinical medical students, the same array and frequency of painful conditions (headaches, backaches, dysmenorrhea, old injuries, and so on) were reported as in a class of law students. What was surprising was that many of the medical students who obviously were familiar with many pains and with the physicians in their hospital and had access to free medical service never consulted a physician. One can only surmise that they must have suffered fear, shame, guilt, or disillusionment with medicine along with their pain. Here is pain as a taboo subject operating on the informed individual. It raises the question of the reliability of the sample, which haunts every aspect of epidemiology.

The other aim of epidemiology is to establish cause. The field of tropical medicine contains many spectacular examples where careful study of geographical distribution and particular habits and habitants led directly to the identification of the causative organism. We do not have enough examples of such studies in painful conditions. For example, we still do not know if low back pain is related to the way in which muscles are used before the pain. A recent large study of low back pain among factory workers found that it related only to job satisfaction. This conclusion was welcomed by those who suspected that workers with back pain were just complainers. Others found the conclusion less satisfactory when it was noted that the sample did not include all workers but only those who complained to the company doctor, who might well be a target of dissatisfaction.

The most obvious unequal distribution of pain occurs between men and women. Apart from the special case of pain from the uterus, ovaries, breasts, and vulva, there is a marked preponderance of women over men in a surprising number of specific conditions. These include migraine, atypical facial neuralgia, temporomandibular joint (TMJ) syndrome, fibromyalgia, postencephalitic myalgia, irritable bowel syndrome, rheumatoid arthritis, and multiple sclerosis. This evident liability of women to a series of very different painful conditions contrasts with the universal longer life expectancy of women. Surely these facts must contain a set of clues worth serious analysis. Instead, there is a subculture of flippant and sexist pseudoexplanations that permits the imbalance to be ignored. The most common myth is that women have lower pain thresholds and a high tendency to complain. The experimental literature both confirms and denies the differences in a horrible confusion. The most familiar sources of confusion are failures to take into account the meaning of the stimulus to the subject, the situation, the familiarity of the stimulus, the sex and social status of the observers, and the presence of peers who set approved standards of response. In a recent example, two male experimenters found no difference between men and women subjected to painful hot and cold stimuli. However, women were significantly more sensitive and less tolerant to electric shocks than men. My reaction is that men are usually familiar with electric shocks in the course of car maintenance and in fixing electrical gadgets, while the most liberated of women still tend to show a sensible respect for bad wires. I am waiting for a resolution of the question, but my reading of the literature is that no difference has been shown between men and women subjected to brief harmless stimuli. I also doubt the other common myth that the difference is explained by hormones. The striking preponderance of rheumatoid arthritis and multiple sclerosis in women is hard to attribute to a major endocrine difference. Perhaps the best case can be made for migraine. When this disease is diagnosed by accepted criteria in children, the sex ratio is equal and only diverges in favor of women after the age of twelve. It is frequently relieved in pregnancy, and after menopause the ratio of women over men declines. For the individual with migraine, the nature of an attack is identical in men and women. Rather than considering hormones as the cause of migraine, it would seem that men and women equally may possess a design defect that explodes as migraine but that hormones secondarily may exaggerate the defect. An alternative hypothesis would be that migraine is a partially sex-linked genetic disease since migraine appears to run in families. There are more than just hormones in the differences between men and women. For example, hypermotility, which is evident in children, is more common in women and is present in a high percentage of chronic low back pain patients. Where a condition is unevenly spread in the population, hard work on critical classical epidemiology can unravel genetic and environmental factors.

Prevention

A surprising number of pain complaints are predictable. The most obvious example is pain after elective surgery. In nerve damage, there is usually a prolonged evolution of occurring pain. In the case of some neuropathies, such as diabetic neuropathy, the condition is usually diagnosed long before it becomes painful. Postherpetic neuralgia slowly emerges from the florid acute state. Even when pain occurs immediately after damage to a single nerve, the pain is at first limited to part of the territory of the damaged nerve and only slowly increases over the months to incorporate neighboring tissue. This means that the physician has time to consider preemptive therapies that might influence the subsequent misery.

The possibility of ameliorating postoperative pain is at present under intense investigation. Since my 1988 proposal that preemptive analgesia might be possible, there have been twenty clinical investigations, the majority positive but with some clear negative results. Briefly, it has become apparent that the arrival of impulses in unmyelinated afferents in the spinal cord sets off very prolonged increases of excitability of nerve cells involved in provoking pain. The nature and chemistry of the long-acting neurotransmitters and of the changes in the cells are becoming defined. These prolonged hyperexcitabilities can be prevented in animals either by preventing the input volley with local anesthetics or by preventing the cell reaction with narcotics or more recently produced compounds. The hypothesis to test in a human subject is that the patient in postoperative pain is complaining partly about impulses arriving over the afferents at the time of the complaint and partly about the long-lasting increased excitability induced during surgery. The clinical trials in progress are testing the relative effectiveness of local anethesia in the various tissues damaged during surgery and of local or systematic narcotics given before surgery and of various anti-inflammatory agents. These prior therapies are being combined with various regimens of continuous postoperative analgesia. It seems likely that no one approach will eliminate pain but that combinations may lead to marked improvement not only of pain but of lung malfunction and other sequelae.

In cases of nerve damage, the time available for intervention is much longer, but the problems are more complex and quite new therapies may be necessary. We do not yet understand the relative role of nerve impulses and of transported substances, both of which may play a part in the subsequent changes in central nerve cells. Furthermore, there may be combined multiple sites of pain-provoking pathology from the site of axon damage to the dorsal root ganglia and on to the central cells. If the prolonged pain is caused by the nerve impulses generated during surgery for elective amputation or during the acute stages of neuropathic damage, it should be controllable by variations of conventional therapy. If, however, transported chemicals are the major source of the problem, a lot of fundamental research and ingenuity will be required. Promising agents are the growth factors that can be made in therapeutic quantities by genetic engineering. The situation is exciting and hopeful, but since combined therapies are the likely outcome, hard and difficult clinical trials will be necessary. For example, acute herpes zoster (shingles), even in the elderly, normally resolves without pain. If it is decided that vigorous therapy of the acute phase will prevent the development of postherpetic neuralgia, as many believe, it will be necessary to treat very large numbers of acute patients in order to prove a significant decrease of the minority who go on to develop postherpetic neuralgia.

Patrick D. Wall

Pain without Peripheral Pathology

Modern medical diagnosis is firmly based on a two-hundred-year development of pathology, initially on morphological pathology and, since the turn of the century, on chemical pathology. Furthermore, classical neurology taught that pain was initiated impulses in nociceptive peripheral afferents activated by a pathological state in peripheral tissue. However, we are faced with a crisis epidemic of painful states where no peripheral pathology has been discovered or, if apparent, is clearly secondary to some primary change. These conditions now include tension headaches, migraine, temporomandibular joint syndrome, trigeminal neuralgia, the majority of neck and back pains, fibromyalgia, interstitial cystitis, among others. To add to this problem, it is emerging that, even where overt pathology is clearly present, the extent of the peripheral pathology is difficult to relate to the amount of pain. These conditions include myocardial ischemia, arthritis, amputation, neuropathies, and so on. The extent of this paradox is emphasized in the same individual where successive episodes of cardiac ischemia fail to indicate the amount of ischemic muscle in terms of pain, and, even worse, where a patient, with two unequally osteoarthritic hips at the same time, complains only of the less damaged hip.

The standard response to this general problem is given by the great majority of doctors in two stages. First, the normal sensory nervous system is seen as a reliable, accurate witness to currently observable peripheral pathology. Second, any deviation from this first rule is deemed a mental aberration. These two rigid rules are simple restatements of Cartesian dualism. I firmly believe that there are three alternative possibilities. First, I find it unwise arrogance to believe that our present techniques of diagnosis are capable of detecting all relevant forms of peripheral pathology. Second, we are now beginning to realize that a peripheral event may trigger long-lasting changes in the spinal cord and brain by way of nerve impulses and transported substances. This means that overt peripheral pathology is capable of initiating a cascade of changes that may persist in the central nervous system long after peripheral pathology has disappeared. Third, we are now beginning to discover that sensory systems are not dedicated and hard wired but are normally held in a stable state by elaborate dynamic control mechanisms. The rules of the physiology of these control mechanisms allow them to be pushed outside their normal working range, in which state they will oscillate or fire continuously. As with all known mechanical and biological control systems, it is also possible for them to drift idiopathically into an unstable state as a pain-control-system disease, as described elsewhere.[1]

The contemporary custom of assigning the cause of pain either to peripheral pathology or to mental pathology is too simple because it ignores the subtle dynamic properties of peripheral tissue and of the nervous system, of which three examples have been given, which could explain many of the diseases listed, and which have previously been attributed to mental disorders.

The Silence of Psychiatrists and the Burden on Psychologists

The problem of pain has failed to penetrate mainstream psychiatry. This is particularly unfortunate when the classical psychiatric subject of hysteria has been shifted to the apparently meaningful term *somatization* and applied to a very large number of pain patients.

The consequence of the progress I have been describing is that a huge burden has been placed on clinical psychologists. The full power of the classical medical profession, which is pathologically based, has concluded that there is "nothing wrong" in pathological terms with the great majority of chronic pain patients. Since this conclusion is unquestioned and since the only generally accepted alternative is that there must be a design fault in human mental processing that permits the generation or gross exaggeration of pain states, then the psychologist is presented with compulsory questions. It becomes the duty of the profession of psychologists to find an answer to the questions, What is the nature of the personality that is liable to create pain? Or, what is the personality that is liable to exaggerate subclinical disorders into crippling states? Most would agree that there has been a failure to answer these questions. Is that because psychology is inadequate or because psychologists were asked the wrong questions? Their problem was exaggerated by the obvious necessity to start with people in pain and to look backward in an attempt to define the personal nature of pain patients. This inevitably required them to attempt to unravel the consequences of pain from the causes of pain. In the course of this exploration, they took on the responsibility for effective therapies such as cognitive and behavior therapies. The rationale for these beneficial treatments is taken either as affecting the premorbid personality or as a pragmatic learning to cope with existing pain. This profession needs and deserves our intellectual support in answering the conundrum we and the patients have presented.

A Scheme for Pain Mechanisms

We live in an age where ideas have taken a minor and tertiary role. Watson with Crick discovered the structure of DNA and they proclaim that science progresses from technique to data to ideas, and most agree. I disagree and believe that old accepted ideas form an éminence grise that covertly drives the nature of the questions and the techniques they are meant to solve, and therefore the data represent self-fulfilling answers to doubtful questions. For that reason, I believe we need to generate new ideas as possible testable solutions to the hugely puzzling questions about pain. The artificial intelligence modelers of the brain produce marvelous new electronics but fail to influence biology. The contemporary philosophers still trudge in the funeral procession of Aristotle[2] and fail to incorporate the neurosciences. Any one thinking inevitably produces a scheme that incorporates cause and effect. Experimentalists also require a plan on which to organize their questions and, usually, implicitly, without statement, adopt one of the philosophical schemata. With almost vanishing rarity, experimental findings have affected philosophical thought. There are four classical plans on which experiments to discover the nature of sensory processing have been based, and I wish to propose a fifth for the future. The following plans (dualism, hierarchies, cybernetics, ethology, and reality/virtual reality) are complementary, and each has generated undoubted facts that have to be incorporated in any plan.

Dualism

This scheme remains the main foundation on which most neurophysiology is based. It predicts that identifiable components of the brain will reliably detect, transmit, and deliver specific fractions of sensation. My own and many others' inability to detect such a system that could be reasonably labeled a pain system led me to reject the plan as a plausible generator of the sensation of pain.[3] Light pressure on the skin usually provokes a sensation of touch, but in other circumstances—for example, tenderness—the same stimulus to the same skin is very painful. The plas-

---

Descartes to Eccles and Popper

STIMULUS → TRANSMISSSION → SENSATION → PERCEPTION

Figure 1. Dualisms.

ticity of the relation of the stimulus to response and the changeable properties of the neurons made it impossible to view this as a line-labeled, modality-dedicated, and hard-wired sensory system as required by the Cartesian system. From René Descartes on to John Carew Eccles and Karl Popper, an absolute separation is made between the reliable body machinery, which produces sensation, and the subsequent mental process of perception (fig. 1).

Hierarchies

Two hundred and fifty years after Descartes and contemporary with Charles Darwin, a scheme for the subdivision of the nervous system into higher and lower levels was introduced (fig. 2), but it has been interpreted incorrectly in three ways. First, it has been taken to mean that "higher" is the same as "more recently evolved." This, in turn, is taken to justify the dogma that the mind is in the cerebral cortex. What a leap (in the dark)! Second, while evolution is much discussed in Hughlings Jackson's

---

Hughlings Jackson and Herbert Spencer to Sherrington

STIMULUS ↔ SPECIFICS ↔ INTEGRATION ↔ HIGHER CENTERS

Figure 2. Hierarchies.

writing, and while his guru Herbert Spencer originated the phrase "the survival of the fittest," they used the term *evolution* to mean something quite different from Darwin. Spencerian evolution relates to thermodynamics and to entropy and is therefore reversible, while Darwinian evolution is not reversible. The third incorrect interpretation was a trivialization that has dominated the use of the scheme in the twentieth century. Three crucial discoveries had been made by Jackson's time: there are anatomically separate inputs and outputs to the central nervous system (Bell and Magendie); there are anatomically separate input and output pathways within the central nervous system (Brown-Séquard); there are reflex pathways within the spinal cord that link inputs and outputs (Sechenow). Even the simplest neurologist and the most sophisticated textbook writer could cope with these three ideas. Therefore, they took Jackson and his subtle followers to mean that there was a short reflex pathway, which ran through the spinal cord; a longer one through the brain stem; and the longest one, which looped through the cortex. In fact, Jackson and Sherrington were very specific that there were internal loops connecting the various levels, which makes the pathways far more complex than a simple set of reflex loops.

Jackson's greatest neurological discoveries came from epileptics. In the most common form of grand mal epilepsy, the convulsive phase of the attack is preceded by a sensory aura in which the patient has a sensory experience. This can vary among patients from a simple tingling in one finger to an elaborate scene with people, music, and a landscape. These are not hallucinations in the sense that the patient believes they are actually happening. On the contrary, the patient is angry and terrified, knowing that he or she is about to have a fit. (Auras are brilliantly described by Dostoyevsky, himself an epileptic, in *The Idiot*.) The importance for our present discussion is that the brain is capable of creating virtual reality without reference to our stimulation from the sensory nervous system. This depends on long-range feedback mechanisms within the central nervous system, which do not reach out into the periphery.

Cybernetics

Claude Bernard was concerned with the maintenance of a stable internal environment. As he and those who followed studied how stability was achieved, they began to realize that a series of components must exist. This was formalized by Norbert Wiener as cybernetics (fig. 3). First there had to be an internal standard that was compared with the actual situation. A comparator measured the mismatch between the sensory input, which signaled the actual situation, and an internal standard, which signaled the ideal situation. When this mismatch signal was amplified, it

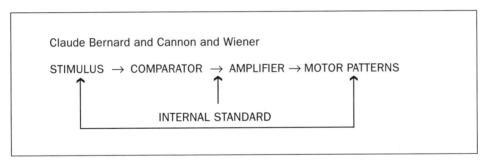

Figure 3. Cybernetics.

triggered a series of graded output patterns, which in turn fed back onto the actual input to reverse its trend and to thereby reduce the mismatch signal. Physiologists have identified many of the components in this process. In cooling, for example, the dropping temperature is the stimulus that deviates from the standard. The mismatch difference signal triggers an orchestrated series of output patterns as the difference grows: vasoconstriction; piloerection; release of thyroid hormone, insulin, and adrenaline to increase metabolism; shivering; rigors.

Ethology

This spectacular development of old-fashioned natural study defined a series of stages between stimulus and response (fig. 4). The sensory input is used twice, to

Hess, Tinbergen, Lorenz

STIMULUS → REPERTOIRE → MOTOR PATTERN → OUTPUT
↑ ↑
INTERNAL STATE STIMULUS

Figure 4. Ethology.

decide first what to do and then how to do it. In the initial stage, a combination of sensory signals from outside and from inside assigns a priority to one feature in the behavioral repertoire. This releases the motor patterns that are most relevant to the biological situation. The successful achievement of this motor pattern requires a second consultation with the sensory system. Where is the enemy, mate, nest, or chick, and is it being approached on the optimal course? Experimental studies have been very successful identifying the sensory patterns and the motor pattern generators but less so the priority-assignment mechanism.

Reality/Virtual Reality

I wish to propose here that advanced brains contain both the Jackson version of the hierarchical system and the Tinbergen-Lorenz version of an ethological system. The ethological sequence of repertoire-priority motor pattern contains an inherent fraction of species-specific components heavily modified by experience and learning. This machinery is entirely responsible for the domestic and skilled actions of everyday life and does not involve consciousness. On occasion, however, a combination of internal and external stimuli occur for which there is no biologically appropriate response available in the repertoire-priority motor pattern system. When this mismatch occurs, an attentional switch diverts the input into quite a different system.

Here are two illustrative examples. The phantom limb has been a challenging paradox for philosophers and neurologists. As he writes in *Meditation on a First Philosophy*, Descartes was aware that he had set a trap for himself in the very rigidity of his proposed sensory mechanism:

It is manifest that notwithstanding the sovereign goodness of God, the nature of man, in so far as it is a composite of mind and body, must sometimes be at fault and deceptive. For should some causes, not in the foot but in another part of the nerves that extend from the foot to the brain, or even in the brain itself, give rise to the motion ordinarily excited when the foot is injuriously affected, pain will be felt just as though it were in the foot and thus naturally the senses will be deceived: for since the same motion in the brain cannot but give rise in the mind always to the same sensation and since this sensation is much more frequently due to a cause that is injurious to the foot than by one acting in another quarter, it is reasonable that it should convey to the mind pain as in the foot.[4]

The brilliance of Descartes here introduces the idea of the false signal but at the same time has to define the mind as a passive slave to the sensory apparatus. Three centuries later, Bromage and Melzack considered the results of adding local anesthetic to nerves supplying a body part.[5] Far from producing signals, these agents block the normal trickle of signals that reaches the brain. A startling phantom phenomenon appears in the area of anesthesia. This phantom is not an imitation of the real limb; it is more real, swollen, and attention grabbing. In the scheme under discussion, the repertoire-priority component of the brain is presented with a sensory input that is simply not in the repertoire. In that situation, the attention switch operates to bring into action the sensation-perception mechanism, which, in the absence of a sensory input, creates a virtual limb. Seeking a confirmatory sensory input, the patient visually explores the limb and palpates it, and the phantom disappears.

The second example comes from the work of Dubner et al. and Duncan et al., which is so startling and novel that it it has yet to intrude on theory.[6] Duncan and colleagues recorded in monkeys responses from first-order central cells, which receive information from nerve fibers in the skin. By all classical criteria, these cells fulfill perfectly the requirements of Cartesian sensory transmission cells—that is, their discharge rigidly and reliably reflects a particular stimulus applied to a unique area of skin. The cells signal in a lawful fashion the location, intensity, and nature of the stimulus with such reliability that the signal was the same in awake or anesthetized monkeys. These workers then trained the animals to use a stimulus in a discrimination task in which the correct response was rewarded. The animal was first given a warning signal that the trial was about to begin; then the stimulus was applied and the animal was rewarded with a drink of orange juice if it reached out and pushed a button when the stimulus was of a particular intensity. When training began, of course, the cell responded only to the skin stimulus and not to the warning signal or any of the other events. However, when the animal had

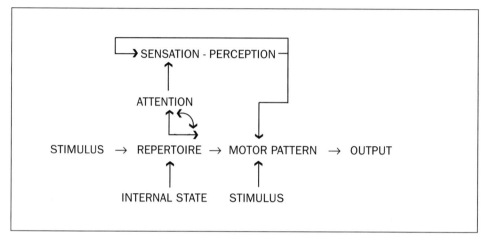

Figure 5. The brain and virtual reality.

successfully solved the problem and was fully trained, many cells produced a brief burst of activity after the warning signal. This novel period of cell discharge mimicked the discharge of the cell that always occurred after the stimulus to be discriminated was presented. This means that the trained brain had created a virtual input that ran over the same pathway as the input provoked by the real stimulus. A precise model of the expected output precedes the input actually provoked by the expected stimulus. The literature contains several examples of this creation of inputs without stimuli in classical and operant conditioning.

Returning to the scheme, it proposes that the brain is capable of generating a virtual reality (fig. 5). It is further proposed that this experimental theater is brought into action only when the repertoire-priority system fails to provide a biologically appropriate motor pattern. The Jacksonian reality/virtual reality experimental theater is simultaneously author, director, stage, actors, and audience. In the situation of a fully mastered discriminant task, the expectations of the stage play precisely mimic reality. That is pantomime. In chronic pain, no amount of rewriting or changing of cast and scenery provides a resolution to match and cancel reality. That is tragedy.

In summary, it is proposed that there are two alternate brain mechanisms superimposed on each other that can use some of the same neural elements. They do not operate simultaneously. The reality circuit, which does not involve conscious perception, operates when one form of behavior has been assigned a high priority. This is the situation during emergency analgesia when a reaction such as escape has been assigned a higher biological priority than attending to pain.

This circuit is also in action during the placebo reaction when expectation has assigned pain a low priority because it is appropriate. The virtual reality circuit operates and continuously reexamines the input as modified by the possible repertoire of alternate behaviors when the normal circuitry can assign no evident priority to the repertoire of behaviors that would remove the stimulus. I propose that the operation of this circuit, which is consciousness, is in action during perceived pain.

Notes

This essay has been reprinted from *Textbook of Pain*, Patrick D. Wall and Ronald Melzack, eds., 3d ed. (London: Churchill-Livingstone, 1994); used by permission of Churchill-Livingstone.

1. P. D. Wall, "Stability and Instability of Central Pain Mechanisms," in *Pain Research and Clinical Management: Volume 3*, ed. R. Dubner, G. F. Gebhart, and M. R. Bond (Amsterdam: Elsevier, 1988). (Proceedings of the Fifth World Congress on Pain, Hamburg, 2–7 August 1987.)

2. J. Searle, *The Rediscovery of the Mind* (Cambridge, Mass.: MIT Press, 1992).

3. P. D. Wall and M. Jones, *Defeating Pain* (New York: Plenum Press, 1992).

4. R. Descartes, *Meditation on a First Philosophy* (Paris: n.p., 1641)

5. P. R. Bromage and R. Melzack, "Phantom Limbs and the Body Schema," *Canadian Anaesthetists Society Journal* 21 (1974): 267–74.

6. R. Dubner, D. S. Hoffman, and R. L. Hayes, "Task-Related Responses and Their Functional Role," *Journal of Neurophysiology* 46 (1981): 444–64; G. H. Duncan, M. C. Bushnell, R. Bates, and R. Dubner, "Task-Related Responses of Monkey Medullary Dorsal Horn Neurones," *Journal of Neurophysiology* 57 (1987): 289–310.

Ronald Melzack

The McGill Pain

Questionnaires

McGill Pain Questionnaire

Patient's Name _____ Date _____ Time _____ am/pm

PRI: S_____ A_____ E_____ M_____ PRI(T)_____ PPI_____
    (1-10)   (11-15)   (16)   (17-20)   (1-20)

1 FLICKERING QUIVERING PULSING THROBBING BEATING POUNDING	11 TIRING EXHAUSTING
2 JUMPING FLASHING SHOOTING	12 SICKENING SUFFOCATING
3 PRICKING BORING DRILLING STABBING LANCINATING	13 FEARFUL FRIGHTFUL TERRIFYING
4 SHARP CUTTING LACERATING	14 PUNISHING GRUELLING CRUEL VICIOUS KILLING
5 PINCHING PRESSING GNAWING CRAMPING CRUSHING	15 WRETCHED BLINDING
6 TUGGING PULLING WRENCHING	16 ANNOYING TROUBLESOME MISERABLE INTENSE UNBEARABLE
7 HOT BURNING SCALDING SEARING	17 SPREADING RADIATING PENETRATING PIERCING
8 TINGLING ITCHY SMARTING STINGING	18 TIGHT NUMB DRAWING SQUEEZING TEARING
9 DULL SORE HURTING ACHING HEAVY	19 COOL COLD FREEZING
10 TENDER TAUT RASPING SPLITTING	20 NAGGING NAUSEATING AGONIZING DREADFUL TORTURING

BRIEF	RHYTHMIC	CONTINUOUS
MOMENTARY	PERIODIC	STEADY
TRANSIENT	INTERMITTENT	CONSTANT

E = EXTERNAL

I = INTERNAL

PPI
0 NO PAIN
1 MILD
2 DISCOMFORTING
3 DISTRESSING
4 HORRIBLE
5 EXCRUCIATING

COMMENTS:

McGill Pain Questionnaire. The descriptors fall into four major groups: sensory, 1 to 10; affective, 11-15; evaluative, 16; and miscellaneous, 17-20. The rank value for each descriptor is based on its position in the word set. The sum of the rank values is the pain rating index (PRI). The present pain intensity (PPI) is based on a scale of 0 to 5. Copyright 1975 Ronald Melzack. Reprinted by permission from Dr. Ronald Melzack.

SHORT-FORM McGILL PAIN QUESTIONNAIRE

PATIENT'S NAME: _____   DATE: _____

	NONE	MILD	MODERATE	SEVERE
THROBBING	0) _____	1) _____	2) _____	3) _____
SHOOTING	0) _____	1) _____	2) _____	3) _____
STABBING	0) _____	1) _____	2) _____	3) _____
SHARP	0) _____	1) _____	2) _____	3) _____
CRAMPING	0) _____	1) _____	2) _____	3) _____
GNAWING	0) _____	1) _____	2) _____	3) _____
HOT-BURNING	0) _____	1) _____	2) _____	3) _____
ACHING	0) _____	1) _____	2) _____	3) _____
HEAVY	0) _____	1) _____	2) _____	3) _____
TENDER	0) _____	1) _____	2) _____	3) _____
SPLITTING	0) _____	1) _____	2) _____	3) _____
TIRING-EXHAUSTING	0) _____	1) _____	2) _____	3) _____
SICKENING	0) _____	1) _____	2) _____	3) _____
FEARFUL	0) _____	1) _____	2) _____	3) _____
PUNISHING-CRUEL	0) _____	1) _____	2) _____	3) _____

NO PAIN |———————————————————————————————| WORST POSSIBLE PAIN

PPI

0	NO PAIN	_____
1	MILD	_____
2	DISCOMFORTING	_____
3	DISTRESSING	_____
4	HORRIBLE	_____
5	EXCRUCIATING	_____

The short-form McGill Pain Questionnaire. Descriptors 1-11 represent the sensory dimension of pain experience and 12-15 represent the affective dimension. Each descriptor is ranked on an intensity scale of 0 = none, 1 = mild, 2 = moderate, 3 = severe. The present pain intensity (PPI) of the standard long-form MPQ and the Visual Analogue Scale are included to provide overall pain intensity scores. Copyright 1984 Ronald Melzack. Reprinted by permission from Dr. Ronald Melzack.

John O'Neill

Two Cartographies of AIDS: The (In)describable Pain of HIV/AIDS

Cell Wars

I PROPOSE to show how HIV/AIDS has been mapped onto the body politic in order to familiarize the public with a disease it might otherwise ignore as a subcultural malady. By examining a series of maps, pictures, diagrams, and flowcharts (fig. 1), I will show how modern science sets up its plan of attack, how it describes its terrain and its population and familiarizes the public with its own procedures in reports of a war of reason (medicine) against evil (disease).[1] This ideology of militant science is shared by the population to which it offers health. In turn, the public demands to be kept informed about the progress of medicine's battle against disease. Thus the strategic *aesthetics of science* are intrinsic to the public representation of pain and to the self-concept of science as a rational agony. At the level of the individual body in pain, there operates another cartography of pain designed to chart the multiple diseases that invade the HIV/AIDS patient's body and the complex "administration" of a polypharmacy designed to "manage" pain, discomfort, and death. Although this is the intimate dimension of pain, it is noticeable that the suffering body is absent from the charts and diagrams. This effect is intentional since it must be shown that the individual patient is overwhelmed by a battery of treatments and sufferings. Medical "management" finally surrenders to the nonrationalizable dramas of palliative care. Thus the two cartographies of pain displace the suffering body in opposite ways: it is "absent" on the level of pain administration and "present" in the graphics of the body politic.

The *body as a site for medical warfare* is inscribed within the metaphors of militarized scientific discourse (war on poverty, war on ignorance). Because the medical sciences must operate within an economy of scarcity (even when relieved by public health and insurance policies), the *body politic*, which is host to the disease attacked by medicine, is "mapped" in accordance with the statistics of class, gender, and race but in such a way as to conceal the social (re)production or the *political economy of disease*, that is, by classification in terms of "risk" behavior.

HIV/AIDS is also "mapped" as both a national and a global disease. Within the national map, the disease is described in terms of "risk groups" and "risk behaviors." As a result, the *body politic* is divided into social groups for whom the medical system assumes varying degrees of responsibility, and who in turn are made responsible for the transmission of the disease. Pie charts, like those typically found in *Scientific American*, function as a comparative means to indicate the ratio of those infected in one of these groups in comparison with their numbers in terms of a "general population."[2] Such mappings operate on the level of the political unconscious to (re)produce the ghettoization and colonization of HIV/AIDS in response to the larger political economy of HIV/AIDS.[3]

The pain of HIV/AIDS is also subject to a mapping exercise in which the metaphors of politics, war, and business administration overlap in charting the history of cumulative illness in the HIV/AIDS complex, as well as the administration of the therapeutic drugs necessitated by the extraordinary combination of maladies suffered by the patient. It is important not to minimize the accumulation of suffering involved in HIV/AIDS and the intensive therapy required. Once again, the (re)presentation of these charts is intended to show how HIV/AIDS is rendered through a *medicalized aesthetics* (i.e., made into a clinical object) in order to fit into the grammar of the health system and its rationalized management of pain. Yet as we have pointed out, the body is absent from this cartography because it is the "site" of a battery of illnesses and treatments whose administration requires that "a case" be treated in a series, in accordance with the rationalized probabilities of modern medicine. The final stage is surrendered to the palliative arts of dying.

John O'Neill

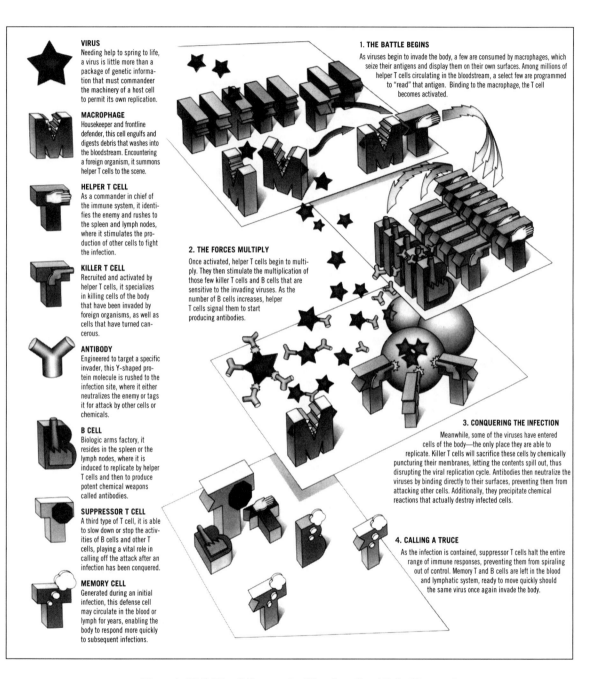

Figure 1. "Cell Wars," diagrams by Allen Carroll and Dale Glasgow, for "Our Immune System: The Wars Within," *National Geographic* 169, no. 6 (June 1986): 708-9. Reprinted with permission from *National Geographic*.

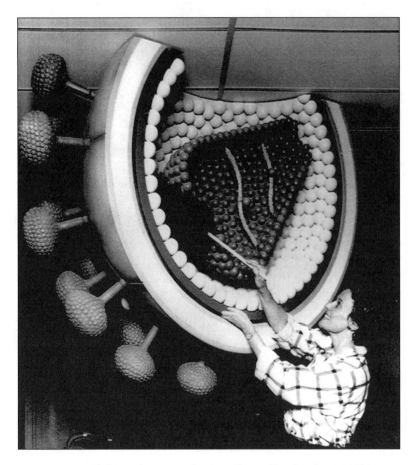

Figure 2. "She" introduces us to the virus. *Toronto Star*, October 16, 1991.
Canapress Photo Service (Ian Gillespie).

Popularizing AIDS

If there is to be a public awareness of AIDS, the public must be taught to see itself
in a variety of social responses to the disease. From a typical sample of images, one
can reconstruct how illness is made into a family narrative. In this photo from the
Toronto Star, a smiling woman points to a giant fiberglass model of the HIV/AIDS
virus.[4] "She" introduces us to the virus (fig. 2). In *National Geographic*, we are introduced to a biologist whose interest is in the genes that contain blueprints for the receptors that trigger immune responses.[5] Chin in hand, Dr. Leroy Hood sits in front
of a range of technical instruments and a computer printout, reminding us of his
status as scientist. He sits beside a model of the gene fragment. "He" constructs a

model of DNA. In a two-page photospread, "kids" get into the cancer game on a video machine.[6] They are being given the hope that they can combat their disease by visualizing their struggle. A 1987 cover of *U.S. News and World Report* presents us with a worried-looking, middle-class, white, heterosexual couple accompanied by the headline, "AIDS: What You Need to Know, What You Should Do."[7] This couple must orient themselves to the statistical grid of AIDS death. Finally, in a RepliGen advertisement, big bold capitalized letters proclaim: **"TO DEVELOP AN AIDS VACCINE YOU MUST CHOOSE YOUR PARTNERS CARE-FULLY."**[8] "They" are the corporate partners in the safe sex game (fig. 3). He, she, kids, couples, and corporate partners all participate in the battle against disease. The semiotic task of these images is to genderize and familiarize, and to make both child's play and science game of understanding the virus. At every stage of life, for men, women and children, in love and in business, the pervasive concern with HIV/AIDS is framed with images of rational control.

Through a combination of science, play, and commercialism, these images have become staples in the representation of HIV/AIDS as a communicable disease to which the community must respond if it is to reduce its risks in the short run while supporting a long-run medical and societal strategy for the conquest of the disease. These representations of HIV/AIDS must be understood as "realist fictions" intended to portray what families and lovers can do about HIV/AIDS to bring it within the parameters of a modern health system and its medical-legal-rational controls. In other words, these public images are essential to the communicative work of familiarization, making it a family affair, thereby reducing the potential for moral panic and an antiliberal state policy in matters of sexuality.

Globalizing AIDS

It is a constitutive practice of modern societies to document, calculate, and report on themselves rather than look to the mirror of nature for their self-image. With the shift from feudal to mercantile-industrial society, it became necessary for the State (thereby inventing the next stage of the State) to institutionalize a *political arithmetic* to keep track of its population, trade, health, crime, and education processes. Of course, these practices did not spring from the head of the State all at once. With regard to health matters, the mapping of illness required a conceptual distinction between illness *in* a body, so to speak, and illness *between* bodies. This distinction was imperative to the articulation of social medicine and its preventive strategies. By now, everyone is familiar with the politics of government agency statistics and their tactical

TO DEVELOP AN AIDS VACCINE, YOU MUST CHOOSE YOUR PARTNERS CAREFULLY.

Repligen scientists are working around the clock to transform our
knowledge of the AIDS virus into a vaccine.
And the scientists we're working with in the private, government,
and academic sectors are among the best in the field.
It's these partnerships that make us believe we'll be the company
to develop the AIDS vaccine.
And hopefully, we'll do it in time to save thousands of lives.

RepliGen

Repligen Corp., Cambridge, MA

Figure 3. The corporate "partner" in the "safe sex" game.

employment in the news of the day. It is against this background that we have to understand the mapping of HIV/AIDS.

The variety of graphic artifacts employed to render the "facts"
on HIV/AIDS is considerable and what I am arguing is that they cannot be read off
with the apparent ease or evidence that their looks suggest. To show this as conveniently as possible, I begin with the cartographics of AIDS in the special issue
of *Scientific American*,[9] in which we have a nice play between science for Americans
(whether they like it or not) and the Americanization of science in the (political)
interest of Americans. A map of the globe purports to show three patterns of infection and the types of transmission endemic to each geographic region. In the first
pattern (which encompasses North and South America, Western Europe, Scandi-
navia, Australia, and New Zealand), 90 percent of the cases are homosexual males
or users of IV drugs. In the second pattern (Africa, the Caribbean, and some areas
of South America), the primary mode of transmission is said to be heterosexual,
making the number of infected females and males approximately equal. In the third
pattern (Eastern Europe, North Africa, the Middle East, Asia, and the Pacific),
there are relatively few cases; those that exist are said to be a result of contact with
countries from the first and second patterns.

I want to stress that the "rationality effect" of the maps and
figures presented on HIV/AIDS is "schizzed" or undermined by the political desire
to locate AIDS *in* a body rather than *between* bodies. This strategy aims to preserve,
on the one hand, the medical model of acute rather than chronic illness and, on the
other hand, to locate HIV/AIDS in a specific subculture (at home or abroad) rather
than to institutionalize a national or global model of health/illness into which
HIV/AIDS needs to be integrated.

The global spread of HIV/AIDS is essential to the political
strategy I shall call "globalizing panics."[10] I understand a globalizing panic to be any
practice that traverses the world to reduce it and its cultural diversity to the gener-
ics of Coca-Cola, tourism, foreign aid, medical aid, military defense posts, tourism,
fashion, and the international money markets. Since these practices are never quite
stabilized, their dynamics include deglobalizing tendencies that will be reinscribed
by the global system as threats to the "world order." Some nations may consider
themselves to be the prime agents in this world order, while others can only maintain an aligned status or else enjoy a toy nationality that can be appealed to in order
to supply neutrality functions on behalf of the world order. The globalizing panics
that confirm the world order rely heavily on the media—television, newspapers,
magazines, films, and documentaries—to specularize the incorporation of all

societies in a single global system destined to overcome all internal divisions, if not to expand into an intergalactic empire.[11]

It is an important function of the media to offer charitable images of First World medicine that remains largely unavailable to the poor in the United States and the so-called Third World, whose infants are ravaged by disease and death amid populations that are continuously uprooted by famine, flood, and warfare. By the same token, media images from the colonized world are exploited on behalf of the promise of the global order, whose own political economy is largely responsible for the natural disasters that ravage the Third World. In addition, the sexual economy, which must be treated as the framework for any grasp of the political economy of AIDS, is subject to every other subsystem of the global economy and national political economy. It is so even though sexuality appears most disengaged. This is because its disengagement is inseparable from processes of disenfranchisement elsewhere in the society, that is, the degradation of gendered economies, family, and church authority, as well as of any politics grounded in these communities.

Class(ifying) AIDS

Whatever the level of public knowledge of virology, immunology, and DNA structures, the looks of these things have been given a certain familiarity through the powerful aesthetics of modern science conveyed not only in *Scientific American* but also, as we have seen, in *National Geographic*, a magazine that has a rightful place in anyone's imagination of the nature of things, animals, and plants that make up the human globe. *National Geographic*'s treatment of the immunological system is remarkable for its employment of the video language of Star Wars, kids' games, "combining fun and therapy" in "zapping" the "Killer T Cell" in order to defend the "kind of biologic democracy" that prevails in the human immune system against cancer cells that "have turned from self to nonself, friend to foe."[12] Like America, the cancerous body is at war with its world or, rather, at war with itself, split allopathically into good and bad self. Thus the central metaphors of war, medicine, and politics miscegenate to deepen our understanding of HIV by reducing our empathy for "the problem." Yet beneath this construction there lurks the suspicion that it may be American society that "stresses" the immune system—in short, that the "lifestyle" of Americans may be autotoxic.

Indeed, I would argue that once any radical alternative to the American lifestyle is foreclosed on the level of politics, anxiety must build up on the level of family, personality, sexuality. Problems such as alcoholism and drug abuse will in turn be mapped in terms of the militarized medical metaphors of the State that will declare its wars on poverty, ignorance, drugs, drunk driving, and the like. Whatever the contradictions in this discursive pattern, its central features, that is, the *individualization and somatization of sociopolitical troubles*, are essential to the administration of the body politic through the complementary techniques of the medicalization of politics and State politics of medicine.

A noticeable feature of the reporting of HIV/AIDS figures is that it does not employ the more usual indices of income or education but does include age and race.[13] However, such reports are distinctly unusual in that they categorize their population according to a mixture of 'risky' sexual and narcotic behaviors, including the risks run by hemophiliacs in a contaminated blood-transfusion system. Here the sociographics of HIV/AIDS schizz (betray while claiming to portray uniquely) the epidemiological data. Here the political unconscious (desire) is at work to identify a sociopathic population whose practices result in a high rate of HIV/AIDS and thereby suggest a target population for treatment or 'benign neglect,' supposing one has any confidence in the immunological properties of being on the right side of the class/race wall. Thus the risk behavior categories are doubly strategic inasmuch as they individualize and 'behavioralize' dangers to life that are endemic in the national society and the international narcotics ring. Worse still, they furnish the basis for weak AIDS pedagogies on the street and school levels where a litany of risk behaviors is recited by 'workers' with little more in hand than the pamphlets in which those categories are reproduced. Perhaps the most significant turn in the risk-groups reportage[14] on HIV/AIDS is the possibility that its incidence has peaked in 'the gay community' (First World white urban males) while it is on the rise in the heterosexual community, that is, First World urban Black/Hispanics and their children, and Third World Africans. Such reports, while encouraging in the sense that they reveal results due to community action and 'behavior modification' (unequally appraised in the medical model and its political economy), nevertheless are dangerous inasmuch as they feed scientifically the social imaginary of the other as the source of disease, trouble, and moral risks of all kinds.

Drug War

Western medicine fights disease; it even fights off other medical cultures that adopt a homeopathic approach to disease and illness.[15] One paradox of Western medicine is that its allopathic treatment model is embroiled in the colonialization of homeopathic cultures whose territories are the main source for its pharmaceutical armamentarium. Western medicine is the principal element in the charitable restoration of the Third World, where it can also conveniently dump its excess pills, milk formula, and the like.[16] Here, however, we must focus attention on the complex *documentary aesthetics* that convey modern medical strategy.

The basic mechanism of HIV is generally represented by the following graphics and table: (1) as an attack mechanism; (2) as a therapeutic anti-retroviral armamentarium[17] and a polypharmacy for HIV/AIDS.[18] Together, these devices illustrate a causal process and a resultant pharmacological prescription, yet among medical workers and HIV patients themselves, involve contested rather than settled science. Once the replicative cycle of HIV has been mapped, it permits the specification of therapeutic target sites. As the first diagram (HIV as an attack mechanism) indicates, the virus appears to bind to the CD4 receptor on the surface of the T4 cell releasing both viral RNA and reverse transcriptase. The latter possesses an inherent enzyme activity that eliminates RNA so that, unless a DNA copy is made immediately, replication ceases and no new HIV cell is produced. At this stage of knowledge, reverse transcriptase is designated as a major target for antiviral therapy. But once HIV develops into AIDS, an extraordinary accumulation of maladies sets in, for which an equally large armamentarium of drugs is required. The two tables chart the treatment regime. The list includes a row for each possible drug to be taken, cross-referenced with its uses, doses, side effects, and possible negative interactions with other medications. At a glance such a representation tries to assist in the management of an extraordinary complex of suffering.

Without pretending to any understanding of the illness, what observers can "see" from the massive armory of drugs administered over the course of HIV/AIDS is a process that is otherwise thoroughly mystified in media reports of AIDS patients demanding a specific wonder drug from their doctor, from the pharmaceutical corporations, and from the government—provided it is available at a reasonable cost.[19] This image seriously distorts the treatment process necessary to care for the extraordinary complex of viral illnessess, organ and skin diseases, as well as brain and psychic traumas that ravage any given patient and in turn require a large medical personnel to respond not only to the illness but to the secondary effects of the various treatments. In addition, one cannot overlook the extraordinary strain that has been placed upon the first-generation front-line medical staff who have worked with HIV/AIDS patients.[20] Thus, as Gerald Friedland has observed, it is necessary to include in the therapeutic armamentarium a serious concern for the medical community's ability to recruit new members to work in the field opened up by HIV/AIDS. This is especially the case since the presumption of medical immunity built into the allopathic model of medical practice has been challenged. The irony here is that "medical warfare" may also involve casualties among the profession no less than the patients (a doubling of the iatrogenic effect). Equally important is the work and knowledge shared among persons with AIDS that have been a considerable factor in the first-generation (prevaccine) response to HIV/AIDS.

Pain Management

Every society will represent to itself its sources of order and disorder. For this purpose the human body offers both the form and content of society's concern with integrity/wholeness/order, on the one hand, and disintegration/impurity/disorder, on the other hand. Indeed, the right and left hand, male and female, white man and colored man all serve to render the same cosmography of good and evil. Given such practices, it is understandable that an industrialized society will represent the order/disorder problem in terms of *the body as a machine* whose operations are maximized by other machines.[21] These assumptions are basic to the practice of industrialized medicine. They require that the body's suffering be reduced to the neurochemistry of *pain*, which is in turn treated by therapeutic drugs whose own invention, testing, and administration are absolutely coded to the rational-legal requirements of industrialized and bureaucratized medicine. In addition, the cartography of pain will represent the statistical incidence and the chronology of a *disease* to show its spread and history in a population and a patient in order that any specific medical intervention may in turn be interpreted as a rational strategy within an appropriately mapped field of knowledge.[22]

On a somatic level, diagrammatic tables in palliative care books list the types of pain that may be experienced in particular parts of the body, giving it a percentage to indicate the amount of pain suffered in that location, and a brief description of where and how it hurts. This diagrammatic representation is a type of HIV/AIDS "pain portrait,"[23] which helps caregivers grasp the unusual accumulation of maladies suffered. On an individual, psychological level another type of portrait is drawn. Pain is rendered into three dimensions that are distilled into corresponding affective responses: depression, anger, and anxiety. In this behaviorist rendering of pain, the psychic and social dimensions of pain interact with a central core of "noxious sensory impulses" that afflict the patient's body. Surrounding this portrait of pain are the manifestations of this depression, anxiety, and anger such as "disfigurement," "financial problems," "irritability," "fear of death," and so on. The patient, however, is more than a sick body whose troubles can be inventoried without any attention to the psychophysical interactions that define illness for a given person. In turn, the psychophysical person is also a sociopsychological member of a community whose material and spiritual support is essential to the patient's humanity. Yet this is the absent subject in the pain portrait that makes the patient a mere site of clinical symptoms.

The medical model of the doctor-patient relationship is inscribed in a code of universal, medical-legal, rational treatments of cases in which the patient is on the low end of the hospital hierarchy. The medical system is designed to eliminate pain rather than to end human suffering. Because of the phenomenological variety of human suffering, the medical system abstracts from the individual's embodied tale of suffering a generalized discourse of pain and therapy. Care is administered from the standpoint of the medical profession's commitment to restore health through its surgical treatments and chemotherapies. The HIV/AIDS patient is a particular challenge to the medical model of disease inasmuch as HIV/AIDS involves a complex multiplicity of diseases, whose incubation period is very long (up to ten years), whose course is variable and highly individualized.[24]

Worse still, the disease strikes relatively young persons, who in the course of a certain death come to know more about their disease than their caretakers. These patients often challenge the medical hierarchy—as well as its morale—while they fight a disease with no vaccine in sight. The result is that the HIV/AIDS patient requires, in addition to considerable and costly pain-management practices, intensive palliative care from persons with a good understanding of AIDS, polypharmacy, and pain control.[25] Such work is extraordinarily demanding of everyone involved. It requires exceptional communication skills between patient, friends, family, nurses in particular,[26] and doctors, including clinicians and clergy. Each HIV/AIDS patient demands his or her own story. Each story must be told and to each there must be a witness. Each story, then, must belong to every other one until one day the disease is survived by the solidarity we have evinced with its sufferers.

Postscript

We have remarked on the effect of rendering embodied pain a fearful presence on the level of the body politic at the same time that it is absent from the cartography of pain management on the clinical level. We have seen how the two cartographies are mediated by the dominant metaphors of military and industrial management discourses that nevertheless cannot quite function without reference to the class, race, and colonialist parameters of HIV/AIDS. One might imagine that a personal phenomenology of HIV/AIDS pain would hardly have recourse to the constitutive metaphors of bureaucratized discourse. Yet this is the very feature of an extraordinary autobiography from a man (a woman's account might well employ another metaphorical principle) in his latter years with AIDS. Thus Emmanuel Dreuilhe rejects the death sentence etched into his body by externalizing HIV as an enemy, a foreign aggressor, destroying every pleasure of prewar life, demanding constant mobilization of ever-weakening resources to escape shameful capitulation:

My personal war began two years ago when I was mobilized by AIDS. All the pleasures of peacetime and my carefree life were suddenly banished, as if an orchestra had stopped playing to let the theater manager announce that war had just been declared, that Pearl Harbor had been bombed. Since then I have devoted myself exclusively to the war effort, because the futility of civilian life (my thirty-six years of good health) is absurd when survival itself has become the main imperative. Proust likened Germany and France to two organisms locked in conflict, and he identified with France in his stormy relationship with the treacherous Albertine, whose scheming he compared to German military strategy. AIDS is my Albertine, a frightful, intimate enemy, like a demon or familiar spirit. Since the moment we met, I've invested everything in war bonds for our Defense Department: hospitals and medical specialists. I might even hoist defiant flags over the already invaded organs of my body, which has become a battlefield like Paris in 1871, torn between the opposing forces of the Commune and the Prussians. On this same corporal survey map, I could also indicate the organs once believed lost to the enemy but retaken after bitter fighting, backed up by an artillery barrage of antiviral and sulfa drugs: chemical weapons in that trench warfare which has kept me pinned down for almost two years now. Soon eight seasons will have come and gone, without a sign of peace or victory on the horizon. I'm already a war casualty, disfigured by my wounds, but I must go on fighting, disabled as I am. What other struggle is so fierce that it rages even inside hospitals?[27]

Dreuilhe sees the enemy not only in the invading virus but in the public opinion that AIDS is incurable and fatal. In other words, his opponent is defeatism against which he adopts all sorts of personae, masks, guises to act out the resistance, the guerrilla counterattack that will win back his body—his eyes, his bowels—to defend his country, his language, and his life after years of cosmopolitan disavowal and homelessness. All around him his friends, and his lover, fall like those poor wretches who are killed in the opening rounds of a battle they never comprehend. In the meantime, this is a different war from the Great Wars inasmuch as the soldiers know they have no weapons and cannot even be sure of the officers in charge—especially if they are in the Black/Hispanic and intravenous-drug regiments. Moreover, although everyone is in it together, each one hopes to be the sole survivor:

Brothers-in-arms who curse their common lot, after all, each one of us dreams of leaving the platoon far behind, of being the sole survivor of a batallion cruelly devastated by the counter onslaught of pneumonia. That's why we stare so gravely at those mysterious X rays of our lungs, aerial views of our situation brought to us by the medical intelligence service.[28]

So the AIDS sufferer lives under constant threat of abandonment in the midst of a "dirty war" in which no one wants to see him come home. He is the perfect corpse, killing time until time kills him. Meanwhile, the war on AIDS falls into the hands of private companies and the free market in pharmaceuticals that leaves what it does not want to public charity, to a few doctors but many nurses, social workers, friends, and lovers all struggling to combat the AIDS patient's abandonment.

Dreuilhe himself found he could hold the enemy at bay as long as he kept his diary. In it he leaves a testament to a New Jerusalem of male lovers who refuse to curse their fate but resolve to wait it out until their tormentor tires of destroying them. It is hard to add words to such a testament. Dreuilhe reveals his own faults: his neofascism, his masculine, militarized defiance. Above all, he is aware that such honesty will not prevail after the war, anymore than after any crisis in which we mobilize our moralities. But that is the ever dark shadow of human suffering.

Notes

1. Peter Jaret, "Our Immune System: The Wars Within," *National Geographic* 169, no. 6 (June 1986): 708–9.

2. *The Source of aids: Readings from Scientific American Magazine* (New York: W. H. Freeman and Company, 1989), 44.

3. Ibid., 53.

4. Andrew Nikiforuk, "Why Forecasts Now Look Like Science Fiction," *The Toronto Star* (Sunday, October 6, 1991): B4.

5. Jaret, "Our Immune System," 729.

6. Ibid., 704–5.

7. *U.S. News and World Report* (January 12, 1987), as in *aids: Cultural Analysis and Cultural Criticism*, ed. Douglas Crimp (Cambridge: MIT Press, 1987), 41.

8. Special Issue, "What Science Knows about AIDS," *Scientific American* 259, no. 4 (October 1988): 39

9. Ibid., 84.

10. John O'Neill, "AIDS as a Globalizing Panic," *Theory. Culture and Society* 7 (1990): 329–42. I draw upon this essay to some extent in this section.

11. John O'Neill, *Plato's Cave: Desire, Power, and the Specular Functions of the Media* (Norwood, N.J.: Ablex Publishing Corporation, 1991).

12. Jaret, "Our Immune System," 704–5.

13. "What Science Knows about AIDS," 78, 80.

14. Panos Dossier, *aids and the Third World* (London: Panos Institute, 1988), 40.

15. John O'Neill, *Five Bodies: The Human Shape of Modern Society* (Ithaca: Cornell University Press, 1985).

16. Dianna Melrose, *Bitter Pills: Medicines and the Third World Poor* (Oxford: Oxfam, 1982). Gabriel Palmer, *The Politics of Breastfeeding* (London: Pandora. 1988).

17. Michael Youle et al., *aids Therapeutics in hiv Disease* (Edinburgh: Churchill Livingstone, 1988), 102–3.

18. Ruth Sims and Veronica A. Moss, *Terminal Care for People with aids* (London: Edward Arnold, 1991), 72-74 (table 13).

19. Gerald H. Friedland, "Clinical Care in the AIDS Epidemic," *Daedalus* (spring 1989): 59–84.

20. Charles L. Bosk and Joel E. Frader, "AIDS and Its Impact on Medical Work," *A Disease of Society: Cultural and Institutional Responses to aids*, ed. Dorothy Nelkin, David P. Willis, and Scott B. Parris (Cambridge: Cambridge University Press, 1991), 150–71.

21. O'Neill, *Five Bodies*.

22. Charles F. Farthing, et al., *Color Atlas of aids and hiv Disease* (Chicago: Year Book Medical Publishers,1988).

23. John F. Tuohey, *Caring for Persons with aids and Cancer: Ethical Reflections on Palliative Care for the Terminally Ill* (St. Louis: Catholic Health Association of the United States, 1988).

24. John J. Bonica, "Cancer Pain," in *R.H.V. Manual on Palliative/Hospice Care*, eds. Ina Ajemian and Balfour M. Mount (Salem, N.H.: Ayer and Company Publishers, 1982), 117.

25. Sims and Moss, *Terminal Care*, 64.

26. Tuohey, *Caring for Persons*; Renee C. Fox, Linda H. Aiken, and Carla M. Messikomer, "The Culture of Caring: AIDS and the Nursing Profession," in *A Disease of Society*, 119–49.

27. Emmanuel Dreuilhe, *Mortal Embrace: Living with aids*. Translated by Linda Coverdale (New York: Hill and Wang, 1988), 6-8.

28. Ibid., 24.

Michael Fernandes

it may be

```
it may be sex
it may be greed
it may be loneliness
it may be dependence
it may be possessiveness
it may be many more things
it may be suspicion
it may be fear
it may be competition
it may be depression
it may be tension
it may be anger
it may be organic
it may be special
it may be toxic
it may be MSG
it may be vascular
it may be alarming
it may be common
it may be stress
it may be contradiction
it may be demanding
it may be schedules
it may be emotional
it may be receiving
it may be illness
it may be constant
it may be pressure
it may be varying
it may be intense
it may be attacking
it may be distributed
it may be primary
it may be devoted
it may be involved
it may be described
it may be tight
it may be stiffness
it may be muscles
it may be dizziness
it may be light
it may be reported
it may be blood
it may be second
it may be migraine
it may be clustered
it may be affected.
it may be 10%
it may be lasting
it may be several
it may be characterized
it may be severe
it may be days
it may be throbbing
it may be on one
it may be accompanied
it may be nausea
it may be sensitive
it may be limited
it may be difficult
```

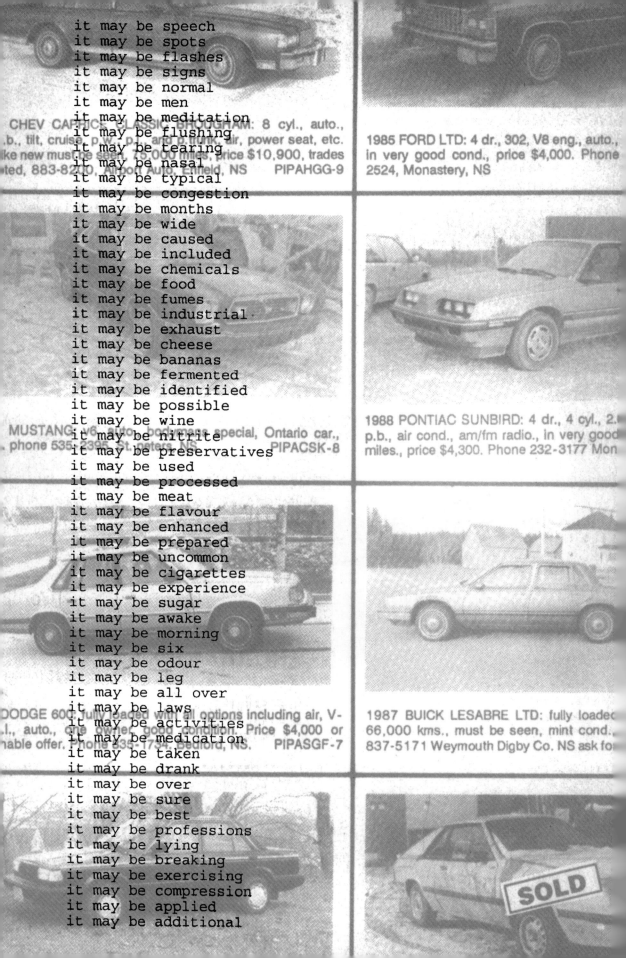

it may be speech
it may be spots
it may be flashes
it may be signs
it may be normal
it may be men
it may be meditation
it may be flushing
it may be tearing
it may be nasal
it may be typical
it may be congestion
it may be months
it may be wide
it may be caused
it may be included
it may be chemicals
it may be food
it may be fumes
it may be industrial
it may be exhaust
it may be cheese
it may be bananas
it may be fermented
it may be identified
it may be possible
it may be wine
it may be nitrite
it may be preservatives
it may be used
it may be processed
it may be meat
it may be flavour
it may be enhanced
it may be prepared
it may be uncommon
it may be cigarettes
it may be experience
it may be sugar
it may be awake
it may be morning
it may be six
it may be odour
it may be leg
it may be all over
it may be laws
it may be activities
it may be medication
it may be taken
it may be drank
it may be over
it may be sure
it may be best
it may be professions
it may be lying
it may be breaking
it may be exercising
it may be compression
it may be applied
it may be additional

3472 Laval #1 - Condo

6227-33 Alma - Duplex

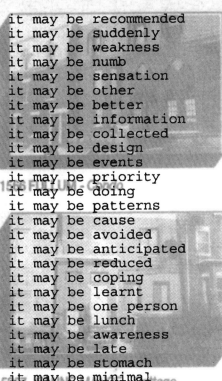

it may be recommended
it may be suddenly
it may be weakness
it may be numb
it may be sensation
it may be other
it may be better
it may be information
it may be collected
it may be design
it may be events
it may be priority
it may be doing
it may be patterns
it may be cause
it may be avoided
it may be anticipated
it may be reduced
it may be coping
it may be learnt
it may be one person
it may be lunch
it may be awareness
it may be late
it may be stomach
it may be minimal
it may be cautionary
it may be profile
it may be ulcers
it may be allergy
it may be people
it may be studies
it may be demonstration
it may be adverse
it may be dosage
it may be appearing
it may be label
it may be poison
it may be injury
it may be necessary
it may be punctuated
it may be touching

5290 JEANNE-MANCE - Cottage

4650 DE MENTANA - Commerce

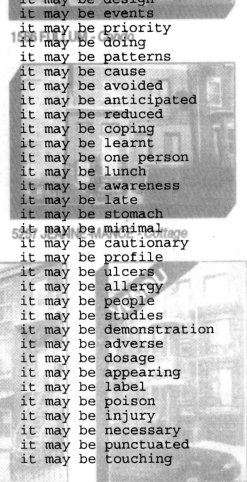

SPLANADE

3476 CARTIER
Condo

4267-75 PARTHENAIS
4-plex

6301-05 ST-VALLIER
Duplex

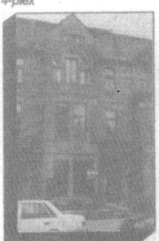

Isabelle Brabant

Reflections on Pain in Childbirth

PAIN IS at the heart of childbirth. Before I began accompanying women during their labor, I had a very dramatic image of it. During my years as a practicing midwife, one of the things that has most surprised me has been to see women simultaneously experiencing pain, joy, excitement, and contentment! I hadn't realized that pain and happiness could coexist.

Pain and Culture

Giving birth is a painful experience for the majority of women. All women think about it during their pregnancy. Every woman who is pregnant for the first time asks herself if and how she will be able to face this ordeal. Pain is a human experience that is both individual and cultural; the perception of it varies not only from one culture to another but also from one person to another, and from one labor to the next.

In so-called primitive cultures, where pain is part of daily life, the pain of childbirth is still real, but it is not considered abnormal. In Mediterranean cultures, one cries out to show pain. In other places, decorum demands that it remain carefully hidden. For the aboriginal peoples of Panama, birth is a shameful event, and labor is very long and painful. The Kahunas, on the other hand, transmit their pain to someone who "deserves" it, and labor is thus made easier!

We live in a society that is programmed to run from pain, a society that thinks anyone who endures a headache without taking an aspirin is masochistic, and that only allows athletes the right to endure pain and illness with dignity. Pain is part of the daily life of millions of North Americans, yet our collective response to it is the unlimited use of analgesics—a strictly chemical answer that is, at best, merely a short-term solution.

We learn from childhood how to react to pain. Some families rush to the baby at its first cry to comfort it from colic, new teeth, or its first scratches. Other families distract the baby with food to wipe away the hurt. Still others prefer to deny the pain, ignoring it. We all receive clear messages from these experiences that provide long-term models for our perception of pain. The stories about childbirth that we have heard as children and adolescents may amplify our fears; our minds often replace the missing details from these stories with an imaginary version far worse than reality.

Throughout our history, birthing pain has been seen as a punishment from God. "You will bring forth children in pain," He said to Eve as she was forced out of the Garden of Eden. But it has also been considered a curse, a deplorable condition to be controlled by assiduously rehearsed breathing or annulled completely with the use of drugs.

We approach childbirth filled with images and memories of pain. This emotional baggage has a direct effect on the way that we feel pain. These emotions often have a more powerful influence than either reason or knowledge when we are confronted with pain. There is no denying that pain exists. An exercise in personal reflection, like that proposed in this essay, however, can help illuminate the extent to which the *emotional* dimension of pain influences how we experience it. Research on pain has shown, to everyone's surprise, that childbirth can be categorized as even more painful than other chronic illnesses such as cancer.[1] Our culture has never differentiated between pain that signals a *pathological* condition or an internal disorder, and pain that accompanies an event like childbirth, where it is the *normal* expression of an extraordinary labor.

> *Experiencing pain.* We have all experienced pain, and most of us have
> been relieved of it. Understanding what has already comforted you will
> help you recognize your own reactions to pain. Do this exercise, either
> in writing or verbally, with someone close to you until you feel

comfortable with the events that you are remembering. Repeat the exercise for several different experiences, whether they are physical or psychological.

—Remember a very painful event.

—Try to remember as many details as possible.

—Where did this take place?

—When and how did the pain start?

—Who was around you?

—How did you show your pain?

—What was the reaction of those around you?

—How did you feel?

—What were your needs?

—Did you ask for help? How?

—Did you receive help? What form did it take?

—What finally comforted you?

It is absolutely essential to prepare realistically for the immense challenge that is labor and childbirth. Certain books and prenatal courses replace the word *pain* with euphemisms such as *discomfort* or *intensity* in a commendable attempt to alleviate women's fears. The unfortunate result is that a woman and her partner find themselves unprepared for the powerful experience of labor. They worry and wonder, with reason, if something serious is happening, because such intense pain is usually associated with a catastrophic event. With this degree of concern, it becomes practically impossible to relax and muster the self-confidence necessary for the birth.

Factors Related to the Perception of Pain during Childbirth

Pain always occurs within a context that influences our reaction to it. Among the conditions that increase our perception of pain are fear, mental stress, tension, fatigue, cold, hunger, loneliness, emotional upheaval, a strange environment, not knowing what is happening, and dread of the impending contractions.

Among the factors that reduce our perception of pain are relaxation, confidence, reliable information, continuous contact with familiar and friendly people, remaining active, rest and good nutrition, a comfortable environment, and focusing on the present, all while taking the contractions as they come.

Responding to Pain

Modifying some of these conditions does not eliminate the pain but greatly contributes to changing its intensity. Women and their companions have the capacity and the power to alter many of these elements. As a result, they are no longer victims but active participants—a change in attitude that, in itself, can alter the course of events.

Vocalization

Allowing oneself the freedom to be "noisy" during labor is an excellent example of how a particular response to pain is capable of transforming it. Women who express themselves vocally during their contractions often find them easier to abide. No one is obliged to moan, but those who feel the need and do so often find comfort in it and see it as an important means of expression. Vocalization helps the body produce its own remedy against pain, namely, endorphins. The production of endorphins is also facilitated by a darkened environment, minimal talking or whispering, and contact with water.

Touch

Touch can be an extraordinary way to help a woman during labor—especially if it is attentive, gentle, and sensitive to the rhythm of her contractions. "Put calmness into your hands," I often whisper to an emotional father who wants to help the mother by massaging her. When the sensations are very intense, women often prefer the warm, immobile presence of hands rather than a rubbing movement that can distract or intrude. Touch is a language that is enriched when explored by the two partners over the course of the entire pregnancy.

Visualization

Although less familiar as a technique, visualization is an effective way to facilitate labor and to induce relaxation. Visualize the cervix opening, the baby descending. Press your stomach against someone, and at the moment when the sensation is the strongest, "send" them part of the pain. Imagine a peaceful refuge between the contractions to regenerate yourself. These are all ways of becoming in harmony with the experience of labor.

Isabelle Brabant

Breathing

Breathing changes and adapts spontaneously throughout labor. When you keep your breathing open, calm, and fluid, each muscle in the body receives the oxygen that it needs in order to stay relaxed. Yoga and other approaches that are designed to make breathing more conscious, full, and invigorating are excellent preparation for labor—as well as for the other moments in life when a mother will need every resource to stay calm!

Movement

Unrestricted movement is essential! Walking, rocking, rotating the pelvis, or sitting, stretching, getting up and down when necessary are fundamental rights at all times and even more important when giving birth. Only very serious medical circumstances justify restricting them.

Rest

When we talk about pain in childbirth, we forget that most of the time in labor is spent without pain! The body has prepared for an enormous task, but it has also provided itself some respite: most contractions, for instance, last one minute, while the intervals last from two to five minutes. Each interval should be an infinite moment of rest and regeneration. When we give life, we also must feed and replenish ourselves with each breath, each shared glance, each word, and each gesture. Are you ready to take advantage of every peaceful moment?

Human Contact

Women in labor need human contact, warmth, and companionship. For example, it has been clearly demonstrated time and again that the continued presence of a midwife during labor diminishes the need to resort to pain killers. How many women will forever remember the tenderness of their nurse or midwife, and the loving presence of their partner during childbirth?

The Best Way to Prevent Pain Is to Enter into It

Talking to someone who was saying how extremely difficult and painful it must have been to have given birth to a 4,500 g baby, the mother replied, with a soft smile, "It's not the weight that hurts, it's the resistance!"

Every cell in our body contains genetically encoded information that tells it, from the first contact of sperm and egg, how to develop an embryo and ensure its survival and evolution. All this allows us to give birth to a baby nine months later. Each phase of labor is inscribed throughout the body. The pain acts as a sign and testament of the important work in progress—announcing the forthcoming birth, as well as the need for intimacy, assistance, and protection.

When a woman's entire being abandons itself to this process, childbirth is a painful but endurable experience. If she resists, regardless of how—whether in her body, emotions, or thoughts—the pain she feels will equal her resistance! Instead of facing a relaxed cervix that can stretch and allow the baby passage, each contraction will fight rigid, tense muscles that do not have enough oxygen and are unable to rid themselves of their toxins. The muscles therefore remain painful even between contractions, prohibiting the mother from resting, and rapidly driving her toward an impasse that only medication or a cesarean can release her from.

When pain is present in the body, the most common reaction is to close oneself upon it. But our resistance, fear, and the apprehension of suffering amplifies the pain. It's like clenching one's fist around a hot coal. The tighter we squeeze, the more it burns. . . . The objective of controlling pain, along with the idea that pain is our enemy, intensifies the suffering, it clenches the fist.[2]

In childbirth, pain doesn't signify danger or disease but the extraordinary, creative work of the body. This pain must be accepted if we want to complete the work. It is the pain of exertion and effort and, rather than resisting it, we must learn to say, "Yes, I want this to work. I want my body to open and allow my baby passage. I want to be one with her." We have the ability to change our initial resistance into acceptance and flexibility. This absolutely incredible process of learning during labor allows a woman to endure, with a relaxed and open attitude, contractions that made her tense only a few hours or minutes earlier.

Marie told me one day how she remembered one little sentence from one of our conversations during her pregnancy: "Love your pain." This juxtaposition seemed incomprehensible to her no matter how she thought about it. But it came back with full force during her labor and guided her. "I probably would never have had the idea of loving my pain if I hadn't spoken to you," she told me. "It's not obvious! It hurts and the first reaction is often to say no! But the more we say yes, the easier it becomes. Having a child is very much an experience of acceptance, and it starts with labor."

Choose pain. Accept it rather than be its victim. This can change everything.

Isabelle Brabant

Opposition in the Social Environment

Women must be able to respond spontaneously to the powerful experience of labor. This immense work requires flexibility and cannot be achieved within rigid boundaries, whether they are dictated by a particular technique, environment, or externally imposed fear. The obstetric practice is organized around goals other than facilitating women's power to bring forth life. It's up to us to reclaim this objective and realize its potential.

The conditions in which deliveries happen have a direct relationship to the way women experience pain. Each form of support described here meets resistance because of the way the medical system perceives the proper procedures for delivering a baby. Women are taught to be quiet because silence is associated with relaxation, moans with panic. The sounds women make during labor may strangely resemble the sounds emitted during lovemaking, which might explain some people's unease and their preference for women who quietly do their breathing!

Breathing has achieved a singular reputation as a supportive practice during childbirth. Techniques developed by Fernand Lamaze and others during the 1950s, and since modified, have popularized this way of experiencing labor. But they are mostly techniques of distraction that force women to follow a rigid model, despite the fact that childbirth requires constant flexibility and complete abandonment to the forces at work in their bodies.

While women are encouraged to walk during labor, the "pushing phase" is still characterized by immobility and uniformity of position, rather than by movement and the right to choose a posture that is most comfortable at a given moment.

The hospital structure does not always guarantee access to a trusted, friendly participant who can provide a human presence and professional reassurance to women in labor, even though it has been shown that this presence diminishes the necessity of medication. When will we relieve obstetrical nurses of their other tasks so that their first priority is to tend to the needs of the woman giving birth?

Anesthetics/Analgesics . . . Is It That Simple?

The use of analgesic and anesthetic medications during labor is not simply a medical problem or strictly a personal issue. Many factors are involved that we must address if we hope to minimize the use of medications. The idea is not to make women suffer, but to decrease the need for medication, which has dangerous side effects.

The pain of a normal labor does not usually surpass the capacities of the laboring woman. However, if there is a blockage—either physical or psychological—the intensity and length of the labor, as well as the necessary medical interventions, can require extraordinary stamina. It is true that there can be moments or circumstances where one may choose momentary relief from the pain. In this way, the discovery of the potential of analgesics was helpful to women, since it liberated them from religious taboos dictating that all women should suffer in childbirth.

Access to anesthesia has gone rapidly from use in exceptional circumstances to generalized, widespread use. In Quebec, for instance, 85 percent of women are subjected to some form of anesthetic during their labor. In certain hospitals, the rate of epidurals is more than 80 percent, which indicates more than exceptional use. If an epidural is not given, the use of analgesics is very frequent. As a result, medication has replaced the touch and human presence that have always accompanied women during labor. This absence is strongly felt, and as a consequence women ask themselves, "Why suffer if I can avoid it?"

This unfortunate substitution occurs in an environment that has profoundly disrupted the process of childbirth: among other things, it inhibits the body's natural responses to pain. In such an inhospitable and unfavorable context, North American obstetrics is incapable of lowering its rate of interventions, a rate that has been judged unacceptable by the World Health Organization: 19 percent of all mothers have a cesarean section; 18 percent have mechanical extractions (forceps, etc.); 85 percent have to be anesthetized in one way or another; 70 percent undergo an episiotomy (cutting the vulva).

It is very tempting to avoid or control pain by using modern techniques such as pharmaceuticals and surgery. Both are useful in facilitating a birth that would otherwise put the life or the physical or psychic health of the mother and/or her baby in danger. These techniques are undesirable when they become direct substitutes for the birthing woman's own resources, or a replacement for human support and companionship during labor.

The ultimate question is one of choice, which must not be merely a choice between different available analgesics, anesthesia, or sedatives. A woman in labor must have the power to choose between several forms of support: that does not pare down the time or human contact given her; that offers real assistance and confidence; that is afraid of neither her pain nor her cries; that yields to her wishes and continues to assist her if and when she consciously decides to be aided by medical intervention. Only when such support is available to everyone will

Isabelle Brabant

unmedicated childbirth be a viable and constructive choice—a choice that reinstates a laboring woman's primary role of power and responsibility. Don't touch her pain: she's dealing with it!

Translated by Wendy Hadd with Kim Sawchuk

Notes

This essay was excerpted and translated from *Une naissance heureuse* (Montreal: Les Éditions Saint-Martin, 1991); reprinted with permission of Éditions Saint-Martin.

1. Ronald Melzack and Patrick Wall, eds., *Le défi de la douleur* (Montréal: Chenelière and Stanké, 1982).

2. Stephen Levine, *Who Dies: An Investigation into Conscious Living and Conscious Dying* (New York: Anchor Books, 1982).

Millie Chen

Demon Girl and Hungry Ghost

A DISTURBANCE of my body that surfaces onto my outer skin, the tale of the demon girl and the hungry ghost unravels on the sole of my foot. The demon girl and the hungry ghost both originate from the spirit world but reside in tangible bodies. In fact, their somatic existence is the locus of their stories. The demon girl is an improvised appropriation from a gothic Chinese ghost story. In my version, she has an extendable tongue, swollen belly, and a demure, maidenly carriage that obscures the fact that she eats human organs. The hungry ghost comes from a twelfth-century Japanese scroll. The hungry ghost is burdened with a cavernous stomach and a constricted throat, condemned to eternal, unrelenting hunger. These two characters are the manifestations of religious, political, and social beliefs of their times concerning the consequences of karma. They are chained to an existence that revolves around mundane bodily functions and incessant bodily cravings; they are at the mercy of their bodies. The demon girl and the hungry ghost are consumers: what they consume constitutes our fears and phobias in the form of lost vital body parts and unwanted bodily wastes (the hungry ghost eats feces, saliva, vomit, etc.). The swell of the demon girl's belly (which signifies *full*) is juxtaposed with the swell of the hungry ghost's belly (which signifies *void/lack/ noxiously* full). Her tongue tip holds a flaming offering that could also be a flaming theft, extracted from the inside of the hungry ghost. She heals and steals.

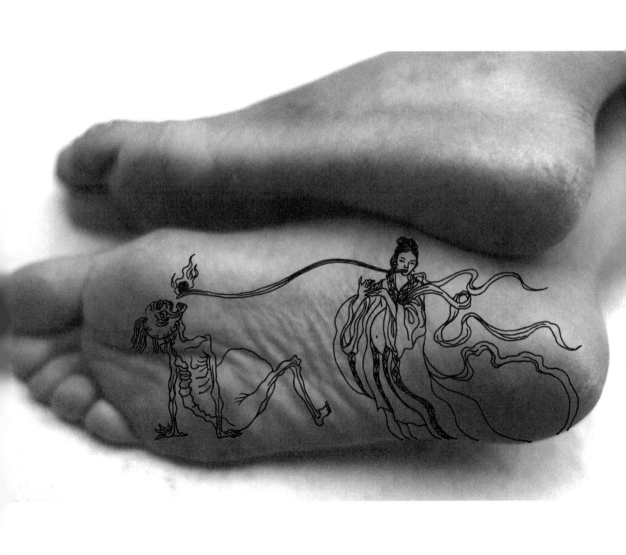

Gerard Päs

Dream Memory of the Brace / Red-Blue Wheelchair

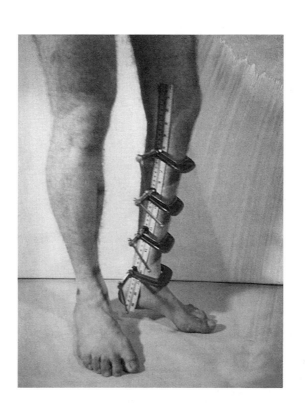

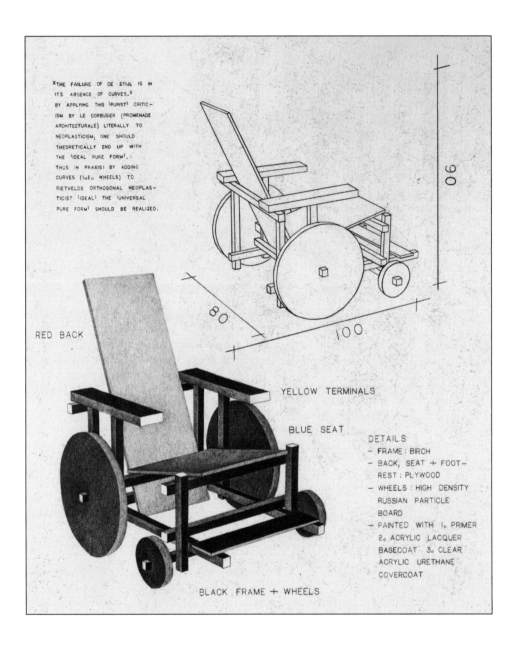

«THE FAILURE OF DE STIJL IS IN
ITS ABSENCE OF CURVES.»
BY APPLYING THIS (PURIST) CRITIC-
ISM BY LE CORBUSIER (PROMENADE
ARCHITECTURALE) LITERALLY TO
NEOPLASTICISM, ONE SHOULD
THEORETICALLY END UP WITH
THE (IDEAL PURE FORM).
THUS IN PRAXIS: BY ADDING
CURVES (i_oE_o WHEELS) TO
RIETVELDS ORTHOGONAL NEOPLAS-
TICIST (IDEAL) THE (UNIVERSAL
PURE FORM) SHOULD BE REALIZED.

90

80

100

RED BACK

YELLOW TERMINALS

BLUE SEAT

DETAILS
- FRAME: BIRCH
- BACK, SEAT + FOOT-
  REST: PLYWOOD
- WHEELS: HIGH DENSITY
  RUSSIAN PARTICLE
  BOARD
- PAINTED WITH 1_o PRIMER
  2_o ACRYLIC LACQUER
  BASECOAT 3_o CLEAR
  ACRYLIC URETHANE
  COVERCOAT

BLACK FRAME + WHEELS

"Mothers cannot get sick!"

"When I have a cold, it settles in my head...I have this feeling that I just can't make it through the day.

Well, mothers can't afford to do this. So, I take a couple of Excedrin®... **2**

Scream and Yell

and then I can go on about my work."*

Cathy Sisler

backwards

I HAVE a big broad back. I've always considered it big for a woman. It measures about eighteen inches across. Is that big? Is that big for a woman? If it is big for a woman, that means it's ugly. If it is big, for a woman that means it's ugly. I used to think it was big and ugly. My back was big and broad and strong, like a man's back. People wouldn't consider me without first considering my size. I was a girl, but I also felt big, like a man. I have believed these things on and off for a long time now, so they're part of me. They're part of my image of myself. My mother would say I have my father's back. I never liked her saying that. Once she told me that my father's back was so hard that she could have hit it with a hammer and he wouldn't have noticed. Nobody would dare hit my father over the back with a hammer. He would have killed you. Most of the time he turned his back to me. It was preferable to being face to face with him. I didn't want to be like my father because, truthfully, we never got along. But I knew I had inherited many of his bodily features. I was big like my father, and there was absolutely nothing I

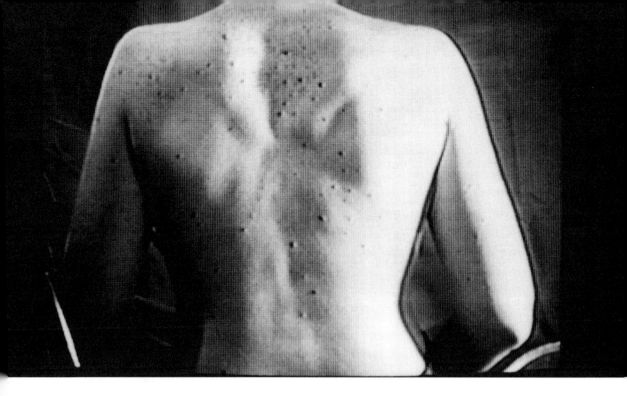

could do about it. I have tried to change my body many many many times through-out my life. One summer, when I was twenty, I lost seventy pounds in approximately ten weeks. I began to call myself by a different name and I moved to a different city. I got a waitress job, though I lost it soon after. I was losing my balance a lot when walking. I had also become very religious. I thought that possibly I could be Christ, the second coming, because I thought this time he should be a woman. It was during this time that I met my first and only male lover. I say *my only* because he was the only one I ever loved, much. He had spent most of his life, since the age of fifteen, in a mental hospital. He did have some very complex fantasies, but without them his life would have been unbearable. I started to suspect I wasn't Christ because I couldn't help his pain. I thought I understood him but I really had no conception of his inside hell. We lived together on and off for about five years, then we lost contact. The last time I saw him he was in the hospital. His throat and stomach were stitched back together after he swallowed glass. A devil had threatened him that if he didn't swallow the glass it would kill his sister. So he swallowed the glass. His sister, who had taken him in, found him in his room and had to rush him to the hospital. They both came from the same family.

What if we could feel each other's pain?
I can't see the glass you've swallowed. You can't see the glass I've swallowed.
I am becoming transparent. Now I am opaque.
You can turn me off now.

Cathy Busby

We Need to Scream to Talk:

An Interview with

Kecia Larkin

CB: You grew up in Alert Bay. Could you talk about the town and what it was like to live there?[1]

KL: Alert Bay is a very small town off the northwest coast of Alert Bay, British Columbia. It's an isolated island about seven miles around whose main industry is fishing. The only way that you can get there is by floatplane or by ferry, and it's about six hours from Victoria. Alert Bay is like most Native communities across Canada or North America in that it has lots of family, drug, and alcohol problems.

Growing up in Alert Bay was nice in that you learned about community and you learned about your families and your culture. But, on the negative side, there were a lot of things in our families that weren't talked about in the open. In my family there was alcoholism, drug abuse, physical abuse, and emotional abuse. And with some of the members of my family there was sexual abuse. This type of thing happened to most people in my community. We have about an 80 to 90 percent rate of sexual abuse, and probably about the same in terms of alcoholism, as well as problems with cocaine and intravenous drugs. It all affects you at some level. When you live in a small town it's easy to get bored. You play sports—soccer, floor hockey, or basketball—and that's about it. For a lot of people it's just boredom. Some people haven't lived anywhere else, so going somewhere else isn't really a choice. A lot of people do leave and go to the city, Vancouver or Victoria.

CB: Do you think the sexual abuse comes out of small-town boredom?

KL: No, I don't think that people get bored and just decide to start molesting kids, or raping or sodomizing children, or each other, for that matter. I think it stems from somewhere in our history. There are generations of victims of oppression, and generations of people who have had these kinds of behaviors inflicted on them. In a sense, people are like children, and they act out what they see and what's happened to them.

Alert Bay never existed before the missionaries came to our area. We lived in the outlying communities. We were supposedly some of the first contacts that white people had when they came on their exploratory trips. Later, they took the children from their families and brought them to Alert Bay and set up a residential school there. Families wanted to be with their children, so they all moved to Alert Bay. So many people in Alert Bay don't really belong there—they're all from different communities that don't exist anymore.

CB: It's now fairly well known that physical and sexual abuse occurred in the residential schools.

KL: Yes, that's a large part of it. It's what we are still dealing with here, and I just happen to be a product. We're talking probably three or four generations now, although these are things that aren't talked about. These things weren't dealt with because the easiest way to oppress people was to keep them silent. So, in a sense, what I'm trying to do now is to get out there and start talking, to start saying what I see and what I feel. I know there's a lot of people suffering who still aren't able to talk about those things and are in real deep denial about what happened in those schools.

CB: In the article [in *Fuse* magazine] you talked about alcoholism in your family and sexual abuse as part of the experience of growing up and, later, related experiences in the sex trade in Vancouver.[2] And now we're on to denial. Do you see denial as a factor in the spread of HIV in Native communities?

KL: Well, there are different issues. When I was growing up, the first thing that started happening in our community was Alcoholics Anonymous. People started sobering up and coming out of their denial of being alcoholics. And, as we went on further down the road, we started talking about sexual abuse; at the time, I was about fifteen or fourteen years old. And then we started talking about family violence and then other addictions.

Now we're into HIV and AIDS, which is very new. People are persuaded by the media and what they see and read in the papers, rather than getting the education and the facts from the right sources. So people are still pretending that these things don't happen to them or can't happen to them. I even know of families who have somebody dying of AIDS, and they say that they've got cancer or some other illness. People still don't see it, but it is happening to Native people at a very high rate. People in our communities have had to leave because they're homosexual. It's a matter of people not being willing to accept differences or different lifestyles. In a lot of ways people have just been brainwashed with a lot of these issues, like homophobia.

Many communities have no idea how to cope with somebody who has HIV or AIDS. Some of my HIV-positive friends have had difficult experiences trying to go home. They've been bribed with money by the chiefs of their councils, or they've been threatened. They've been isolated and alienated. There's a lot of fear associated with AIDS and HIV.

CB: What made it safe enough for you to go back to your family?

KL: For me, my mother was the safest person—although in many ways she wasn't able to protect me from a lot of these experiences. But at this point I have to understand that it comes from the way that she grew up and the parenting skills she got, and the parenting skills that she's seen.

CB: So she supported you coming back?

KL: Yeah, she did. You have to understand that my family lived in the city when I came back, not in Alert Bay, so I didn't have to deal with a small town where everybody knows you and what you've done, what's wrong with you, and who you are. I had to deal with that on a level that was safe for me, in the sense that I live in the city and I go to Alert Bay when I want to and when I feel it's safe enough to go home. I have been back to Alert Bay many times, and people have been very supportive, people who knew me while I was growing up and still see me as that person rather than this person with this disease. So there has been a very positive reaction from my family, though there are still some areas that are hard to deal with. If it wasn't safe, I wouldn't have come back to my mother in Victoria. I needed my mother and she needed me just as much, so it seemed, emotionally, the best thing for me to do at the time.

CB: When did you first leave home?

KL: I was fifteen. My mother was there with my three younger siblings—my two younger sisters and my younger brother—and there had been some things in the family that happened. It was after those experiences and after the crisis of sexual abuse in my community that she decided to leave Alert Bay. She left as a single parent, went to Victoria with her family, just sort of continued living, and that's where we are now.

CB: And now you have a child. I wonder if you can talk about your decision to have a child, particularly the kinds of attitudes you come across, speaking and standing up for yourself as an HIV-positive mother. Do you think that there is a taboo around talking about HIV-positive families?

KL: Oh, there's a big taboo. It's one that I don't even think people are ready to deal with at this point. They have a hard time with it. People know who I am in the smaller communities, so when I decided to have my baby it was a really hard decision in itself because the pregnancy was unplanned. When I found out that I was pregnant, I had a very short time to decide if I was going to terminate the pregnancy. When I did decide to go through with the pregnancy, many people were supportive but a lot of people were very uptight about the whole issue. It was distressing because there were people who didn't want me to speak because of the mixed messages that I would be giving to people. I'm an HIV-positive person who has gotten pregnant; I possibly had unsafe sex, and that's what people were so uptight about.

CB: And what was your response to that?

KL: Well, the people that were talking and reacting this way knew nothing about me, or who I was, and I had no idea who they were. So it was really kind of hard to respond. But when I would go out and talk, I really clarified a lot of things. I wasn't there to apologize or explain why or how I got pregnant. I was there to say this is what's going on in my life, and it's a choice that I've made and a choice that I have to accept responsibility for, whether I like it or not, whatever the outcome may be. The biggest issue was the mixed messages. A woman having a child, I think, is not unusual. The way that I put it was that if I was a pregnant woman who had found out that she was HIV-positive *after* she got pregnant, people would treat me as a victim. But I'm an HIV-positive woman who knew she was HIV-positive when she decided to have a child, and because of that I've become a moral derelict or something.

CB: Was the well-being of the child put to you as a concern as well?

KL: Oh yeah, people just went nuts. I mean, if they had gotten the chance they would have laid the boots to me. I had no right to make that decision, I had no right to have a child. I'm saying that it comes from the lack of education around HIV and pregnancy. A lot of people still believe that every woman who's HIV-positive automatically infects the child; in fact, the odds are in the favor of the baby. You know, there's one in four women who infect their children, which works out to be 70 to 80 percent of the children who are healthy and normal and go on to live a good life. All of those things were voices around me having a baby and me giving that baby AIDS. People really believed that I had no right to make that choice; I had no right to be a mother; I had no right to have a family.

CB: Do you think that was a part of a punishment mentality, like, "You're bad for having HIV"?

KL: Exactly. I was a bad person.

CB: Despite the statistics . . .

KL: Well, people didn't know the statistics. When you say the baby has a 70 to 80 percent chance of being healthy, they just say, like, "Oh really? I didn't know that." When they actually see you and the child, they take on a whole different attitude. Of course, there are the ones who still stick to their guns and say that I had no right to make that decision. And they are the ones who would be more than happy to come up and say, "See, I told you so," if that child was sick. They wouldn't pull any bones about saying, "Serves you right."

But I've had more of a positive than a negative response. There are lots of women out there who make this choice. There are lots of families who have children, and there are many people who decide that they don't want to take that chance. So it's a very individual and personal thing.

People still don't seem to understand that they can't judge people unless they've been through that experience themselves. I think that's one of the biggest problems with this HIV and AIDS situation. There are many people who are very caring and compassionate, but there are others who really believe that it's a punishment: "You deserve to have it. You don't deserve to have any kind of a normal life after being diagnosed with HIV or AIDS." And that has a real big effect on where we're headed on this issue. One of the biggest things that I've really tried to portray to people is that I'm making choices and they are mine and I have the right to those choices and I have a right to my life, and that's all I can do.

CB: Why did you decide to talk about your life publicly?

KL: July of 1990 was the first time that I ever spoke to my family about HIV and AIDS. At first I told my mother and I didn't want anybody else to know, because I was very ashamed and scared, and I guess I was very afraid of the judgments, about my lifestyle: I was a junkie and a streetperson. My mother couldn't really hold the knowledge that I was HIV-positive for long, so I decided after quite a while that it was time to talk to other members of my family about it. What came out was that I needed to talk about why I was very afraid for the people that weren't hearing about it or talking about it. When I left home, they didn't have any AIDS education in school, or anything in place for people who were coming home. They had nothing. There was a lot of pain in my family because of me, and when I talked to my family about it, I said, "I wish there was a way to get out there to tell people about this, that it can happen, and it is happening to us."

There was a woman who was very interested in what I was talking about, and she was also a friend, or connected to my family somehow, and she worked in the ministry [BC Ministry of Health]. She asked if I would be interested in going around with this doctor she knew of who was talking about AIDS. She thought that it would probably be very good for the communities, hearing from somebody who was HIV-positive, because it would drive the message home. I guess I became this sort of scare tactic in the sense that I was putting a face to it. So I started traveling with this doctor, and it just continued. I was told that I was the first Native woman to come forward in Canada. I was this young, straight, Native girl who represented a lot of our communities, and people wanted to hear about it and wanted to see it. That's how it started because word travels around. I was on the news, so people started hearing me.

CB: What kind of places do you speak at?

KL: I speak mostly on reserves. I have been to many other places; I speak at a lot of conferences, in a lot of forums. I've been to the United States; I've been across Canada—mostly small communities that are isolated or have just begun to do AIDS education. They try and get somebody who is HIV-positive to come in and talk about their experience with HIV and AIDS. So in that sense it's been really useful to the communities because they get to see somebody with this disease. Usually they're quite surprised because I look like everybody else. There's a lot of barrier breaking to do, but a lot of barriers have come down because of the work done by these people who are dedicated to getting the messages out there.

CB: Both about prevention, but also about not being afraid of AIDS when it comes home?

KL: Yeah, AIDS educators have been working on the prevention part for quite a while now, and that's wearing out its welcome because people know it and there's only so much you can take in.

CB: So your work is shifting?

KL: Yeah, what needs to be worked on now is the support. They have nothing in place in a lot of communities. Some communities that I've been to have had a few deaths, and a lot of people have family members who are HIV-positive, but they have no support. They're isolated and they're alone in this situation. If you go to Vancouver or Toronto or even Victoria, you can go to AIDS resource centers and have a place where people can connect. But when you're up north or you're out of the city, there's nothing.

An Interview with Kecia Larkin

CB: You said before [in the *Fuse* article] that we need to "yell and scream," rather than sit and suffer in silence. Who would you like to speak to?

KL: I like yelling and screaming to anyone who will listen or anyone who's not listening. It's just that there's so many different issues in that yelling and screaming, and we're not just talking about AIDS and HIV. We're talking about racism; we're talking about oppression; we're talking about all kinds of things . . .

CB: So are there particular groups of people, particular government bodies, particular kinds of people that you are targeting? When I think of *yell and scream*, I think of anger and force behind the speaking.

KL: In some of these conferences and things that I've been to, people often do a lot more pencil pushing and lip service than anything useful. So that's where I'd like to focus that energy. I guess it covers a lot of people in that sense. I'd also like people in the communities to listen a little more and try and hear what we're saying because there are a lot of people going home and wanting to be with their families.

CB: What could be the results of this? Are home and community better places for people to be when they're sick?

KL: I'd like to see people going back with their families. I'd like to see families healing together. I'd like to see communities accepting people back. So I don't really want people to go out of their communities to have to get the love and compassion and caring they need. They need to have someplace to go. They need to have people there to give them hugs and give them love and take care of them, but also empower them to take care of themselves. You have to rock a lot of boats in order to get what you want, where people start hearing. And I guess it's sort of shaking them out of their denial.

CB: So you think that speaking, your speaking, can help to shake them out of their denial?

KL: I'm hoping it will. I'm hoping that when they see somebody in my shoes and hear about my stories, they'll listen a little harder and they'll hear a little bit more. It's going to take a lot for them to change their behaviors, and that's a whole other issue that needs to be dealt with. But at least they're listening a little more, so I guess that's the payoff.

CB: When we're talking, I feel like you're a really deeply feeling person, like you really feel for other people and really feel for communities, specifically Native communities. And so my question is, how have you moved? What's enabled you to move from being someone who was in denial of feelings and doing everything you could do not to feel, to being a feeling person?

KL: I think a lot about pain. In respect to this disease, that's where all this comes

Cathy Busby

from. I had to decide at some point if I was just going to lie down and die spiritually and emotionally and just walk around like a shell, or if I was going to try and change, to try and live. It's a constant, never-ending thing, learning how to live. This disease woke me up in lots of ways. I owe a lot of it to my child, too, because up until I was pregnant with her I was still taking drugs or whatever, and she's come along and helped us to make a lot of positive changes in our lives. We have something. I guess when I first found out I was infected, I didn't think there was anything to live for. My family was there, so that helped me along a little bit. I had a person in my life who loved me and cared for me unconditionally. And then a few years later when I had the baby, there was something more. I think that I realized for myself, for my own health, that I had to stop doing this to my body. Otherwise, I would die a lot quicker, just because of a lot of things that have been found out about taking care of yourself if you have a life-threatening illness. So in that respect, I guess the disease and the love from other people helped me along. I've had a lot of support from people.

The work that I've been doing has helped, too, because there's been a lot of empowering and things that have come out of that. I know people really have a lot of feelings in their heart, and I guess trusting them started me trying to be a little happier and a little healthier and a little stronger than I was before. I knew that if I stayed in that lifestyle, there was no way that I'd survive very long. You get to the point where you hurt too much. You hurt so much that you're either going to change or you're just going to stay in that constant state of pain. I didn't really want to stay there because I knew that if I wanted to get off the drugs, I had to change my emotional set of behaviors and the way that I was feeling inside. So I had to start looking at some of the problems that were affecting me. I'm not taking life too seriously, though. You don't have a lot of time here, so you just got to do what you can while you can.

CB: Is there anything else you want to say, anything else that's come to mind for you while we've been talking that hasn't come out in specific questions?

KL: I think I just want to encourage myself and other people to keep going and to stay strong and feel whatever they're feeling, and to yell and scream about it. Just keep going. Something I've learned in my life is that often you become very sedate and get to a point where it seems like you're always going against the grain. When you stop yelling or you stop talking, that's when you stop living. That's what I've been trying to practice and trying to learn and trying to keep in my heart.

Notes

1. This telephone interview took place on November 1, 1993. In the five years since this interview, Kecia Larkin has stopped talking about her life publicly. She thinks responsibility for AIDS education should be shared with those who are not living with HIV. She went back to school to train as a lifeskills coach and now works as a consultant.

2. Kecia Larkin, "We Need to Yell and Scream to Talk," *Fuse* 15, no. 5 (summer 1992): 31–32.

Fred Wilson

About Face II

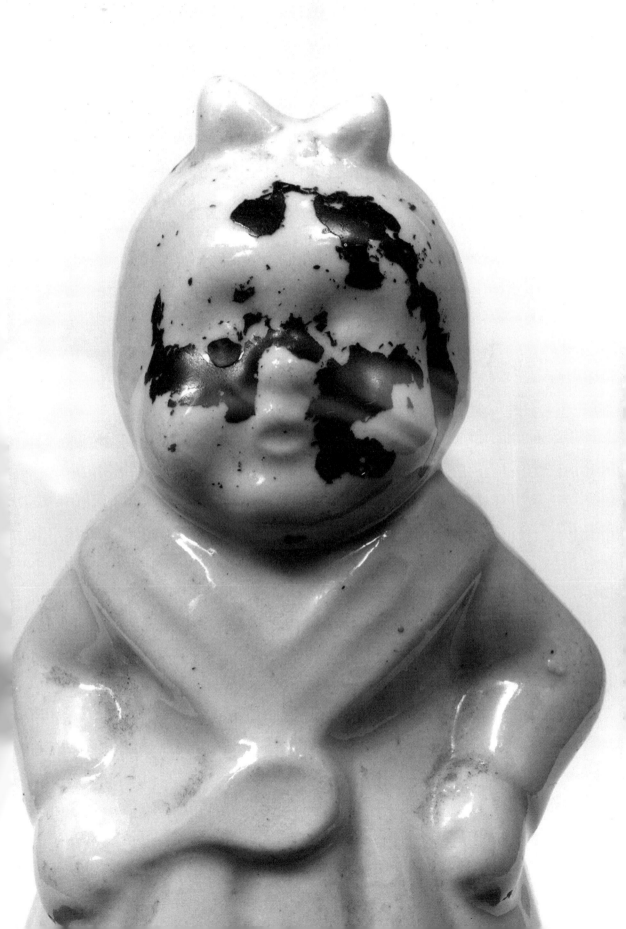

Cathy Busby

The Lure of Roseanne's Autopathography and Survivor Identity

IN HER BOOK *My Lives*, television star Roseanne dis-closes that she was sexually abused as a child, that she has never recovered from it, and that her suffering is severe and enduring.[1] This story of pain and survival contrasts with the themes of her earlier book *Roseanne: My Life as a Woman*, in which she documents her up-ward mobility out of her working-class origins through to television stardom.[2] This first book hovered for four months on the best-seller list of the *New York Times*, but in it Roseanne does not mention that she is a sur-vivor of child sexual abuse. It tells a funny, upbeat, and caustic story of Roseanne's life. In *My Lives*, the story of survival displaces the story of her success. As the title indicates, she is referring to her many identities, including wife, mother, comedian, big-bodied, loud-mouthed television star; other lives or incarnations; and her multiple personalities or lives, which she claims she invented to protect herself from the pain of the abuse she experienced as a child. This multiplicity de-scribes her career and emotional struggles, attributing depression, substance abuse, and eating disorders to a traumatic childhood.

In the five years between the pub-lication of these two books, a social space and market was created for the reception of stories of sexual abuse and recovery. In this space, feminism, therapy, and the self-help genre intersect. The proliferation of stories of pain and suffering is a marketer's dream and a reader's relief, and these books are often highly publicized best-sellers. In my definition of *autopathographies*, written disclosures of suffering, recovery, or healing involve neither a tragic nor a happy ending. Autopathographies document one individual's ongoing emotional struggle, not necessarily in a linear manner. These stories are found, for example, in Gloria Steinem's *Revolution from Within*, Kitty Dukakis's *Now You Know*, and Dennis Rodman's *Bad as I Wanna Be*. [3]

Roseanne's autopathography *My Lives* embodies the social and cultural tensions in public debates around the veracity of memories of child sexual abuse and the degree of damage that sexual abuse causes. In it she describes her recovery process and speaks as a survivor. She writes convincingly about her suffering, its relationship to sexual abuse, and her coping strategies: "I survived my childhood by birthing many separate identities to stand in for one another in times of great stress and fear" (240).

The autopathography is a way of thinking about a discursive form, enabling a crossing of categorical boundaries: autobiography (celebrity and otherwise), the testimonial, and survivor stories. While David Remnick defined *autopathography* as desperate authenticity in discussing gender-bending basketball star Dennis Rodman's *Bad as I Wanna Be*, the use of autopathography as an analytic tool enables the spotting of a regularity within the discourse of emotional suffering and recovery.[4] Autopathographies document struggles with emotional problems over a lifetime and chronicle the writer's never-ending recovery process, distinguishing them from self-help books, which are always about achieving self-improvement. Take, for example, the self-help book *The Courage to Heal: A Guide for Women Survivors of Child Sexual Abuse* by Ellen Bass and Laura Davis.[5] This best-selling manual has defined survivor identity and set the tone for subsequent courses in healing, requiring the reader to remember and tell her story of abuse and survival, defining a procedure for the reader to follow in order to come to terms with what she lost by being sexually abused. Influenced by the feminist practice of working collectively toward accepting and loving oneself as a first step to improving social conditions, this book encourages women who have been sexually abused to tell their stories and identify themselves as survivors rather than victims (59). Survivors' stories clarify that home can be a dangerous place. They highlight the vulnerability of children, particularly girls, in the family and voice the extensiveness of the pain caused by sexual abuse. This finger-pointing has simultaneously brought perpetrators to task and resulted in widespread uncertainty as to the believability of memories of abuse, and denial and doubt of survivor stories from the past and related present pain.

In both her mass-market books, Roseanne credits feminism and therapy for her survival and success and validates women who tell their stories. What she adds to survivor discourse is that the healing process may exceed the limits of descriptions, disclosures, and processes found in a self-help book such as the *The Courage to Heal*, and, further, that you may not heal. In the midst of debates over the pain of the survivor and whether or not to believe her, *My Lives* lends credibility to the discussion of survivor identities, linking it to mass-market self-help literature.

Survivor Identity in *My Lives* and *The Courage to Heal*

While survivor identity is used to specifically define those who have survived child sexual abuse, its broader application—referring to the journey from despair through emotional transformation—allows a pattern of media representation to emerge. The autopathography is the dominant narrative form through which survivor identity is described. It tells us much more about mediations of emotional experiences and transformations than a story that simply makes desperation authentic. It documents the emotional climate of a cultural moment and enables the dissemination of a series of related narratives in a form that has much more room than the self-help book for contradiction, inconsistency, and inconclusiveness. Autopathography is found in both celebrity autobiographies and recovery books. The form draws on Alcoholics Anonymous, psychotherapy, and feminist consciousness-raising practices. Since the publication of *Alcoholics Anonymous* in 1935, self-help books have been advising readers step by step on how to transform themselves emotionally and recover. Dominant themes have emerged: self-help books of the 1960s and '70s catered to the anxieties of the New Woman, while those of the 1980s and '90s have offered stress and burnout remedies as a way to counter the effects of overwork, unemployment, and economic insecurity. They are one recovery aid the consumer can use to become more self-aware and to make behavioral and attitudinal changes, ultimately relieving emotional pain and creating survivor identity.

The Courage to Heal is the most influential book available on the subject and is key in the genre. The 1994 revised and updated third edition is a bulky 604 pages with a layout dividing the chapters into subsections in double-column page format. It resembles a textbook, a user-friendly manual, offering a pragmatic course in healing to the female reader, with a collection of testimonials to help her identify herself as part of a community of survivors. In this way, it substantiates and validates survivor identity. According to coauthor Ellen Bass, the naming

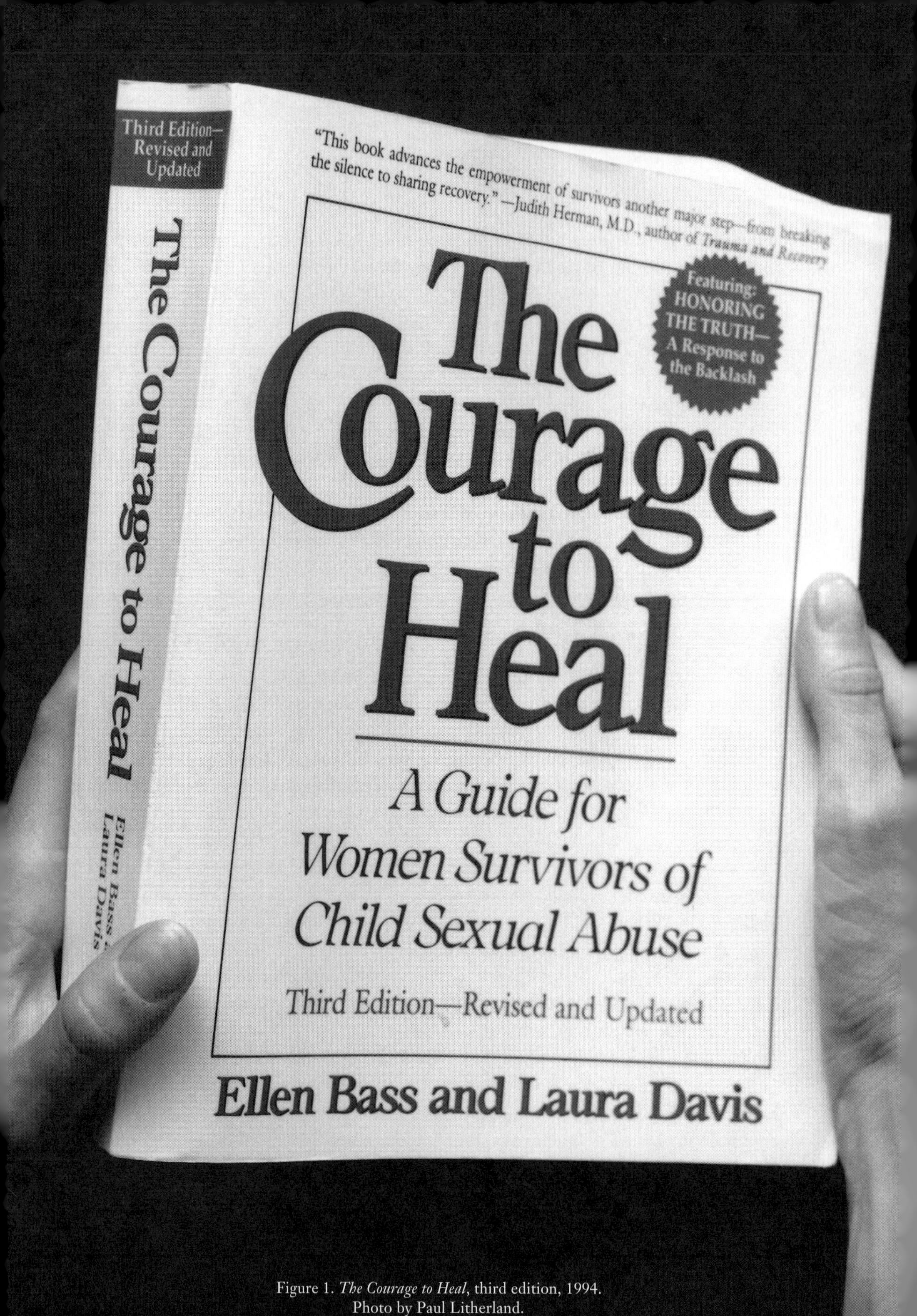

Figure 1. *The Courage to Heal*, third edition, 1994.
Photo by Paul Litherland.

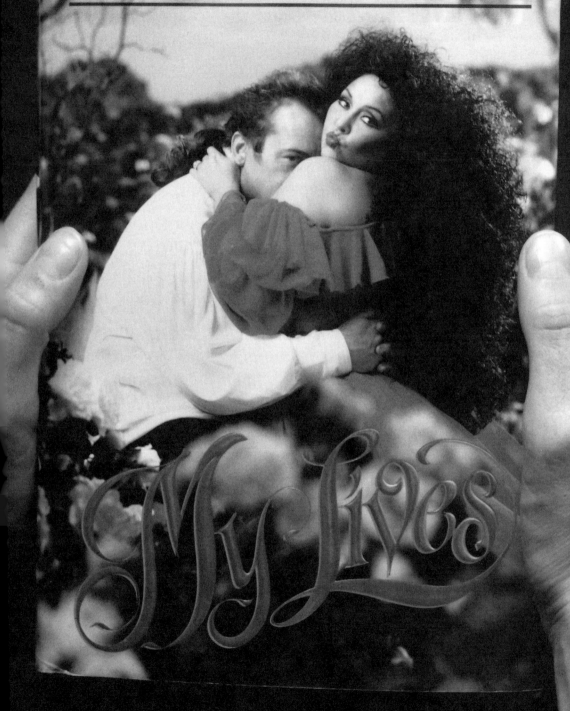

Figure 2. *My Lives*, 1994. Photo by Paul Litherland.

of the "survivor" of child sexual abuse emerged in 1974 in women's writing work-shops, designed to enable recovery. Since then, it has been claimed by women re-covering from incest and other sexual violence. Along with this naming of a specific abuse came the recognition that survivors are in pain and that in order to relieve it they must go through a healing process and construct themselves within a survivor identity. The chapter titles in the book name the stages in this process: "Recogniz-ing the Damage," "Anger—The Backbone of Healing," "Believing It Happened," "Breaking Silence," and "Trusting Yourself." Each chapter is flagged with a quote, usually from a survivor. The chapter "Remembering," for example, is followed by "I've looked the memories in the face and smelled their breath. They can't hurt me anymore." The reader is drawn into a community of survivors, in the midst of a dis-cussion. Throughout the book, the authors assert that the healing process cannot be accomplished alone—talking to others is essential. The survivor can intention-ally change her life, but she must first become aware of what she wants to change and examine why she needed that behavior: "Deciding to heal, making your own growth and recovery a priority, sets in motion a healing force that will bring to your life a richness and depth you never dreamed possible"(77). The book advises that the survivor must have compassion for what she's done in the past, even if she didn't make the best choices, and she must realize that change often reveals unmet needs. Then she must work at finding new ways to meet her needs. For all of this she needs the support of people who can encourage her:

And then I started to take care of my life. I changed my relationship. I changed my job. I changed my home. I started taking care of business! . . . I started getting angry. I started to cry. I've really changed. I look different. I sound different. I changed my life intentionally. (184)

The book proposes that by following the recovery process, the survivor can feel compassion for herself and anger at the abuser and have a greater capacity for inti-macy with others. There is a complexity to the negotiation of these feelings, but the implication is that she can bring about positive change in her life.

Roseanne corroborates this survivor narrative, expanding and giving voice, not only to her rage, but to her utter inner despair:

I set out to write a book about surviving incest and abuse. I so very much wanted to write a happy and inspiring story. Tonight, again, I know there is no happy or inspiring ending to any of this. Only that I lived through it, and that in spite of its hovering and crushing weight, just the reality of it, just the possession of my body and mind and soul in its aftermath, somehow, I, like millions of others, carried on. . . . Some days I feel as though I have lost too much, and nothing will make it better. Nothing at all, not drugs, not alcohol, not even speaking out as an advocate, not therapy, not writing, just nothing. Nothing. (240–41)

The narratives in *The Courage to Heal* present desperation as a "low" that can be overcome. Part of Roseanne's version of survivor identity is the insurmountablity of her emotional struggles.

       The contrast that is found in these two different kinds of survivor stories is carried through in the visual representation of the books themselves. Where the cover of *The Courage to Heal* presents an earnest, no-nonsense design with a clean and clinical edge (fig.1), the cover of *My Lives* suggests a mass-market romance novel with Roseanne photographed in a free-wheeling, sexy, gypsy fantasy of romanticized pleasure, footloose and fancy-free (fig.2). Roseanne looks directly toward the reader with pursed lips while embraced by her lover. The title in playful gold type announces *My Lives*. In contrast to the romance novel's typical dust jacket, the contents describe Roseanne's struggle to live and overcome her depression and self-abuse. She reveals that since her first book, *Roseanne: My Life as a Woman*, she has been "in recovery" for four years. In *My Lives*, she gives due credit to feminism, reveals the details of her recovery process, and documents her memories of abuse by her parents. She talks about the profound depth of injury she attributes to abuse, as she exposes her pain. She describes the traumas of her childhood and claims that feminism has helped her be angry and disgusted at the victimization of women and children. Alternately confiding in and providing advice to the reader, Roseanne offers in *My Lives* a remarkable telling of the traumas of her childhood, the failures in her emotional life, and the successes in her career. In expressing her pain and its management, she questions the notion of progressive improvement through programs of self-help and recovery while maintaining a vision of playful provocation. On the other hand, *The Courage to Heal* earnestly coaches its readers toward step-by-step improvement. For example, opening the 1994 edition, the reader is greeted with a page of endorsements: "Your book has revolutionized my life. In one year's time I have changed from a repressed, terrified, lonely, angry, victimized, suicidal drunk into a healthy, vibrant, warm, loving, nurturing, contented, active, happy woman." In *My Lives*, Roseanne's story is one of recurring dysfunction. Nothing can make it better.

       In *The Courage to Heal* the healing process is described by seventeen survivors of different abuse backgrounds, classes, and racial and ethnic origins. The stories help the reader place herself in a spectrum of sexual abuse circumstances. One woman was molested on the subway as a sixth grader and was told she should expect this kind of thing; another had her vagina sucked by her father every night before she went to sleep and thought these violations were normal, like being kissed goodnight on the forehead; another recounts how her mother used her body for masturbation and then beat her regularly throughout her childhood. As the stories unfold, the women get better despite panic attacks, eating disorders, and difficulties with intimacy and trust, overcoming the horrific range of violations. According to *The Courage to Heal*, you can always survive.

In *My Lives* Roseanne discloses her childhood traumas and symptoms and confronts her parents, who claim it was all a joke and did not mean anything by it. She is connected with and fueled by her pain and the knowledge that there is an audience for her story of suffering and survival. She writes that it hurts to be abused and when it happens as a child, it injures your whole being for your whole life: "Being abused leaves a child with a whirlpool of self-hate funneling down into numbness. You lose your ability to judge places and people. You no longer know who or what is safe. An abused child becomes a perpetual victim in situation after situation, time and time again" (229–30). Roseanne describes and analyzes the extent of damage, while expressing continuous rage, which distinguishes her story from the testimonials in *The Courage to Heal*. Roseanne remains in her television star character as a loud-mouthed, working-class spokesperson, adding her particular story to survivor discourse. In *The Courage to Heal* the reader isn't following the entire life story of a survivor but gets the piece that frames the abuse: current circumstances, some family history, symptoms, survival strategies, and usually a progress report at the end. While in *The Courage to Heal* pseudonyms are used for legal protection, Roseanne adds a celebrity face and body to survivor discourse. She can afford to flaunt her public identity as a survivor. Not only does she contribute her name to survivor identity, Roseanne consciously constructs a visual embodiment of the female survivor.

At the time of Roseanne's launching of *My Lives*, *Vanity Fair* featured her in an article titled "Really Roseanne."[6] The accompanying photo spread by Annie Leibovitz opened with a picture of Roseanne lying passively, half on and half off a child's bed. Roseanne looks out at the viewer, and the accompanying narrative describes her "battle to survive" as she emerges from the "nightmare that she says began with childhood molestation and became a cycle of drug abuse and depression." The photos show the big-bodied Roseanne in sexually ambiguous poses and clad in lingerie. She looks sexy, desiring, child-like, hurt, confused—the photographs represent pleasures specific to survivor relationships to sex. Her images and poses in the article suggest the hurt of a child and the sexual desire of a survivor, balancing pleasure and pain. Here, she talks of reading a lot of recovery books and her role as a warrior in the fight against child sexual abuse. This metaphor is repeated in *My Lives*: "I've chosen to become a soldier in a terrible war against children, innocence, ultimately a war against ourselves" (229). Her updated image of survivor enhanced her market viability and launched a celebrity survivor into popular culture. What distinguishes the autopathography is its disclosure of unresolved emotional excess, including photographs such as these.

The popularization of survivor identity took place in the wake of legal battles over repressed memories and related media stories. Roseanne publicly disclosed that she was sexually abused as a child in September 1991 after six weeks of preparation with Marilyn Van Derbur Atler, the former Miss America who came out as a survivor in May of that year. Roseanne saw going public as a way to advocate for women and demonstrate her solidarity with other survivors by making the link between herself, of working origins, and Van Derbur Atler, a woman born into wealth and privilege. Roseanne continues to work with her celebrity survivor identity, speaking about her feelings of shame, anger, and loss. She connects her recovery with higher powers, or a god, and wants to leave guideposts for other women, as women have done in the past. It is clear in *My Lives* that while she adopts a pagan-matriarchal spirituality and appropriates other worlds, idioms, religions, and goddesses, she also successfully embraces life as a businesswoman, television star, and survivor.

According to *Publishers' Weekly*, books on sexual abuse and incest were strong sellers in 1991 in part because a former Miss America and Roseanne Barr came "out of the closet."[7] While Roseanne and Marilyn Van Derbur Atler are public about their pasts and are victim advocates, their presence also carves out a market and a discursive niche that may in fact create and enlarge the community of survivors through audiences' identification with their stories. Jackie Stacey argues in her essay, "Feminine Fascinations," about women's identification with Hollywood stars, that stars serve a normative function in being read as rolemodels, thus contributing to the construction of ideals of feminine attractiveness circulating in culture at any one time.[8] If this is so, then the identification of an ideal feminine attractiveness includes the survivor, or is interrupted by her. Stacey goes on to discuss the pleasure of feminine power and identification with the star's personality and behavior: "Some female stars represented images of power and confidence. These are frequent favorites because they offered spectators fantasies of power outside their own experiences" (151). Roseanne expands what power and confidence might be when she identifies herself across the pages of *Vanity Fair* as a survivor while simultaneously continuing her emotional struggle with no end in sight and playing with her multiplicity of lives and roles. In a *Newsweek* article about a sexual abuse case, a head shot of Roseanne is captioned, "The culture of abuse." It calls Roseanne a "walking billboard for the culture of abuse," aiming its critique at adults who charge those who sexually abused them as children.[9] In this instance, Roseanne is a target, someone to blame in the controversy over the validity of survivor stories.

Do You Really Remember, or Are You Making This Up? Roseanne Intervenes

> **Every day is a struggle to remember, to hold on, to choose to live. I am an overweight, overachiever with a few dandy compulsive-obsessive disorders and a little problem with self-mutilation.**
> Roseanne Arnold
> *My Lives*

In the early 1990s, debates were raging in both therapeutic and legal contexts around the truthfulness of memories of child sexual abuse, and the degree of harm such debates caused. Many columnists proclaimed that survivor stories were a "glorification of neurotic behavior." For example, in a 1991 column in *Maclean's* magazine, Barbara Amiel, noted for her conservative views, complained about being exposed to the tiresome stories of "women's inner turmoil." After noting recent celebrity disclosures of abuse and battering, she concludes that these "preoccupations" are shared by the general population: "The problem is not simply the glorification of neurotic behavior itself: the larger problem is the acculturation of such behavior. By now it is virtually normative to describe oneself as a victim of some sort."[10] Amiel claims that as a result, "we are suffocating in our own pain." She advises that as a solution we buoy ourselves, take greater individual responsibility for our behavior, and "build character." In *Harper's* magazine that same month, an article titled "Victims All?" by David Rieff links the recovery movement to long-standing traits of American national identity. Narratives of rags to riches are now translated to a central metaphor of addiction to recovery with its "self-improvement," "know-how," and self-transformation, coming out of "chronic inner pain."[11] Rieff, from a left-wing perspective, bemoans the self-indulgence of the movement and claims that in the 1960s at least there had been a tension between healing oneself and healing the world. However, in lumping together all approaches to emotional self-care, Rieff does not give credit, for instance, to the legal action taken by sexually abused women, a clear example of a political action coming out of what he might call the self-indulgence of healing oneself. He also defines the recovery consumer as affluent, a definition that does not concur with the people profiled in *The Courage to Heal*, whose class, racial, and ethnic origins are diverse.

Meanwhile, George Pransky and other "psychology of the mind" advocates argue that the concept of the unconscious is harmful and that we need to acquire self-esteem, invoked at will. He, along with five hundred like-minded therapists in the United States, believe that "dwelling on painful past experiences keeps people from experiencing the innate mental health we all possess. . . . The best way to deal with your problems is not to analyze them."[12] From this position, the analysis of feelings demands too much social space. Pransky and other critics explicitly attack feminist grass-roots and professional mental health work that advocates for women to become more healthy through looking at their "inner turmoil." However, it is precisely addressing this turmoil that leads to improved mental health through the reduction of self-destructive behaviors. These attacks are an attempt to close down the emotional and feeling space that therapy and recovery offer. Even with its programmatic limitations, *The Courage to Heal* invites the survivor to take her pain seriously, remember what happened, and give herself time to work through the emotional damage. Roseanne in her survivor identity similarly advocates for emotional recovery space and legitimation of the pain—she didn't, and we didn't, make it up.

In this social climate of impatience and doubt as to the healing potential of psychotherapy, the landmark *People v. Franklin* case opened the debate around the belief in repressed memories. In this case, Eileen Franklin Lipsker, the accuser, had been in therapy for her troubled marriage when she looked at her six-year-old daughter and had a horrific memory come to her. She remembered seeing her father rape and murder her best friend twenty years earlier, and being sworn to secrecy by him. In November 1990, based on Eileen's recovered memory, George Franklin Sr. was convicted of murder. In the wake of this case, many women began to turn to the law to seek retribution for abuse.[13] This turn of events threw the repressed memories of survivors into the limelight. The debate over the veracity of repressed memories recovered in therapy soon became confrontational, and the question was reduced to whether or not survivors' stories should be believed. In "Beware the Incest Survivor Machine," a feature article that first appeared in the *New York Times Book Review* and was soon after reprinted in the *Montreal Gazette*, social psychologist Carol Tavris emphasizes the widespread suspicion and doubt of incest survivor's stories.[14] She asserts that incest-survivor construction is based on the work of nonscientifically trained therapists and survivors who are validated by the books they write within the marketing terms of the industry. She attacks feminist-influenced recovery manuals, primarily *The Courage to Heal*, suggesting that while research psychologists are skeptical of memories of child sexual abuse, the authors of the incest-survivor recovery books accept them as truths. She argues that in order to self-diagnose child sexual abuse, the authors of *The Courage to Heal* ask questions of the reader that could fit anyone. She paraphrases from the chapter, "Effects: Recognizing the Damage":

> You feel that you're bad, dirty or ashamed.
> You feel powerless, like a victim.
> You feel that there's something wrong with you deep down
>   inside; that if people really knew you, they would leave.
> You feel unable to protect yourself in dangerous situations.
> You have no sense of your own interests, talents or goals.
> You have trouble feeling motivated.
> You feel you have to be perfect. (B1)

Significantly, Tavris introduces the list asking the reader how often they suffer from these symptoms in order to assert that the list is general enough to include everyone. The original list in the book identifies more severe symptoms and situations to which the survivor is vulnerable, which Tavris fails to include:

> Do you ever feel self-destructive or suicidal? Or that you
>   simply want to die?
> Do you hate yourself?
> Are you often immobilized?
> Have you experienced repeated victimization (rape, assault,
>   battery) as an adult? (*The Courage to Heal*, 35)

The reduced version of the list bolsters her argument that many people could misdiagnose themselves using these questions. In this way her position resembles Rieff's generalizations concerning the ease with which the affluent identify themselves as victims.

In this climate of skepticism where recovered memories are under attack and psychotherapy is an "indulgence," Roseanne's autopathography is an important intervention into the survivor identity and the recovered memory debate. Despite her courage, Roseanne often feels desperate and says so with unreserved certainty and rage, as the interview in the *Vanity Fair* article indicates:

> ROSEANNE: I'm still in heavy-duty psychotherapy. I'm in my fourth year of it. I'm fucked-up. I'm just trying to hang on.... I'm at a real scary time in my life.
> INTERVIEWER: I'm sure the Prozac does help, but there are some in the drug-recovery movement who would say you are not sober if you are taking pharmaceuticals.
> ROSEANNE: Then they're fucked-up. Then insulin means you're not sober, too. They're just fucking idiots. I'm thankful I got on that drug—goddamnit—or I wouldn't be here.
> INTERVIEWER: Do you really think you would have killed yourself?
> ROSEANNE: Which of the thousand times?[15]

Roseanne makes use of psychotherapy and antidepressants yet still claims to seriously suffer emotionally. The mediated display of her pain serves to counter the kind of blatant charges of victimhood made by the likes of Rieff and Tavris. Roseanne in her survivor identity also counters the claims of the False Memory Syndrome (FMS) Foundation, an organization formed in March 1992. It was spearheaded by Pamela Freyd, an educator whose daughter, Jennifer Freyd, a professor of psychology, claimed her alcoholic father had sexually abused her when she was a child. Both mother and father deny that the incest occurred. The organization focuses on ill-founded repressed memories of child sexual abuse and includes professionals and affected families. The FMS Foundation blames the therapist and claims therapeutic victimization of the client. Therapists are accused of working under assumptions from unscientific research findings, planting memories in the minds of vulnerable clients in order to generate business, while those in therapy are accused of inventing memories of child sexual abuse to please therapists.

In lending celebrity presence to the damage, Roseanne is targeted in the heated debate as to whether such claims are true or fabricated. Her autopathography validates the experience of felt, inhabited pain and suffering in popular culture not only through her uncompromising and unapologetic recounting of emotional suffering, but also through her body. In *My Lives* she talks about her "tummy tuck." The weight gain and loss over many years had left apron-like skin that hung, covering her genitals. Once she was ready to see part of herself again, she decided to have it removed in the course of her healing process. This discernment of her body and its positioning in the discourses of sexual abuse and eating disorders help to put the survivor body in the foreground. Eating disorders and sufferers' attempts to control the body are commonly associated with sexual abuse in recovery discourse as found in medical and psychological research, and self-help books. Roseanne's visible articulation assures her readers that her pain is connected to her body, which she has relentlessly expanded and contracted over her years of bingeing and purging. She frames her physical alterations through cosmetic surgery within the emotional "makeover" of her recovery. *The Courage to Heal* also recognizes that the body is damaged by sexual abuse. The chapter titled "Your Body" recognizes difficulties with eating and self-mutilation and proposes the possibility of changing from hating, ignoring, and being numb to loving, listening, and feeling the body (217). Both texts offer insight into the legacy of bodily damage resulting from child sexual abuse. Roseanne's autopathography, however, circulates within popular audiences, outside those specifically addressed by *The Courage to Heal*.

Conclusions

Roseanne has replaced Madonna as the epitome of the tough-minded woman always reinventing herself. Madonna's litany of costume-and-role changes has been supplanted by an equally long list of Roseanne's woes, ranging from alleged childhood incest to drug, alcohol and now alleged spousal abuse. . . . If you want to be a star today, admit something, anything, show us your struggle, get some recovery coverage.
Dan Bischoff and Leslie Savan
" *Celebrity in the '90s: No Pain, No Fame,* " Us

"Celebrity Pain in the '90s: No Pain, No Fame," in *Us* magazine, writes off emotional pain as the latest market-driven celebrity-maintenance program. Roseanne, her autopathography *My Lives*, and *The Courage to Heal* insist on emotional or feeling space for women. They argue, in their own ways, that women who are in pain and don't have the language, time, or support to work through it will act self-destructively because of unresolved feelings left over from their abuse experiences as children. Self-hatred and self-destructive patterns of behavior do not change without conscious effort, which requires emotional validation. It was in a climate of openness to emotional healing and its methods that the naming of child sexual abuse came into being more than twenty years ago. The autopathography is an addition to the discourse that validates emotional struggle. In this period of attack and challenge to the validity of stories of sexual abuse, Roseanne and the survivor identity she projects acknowledge the pervasiveness of abuse damage, its consequences to emotional well-being and the body, and its origins in the family, while refusing a victim identity. Tempered with playfulness, she asserts a position of power and control and insists on representing her body as desiring sexual pleasure. As Jackie Stacey argues, star identification means women see stars as role models, so Roseanne is providing a bold addition to the discourse of survivor identity. As this analysis demonstrates, survivor identity does not necessarily adhere to a progressive narrative—for example, emotional rags to riches, desperation to recovery. It is a complex model of coping with survivor subjectivities and takes into account individual biography, memory, loss, and the consequences for the body.

Notes

1. Roseanne Arnold, *My Lives* (New York: Ballantine, 1994). All further references will be cited in the text parenthetically by page number.

2. Roseanne Arnold, *Roseanne: My Life as a Woman* (New York: Harper and Row, 1989).

3. Gloria Steinem, *Revolution from Within* (Boston: Little, Brown, 1992); Kitty Dukakis with Jane Scovell, *Now You Know* (New York: Simon and Schuster, 1990); Dennis Rodman with Tim Keown, *Bad as I Wanna Be* (New York: Delacorte Press, 1996).

4. David Remnick, "Raging Bull," *New Yorker* (June 10, 1996): 86.

5. Ellen Bass and Laura Davis, *The Courage to Heal: A Guide for Women Survivors of Child Sexual Abuse*, 3d rev. ed. (New York: Harper Collins, 1994). All further references will be cited in the text parenthetically by page number.

6. Kevin Sessums, "Really Roseanne," *Vanity Fair* (February 1994).

7. Maria Heidkamp, "Beyond Therapy," *Publishers' Weekly* (December 6, 1991): 32.

8. Jackie Stacey, "Feminine Fascinations: Forms of Identification in Star-Audience Relations," in *Star Gazing: Hollywood Cinema and Female Spectatorship* (London: Routledge, 1994), 154.

9. "Was It Real or Memories?" *Newsweek* (March 14, 1994): 55. This particular article is about Steven Cook, who accused Cardinal Joseph Bernadin of sexually molesting him as a teenager, a charge he later dropped. According to this article, it was a case of false memory.

10. Barbara Amiel, "The Noise of Women's Turmoil," *Maclean's* (October 28, 1991): 13.

11. David Rieff, "Victims All?" *Harper's* (October 1991): 49–56.

12. Quoted in Teo Furtado, "The Listening Cure," *Utne Reader* (January/February 1992): 89–96.

13. Lenore Terr, *Unchained Memories: True Stories of Traumatic Memories Lost and Found* (New York: Harper Collins, 1994), 32–60.

14. Carol Tavris, "Beware the Incest Survivor Machine," *New York Times Book Review*, vol. 142 (January 3, 1993): 1; reprinted in *Montreal Gazette* (January 30, 1993): B1.

15. Sessums, "Really Roseanne," 116.

Jana Sterbak

House of Pain:
A Relationship

Dedicated to General Idea

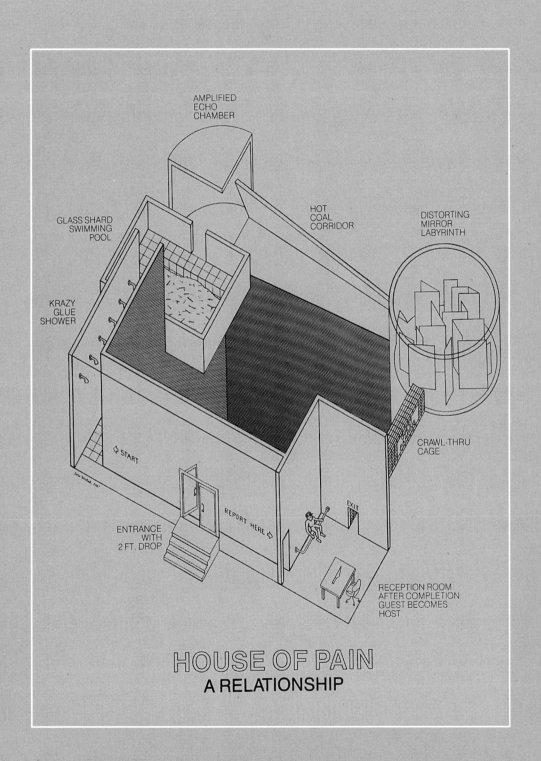

AMPLIFIED
ECHO
CHAMBER

GLASS SHARD
SWIMMING
POOL

HOT
COAL
CORRIDOR

DISTORTING
MIRROR
LABYRINTH

KRAZY
GLUE
SHOWER

CRAWL-THRU
CAGE

⇦ START

ENTRANCE
WITH
2 FT. DROP

REPORT HERE ⇨

EXIT

RECEPTION ROOM
AFTER COMPLETION
GUEST BECOMES
HOST

HOUSE OF PAIN
A RELATIONSHIP

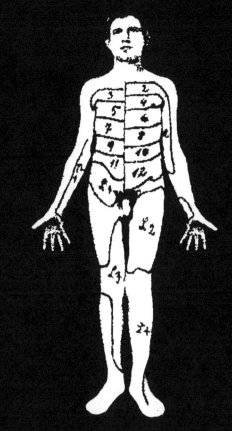

3

Cut It Open

Kim Sawchuk

Wounded States: Sovereignty, Separation, and the Quebec Referendum

> Yes, the nation is sick, and what is worse, it is trying to become accustomed to its sores. This is the aim of my explorations: examining the traces of happiness still to be glimpsed, I gauge its short supply. If you want to know how much darkness there is around you, you must sharpen your eyes, peering at the faintest lights in the distance.
>
> Italo Calvino
> *Invisible Cities*

Pain and the Body Politic

LIKE MOST of the citizenry huddled north of the forty-ninth parallel, I sat in front of the television on October 30, 1995, the night of the Quebec referendum. The voter tally mesmerized me as it rolled in across the province and onto my screen. Minute by minute the results were measured and graphically displayed by a barometer symbolically divided and color-coded into blue signifying a "Oui" to Quebec sovereignty, and federalist red indicating a "Non" to separation.

The second referendum to be held in fifteen years, this latest call for Quebec to secede from Canada and gain status as a nation-state rather than remain one of ten provinces officially began with the 1994 election of Jacques Parizeau and the Parti Quebecois (PQ). The PQ had campaigned on the grounds of sovereignty for Quebec and on September 7, 1995, they placed a seventeen-point bill before the provincial legislature detailing the referendum question and the terms of a "new partnership," known as sovereignty association with Canada. The bill was contingent upon a successful yes vote.

The "Non" side won the referendum by less than one percentage point, a slim majority of fifty-four thousand votes (50.6 percent) leaving analysts to wonder if Canada could "survive" after such a "near-death" experience." [1] Voter turnout was phenomenal (93.5 per cent) bolstering the claims of Quebec nationalist politicians that "democracy in Quebec is healthy." Despite this dramatic finale, the summer campaign that preceded the autumn vote was sleepy until the final thirty days, when the sovereignty movement began to increase its popular support across the province.[2] Common wisdom, both scholarly and anecdotal, attributes the turnaround to the replacement of the portly and academic Jacques Parizeau by the charismatic Lucien Bouchard as the titular head of the "Oui" coalition.[3]

As the referendum campaign unfolded, particularly as the "Oui" began to overtake the "Non," shaking confident and complacent federalists out of their dogmatic slumbers, I became fascinated by the affective language and visceral images that emerged on the street and in my local mediascape. Frantic Canadians called Quebeckers warning: "People's lives are going to be hurt by a YES vote, their mortgage rates, their mutual funds. And their anger, you want someone else to suffer. You want them to be hurt as much as they have hurt you."[4] Federalist politicians spoke of Quebec sovereignty as "dismemberment" and a "tragedy." [5] Opinion pieces and editorials debated how best to resolve "la malaise." [6]

The most striking example of the corporeal dimensions of this debate, perhaps, was the advertisement for the Woundmate Surgical Zipper, manufactured by Woundcare International. The advertisement appeared just two weeks before the vote, on a billboard in the center of Toronto's hospital district in the neighboring province of Ontario. It featured photographs of the heads of Lucien Bouchard and Jacques Parizeau, the two most prominent leaders of the "Oui" campaign, with the surgical zippers across their mouths accompanied by the slogan, "Pity we can't heal all wounds." According to company president, Jerry Lagan, the slogan was not intended as a political statement, but was meant to imply the product's limitations: "the Woundcare Surgical Zipper can only heal physical wounds, it cannot cure the intangible traumas caused by politicians' speech." The billboard was only intended to "use the referendum as a vehicle" to bring attention to the product (fig. 1). [7] In this particular example, the ad does not feature heads from both sides of the debate. Catering to an audience unsympathetic to sovereignty, the advertisement locates the cause of the injury in the mouths of Quebec politicians. Language, central to debates on Quebec national identity, is imaged as a problem invented by these disembodied talking heads rather than a legitimate aspiration rooted in a significant proportion of the population.

While it is true that the traumas caused by political speech often are intangible, the company did find a way to give the political situation a form that illustrates the central claim of my essay. We make our political world through the deployment of these corporeal terminologies, particularly tropes of bodies in crisis. Charting the occurrence of these images and words of the political body in pain provides a clinical history of the body politic that reveals the shape, the locations, and the depths of the trauma.

Philosopher of pain Elaine Scarry suggests that the use of visceral language becomes more pronounced in times of crisis.

When some central idea or ideology or cultural construct has ceased to elicit a population's belief either because it is manifestly fictitious or because it has for some reason been divested of ordinary forms of substantiation the sheer material factualness of the human body will be borrowed to lend that cultural construct the aura of "realness" and "certainty." [8]

Think of the nation-state as one such ideology, belief, or construct. This construct, Canada, is in a legitimation crisis, to quote Jürgen Habermas, because one of its parts wants to break away. This will to secede indicates a crisis in belief in Quebec and instigates a crisis of confidence in Canada, a country that may never have had a strong sense of its own identity except in its difference from the United States. [9] The Canadian people and their federalist leaders feel "angst-ridden," "hurt," "angry," and "held hostage" because despite their efforts to accommodate Quebec's desires for a maximum of political autonomy, they now face rejection. [10]

Scarry's phrase suggests that such a crisis of belief has two possible causes: either the construct was "manifestly fictitious" in the first place, or the construct has been "divested" of its power to elicit belief. At first glance Scarry seems to separate the fictitious and the real, but her subtle distinction between the "manifestly fictitious" and "the delegitimated" calls attention to a similarity

Figure 1. "Pity we can't heal all wounds." Reprinted from Copperfield Advertising, Inc., creative directors David Ernst and Darryl Gordon.

between the structure of perception of committed sovereignists and federalists. Both sides understand their own position as real, but temporarily delegitimated and the position of the other as inherently false or "manifestly fictitious." Both deploy the image of the human body "to substantiate" or to lend an air of "reality" to a shaky ideology, as Scarry suggests happens in moments of political crisis. Discourses of pain, I would add, assist in this transubstantiation.

The extensive vocabulary and images associated with the political body in pain operates as a diagnostic tool that puts the extremely fluid, pliable corporeal contours of the nation, as it was imagined and experienced by its citizenry during the referendum, into relief. The language of pain constitutes the body politic for its citizens, but it did more in this instance. It was used to threaten and assert blame by politicians. It was deployed to establish the reality of the potential hurt and the right solution. It not only humanized the body, but it gave it an age, a gender, and a life in a traditional heterosexual family structure; finally, it is used to give a narrative form to a collective grievance and impart a sense of history that is akin to an individual's own life story.

Like Marco Polo in Italo Calvino's *Invisible Cities*, I want to know why the citizens of this empire think that they are sick and what their affective, visceral manner of speaking of their affliction can tell us about our national disease. The goal of my exploration is not to prescribe a remedy for this trauma, but to chronicle these enunciations of pain in our highly mediated political language and imaging practices.[11] It is a way to make sense of the affective intensity I experience living in a place that, in all of its political contradictions, has become home.

Establishing Blame: Our Constitutional Toothache

> **When you have 70% of your French population that feel in their hearts and their souls that they are Quebeckers first; and when they want all decisions taken in Quebec City, only two things can happen. Either they leave and give themselves a real country; or they stay and they provide you with a never-ending visit to the dentist.**
> Jacques Parizeau
> "Our Constitutional Toothache"

The language of bodies in pain may be used in a threatening manner to invoke a past trauma and a future worsening of the hurt. Deploying a pain-filled vocabulary allows politicians to assert blame and offer a diagnosis and a cure for this ailing body.

Just after his election in Quebec in 1994 Parizeau delivered a speech to the Canadian Club in Toronto, later printed under the title "Quebec Is Canada's Constant Toothache Until It Leaves."[12] In the course of promoting the irresistible force of Quebec sovereignty on the grounds that a common identity shared by a people must be translated into independence, he asserted that "our national will and your national will no longer converge." This nonconvergence or collision has produced a "deadlock" or a constitutional impasse with three relatively recent manifestations: the 1982 unilateral repatriation of the constitution and the betrayal of René Lévesque in what is known in Quebec as the Night of the Long Knives; the 1990 defeat of the Meech Lake Accord, initiated to bring Quebec back into the constitution; and, finally, the 1992 defeat of the Charlottetown Accord in a national referendum. These three defeats became the obsessive focus on both sides of the referendum fence, with one crucial difference. The Francophone presses subtended and supplemented these more recent historical reports by the frequent inclusion of a long-standing list of grievances that begins with the defeat of the French by the British in 1760.

To return to Parizeau's speech to the Canadian Club, Parizeau's analysis of the current manifestation of "the malaise" between Canada and Quebec has a much more immediate goal: to persuade his audience of the logic of a position that has been categorized within much of English Canada as irrational, emotional, and therefore prone to "tribal forms of nationalism" that may lead to ethnic conflict.[13] In order to bypass these accusations, Parizeau deploys a rhetorical logic that calls for an affective understanding of these grievances. But he cannot make an argument based on the assumption of his audience's sympathy. His cause, the sovereignty movement, is understood as fundamentally untrue. To make his argument real to his audience, Parizeau utilizes the threat of a never-ending ordinary pain that most of us have shared: the pain of a toothache.

I put myself in your shoes. This Quebec problem is like a never-ending trip to the dentist. Quebec wants more power, more autonomy—you never say yes, the drilling doesn't stop....[14]

If the problem is defined as a constitutional toothache, then the solution is surprising. Parizeau does not advocate more constitutional talks but nationwide support of a "yes" vote in Quebec, a vote that finally will allow Canadians to leave the dentist's office behind so that the drilling might stop. The yes in Parizeau's sentence is a multireferential, triple yes: yes to Quebec autonomy and self-determination; yes in reference to the past unfulfilled promise of the 1980 referendum; yes in anticipation of a positive response in the referendum to come.

More wondrous than his optimism is Parizeau's verbal maneuvering. Parizeau deftly reverses subject positions and shifts from the people and the nation ("Quebeckers") to politics and the state ("decisions taken in Quebec City"). He thus empathetically occupies the anticipated place of his audience for strategic ends. The intent is to reverse and conflate "us" and "them," while still engaging in the dichotomy. The hostile Anglophone members of the Toronto business club must feel what Jacques Parizeau, elected representative of the majority of Quebeckers, feels. To paraphrase Parizeau, such an argument works like this: You think that I am the source of your problem. I say that I understand how you feel and in doing so, I legitimate my claims to know what you need, even if it is not what you think you want. The medicine may taste bad now, but it will make you feel better later.

The threat of never-ending drilling literally implies a specific body part, a tooth, that acts as a synecdoche for Quebec in this analysis. But Quebec is not the direct cause of the pain; the source of the pain and its cause are located elsewhere. For Parizeau, the constitutional conflict and the quibbling over Quebec as a "distinct" society within Canada may be creating an immediate ache,

Figure 2. "Enfantillages." Reprinted from *Le Devoir*, May 16, 1996.

but the actual source of this discomfort lies in the history of these two particular subjects and, in the case of Quebec, in the chronic fissure between cultural identity and political power.

       Parizeau's diagnosis of the issue contains a solution: The Quebec issue will only be resolved by accepting a fully sovereign and independent Quebec, a Quebec that nationalists describe as a country that only wants to be "normal," a country that is mature enough to care for its own affairs, a "real" country that exists de facto if not de jure because the Quebec people share this distinct history, language and culture.[15] In sovereignist versions of this narrative, the body politic is depicted as an adult who has grown from infancy who wants to achieve autonomy, or "normality" in order to complete the process of growth and change. Sovereignty is seen as healthy.

       The cartoon that appeared in the Montreal paper *Le Devoir*, whose editor Lise Bissonette is an avowed sovereignist, makes this point (fig. 2). In "Enfantillages" a clearly adult male body is in a baby-carriage that is being pushed by a caricature of Prime Minister Chretien. In this image, the federalist position is depicted as infantilizing Quebeckers, implying that independence is about growth, and like the development from infant to adult, it is natural.

These compelling, potent metaphors persuade through the invocation of a shared painful experience but they are highly unstable. As Ken Dean and Brian Massumi suggest in their reading of the first emperor of China, Ronald Reagan, and George Bush:

> *tracing when and where the image circulates, by which institutions or individuals, in whose direction, to what end, yields a non-visceral map of bodily potential, a complex flow of collective desire. The propagation depends in particular bodies becoming hosts for images and the embodiments of at least certain of the dynamics it lives by.*[16]

Any analysis of the language of pain and politics must remain attuned to their ability to be rearticulated in another syntagmatic relation that may produce another meaning.[17] In this particular case, the toothache and dentist metaphor was responded to immediately by a federalist supporter, Marcel Coté, a Montreal corporate economist. Coté appropriated and mobilized Parizeau's trope with a twist in an attempt to spin it into another direction. According to Coté, Parizeau's comments infer that "separation itself will be no more painful than a trip to the dentist," a statement that Parizeau would never have made and a word, *separation*, that the sovereignty movement studiously avoids first, because of its negative connotations and second, because the emphasis is on separating from something or someone rather than on growing out of one's own potentialities. Coté bluntly argues with a statement that he himself makes in ways that are telling:

> *I dispute this assertion. Canada might have a toothache, and it might be a good idea to visit the dentist. But pulling out one, not two, not three, but several large teeth, without any local anesthesia, is not the way toothaches are taken care of in today's society. Separation is harsh and cruel medicine, indeed totally unacceptable medicine for our constitutional toothache.*[18]

Coté employs a panoply of pain-filled metaphors, mixing talk of divorce with open heart surgery in tandem with dental work to underscore the cruelty of the "separatist solution." Coté emphasizes a diagnosis reiterated in the federalist and Anglophone media throughout the campaign: suicide, death, and the potential survival of the country in the case of the unthinkable—a "Oui" majority. In his speech, the suicide is usually figured as a double one: such measures will not only "kill" Canada, but they will "kill" Quebec. The patient, Coté asserts, could not live through the "post-separation trauma" without severe risk and neither country could survive alone against the economic, political, and cultural power of the United States. The purpose of the federalist referendum strategy, which failed miserably, was not to offer a solution but a stern warning. Sovereignty is renamed separation and aligned with the idea of a painful amputation, in corporeal terms, or divorce and given familial associations. Quebec, like a patient who is suicidal, must be stopped before it harms itself. Within federalist discourses, the body politic emerges as a fully formed adult about to be dismembered by political change. The changes proposed by a potential "Oui" vote are seen as disruptive to the health of this nation.

Coté puts forth a solution that he understands as a more reasonable, less emotive answer to the problem of the constitutional toothache.[19] Paraphrasing Alain Dubuc, Mr. Coté opines that "decentralization is the best way to cure the toothache."[20] For Dubuc and Coté the *real* pain is not caused by issues such as identity or culture. Real pain is economic and political and is caused by the juridical division of political power and the current economic mandate of Canadian federalism. In this analysis, the real problem with the country is "a welfare system of federalism" that tries to redistribute incomes across the provinces, leading to resentment among the haves and dependency among the have-nots. In Coté's reading of the situation, this is the "dental treatment" that all Canadians have been avoiding. In this strategy, the debates on language and culture are epiphenomenal and subsidiary to our sorry economic ailments.[21]

Every act of describing pain, suffering, and disease in political debate simultaneously locates the location of the hurt, the source of the problem, and either implicitly or explicitly advocates a treatment. As Elaine Scarry again argues, sometimes this cause is seen to be beyond direct human agency, as in a disease. At other times, the causes are directly attributable to human agency. At such times, a weapon such as a fist, a hammer, a knife, a gun, or a dentist's drill becomes part of the scenario. In the case of a political cartoon that appeared in the *Vancouver Sun*, the state has taken the form of its national symbol, the beaver. The beaver is in a headlock, a gun held to its head by the recognizable and portly figure of Jacques Parizeau (fig. 3). Federalism is not infantilizing Quebec in this image; Quebec is holding Canada hostage.

The act of describing pain, suffering, and disease in the body politic simultaneously contains a diagnosis and prescription. To say "you are hurting me" is to forward that you are responsible for my pain. In the case of the argument between sovereignists and federalists, a singular solution is advocated to treat a complexity of symptoms, and for many political leaders, the bottom line is economic. To give another example, after the referendum provincial liberal leader and head of the "Non" coalition, Daniel Johnson, proposed that "the *sovereignty option* is hurting the economy." Sovereignists and PQ Minister Bernard Landry replied that "the *unresolved* political situation" is the source of the trauma. [22] Politically divisive in their logic of cause and effect, these binarisms nevertheless fit the generic structure of news reporting, which thrives on conflict and fashioning dramatic, colorful headlines to sell papers. [23]

While a shared discomfort with the current constitutional arrangement and with the economy is acknowledged by most Canadians and Quebeckers, the source of that hurt is not named in the same way. The struggle to claim that one is injured and victimized, and to name the cause of that pain, constitutes the field of discourse and the relation of these terms to each other. *Separation, dismemberment, death*, and *tragedy* circulate in the federalist position, a position largely shared by the English language media. *Autonomy, independence, liberation*, and *growth* circulate from the position of Quebec nationalists, a field of terms replicated in the Francophone news media—even among those who are explicitly federalist in politics. Telling in this respect is the campaign literature put out by the "Non" side during the referendum that addresses its Francophone readership differently from the way it speaks to its Anglophone readership. On the French side of the brochure, Daniel Johnson distinguishes between "identity" and "citizenship," saying that he has pride in both, arguing that Canadian federalism can accommodate this duality. They are not in conflict or contradiction. In the English version, no such distinction is made. In the arguments put forth to an Anglophone audience, the emphasis is not on the split between citizenship and identity but on the negative, painful aspects of political change.[24]

Let me return to what I suggested earlier as a major side effect of this language. The idea that something hurts implies that there is a body that has been hurt or a person who has been psychically wounded as well as someone or something that has done the damage. It is by invoking the sensation of pain that this mediated political language makes that abstract entity known as the nation-state real to its citizenry. To follow up on Dean and Massumi's reading of this incorporation, this language gives the nation-state "quasi-corporeal attributes." These attributes inhabit the media images and speech of the political leaders and spokespersons for the various sides, who are called on to take up these positions: a classical case of Althusserian interpellation.

A Bad Marriage: Gender and the Body Politic

This anthropomorphization of the body politic is not a new phenomenon. Since Thomas Hobbes, at least, liberal social contract theory has personified political authority and allegiance:

Figure 3. "Let the beaver go." Reprinted with permission from Ingrid Rice.

By art is created that great leviathan called a commonwealth, or state, in Latin civitas, which is but an artificial man; though of greater stature and strength than the natural, for whose protection and defense it was intended; and in which sovereignty is an artificial soul, as giving life and motion to the whole body.[25]

In the fifteenth century the body of the monarch was represented by the Leviathan, whose authority was based on the doctrine of the Divine Right of ascension. In contemporary liberal democracies this monarchical authority has been usurped and displaced by the will of the people. Sovereignty lies in the representation of this will in a parliament or congress, but the corporeal terms live on. In the words of our former prime minister, Pierre Elliot Trudeau, "Parliament is the only body which represents the whole and is therefore the only body which can deal with problems on a national basis."[26]

The question of the divisibility of such a body lingers in present political discussions. States, as Dean and Massumi playfully demonstrate, strive for a "unity of substance" that is difficult to maintain.[27] The partition movement in the province, for example, claims that if Quebec can separate, then other parts of Quebec can be partitioned off so that those sections that are predominantly Anglophone or federalist can remain within Canada. The Cree and the Inuit state that if Quebec separates, they will claim sovereignty over the North.

No body is ever neutral in these discourses. Feminist political theorists such as Moira Gatens have commented that the predominant image of the body politic within liberal democracies is not gender neutral, but is a masculinized image of "unity and independence." Gatens suggests that slogans such as "Liberty, Equality, Fraternity" disguise the exclusions of specific bodies from full citizenship.[28] In the case of the Canada and Quebec conflict over sovereignty one witnesses the recurrent absence of other positions and issues from the debate. Meech Lake and Charlottetown, for example, were opposed by representatives of women's groups and Aboriginal communities, who both expressed profound dissatisfaction with their exclusion from the process of constructing these accords as well as silences within the final text. In the case of First Nations peoples in particular, the conflict over language and power between Canada and Quebec is seen as a fight between two colonial regimes. The debates over sovereignty are rightly understood as a conflict between two white settler cultures.

Theorizing the political from a feminist perspective also calls attention to the recurrent metaphor of the family and the gendering of the nation-state that takes place at the moment when there is a struggle for legitimate power. During the referendum, divorce and the breaking apart of the household was an analogy that intersected with the language of pain and disease. For example, *Maclean's* financial columnist Diane Francis deemed that Canada is like a "sick marriage": "The spouses are arguing about the symptom of marital breakdown rather than working on a real solution." The separatist claims of representing the spouse who wants to leave are illegitimate, in her estimation, because they are deceitful to their own populations. The only way to "institute clarity" and bring an end to "the never-end-it" is by forcing Quebeckers to answer the simple question of citizenship.[29] Sovereignty association is depicted as an illogical solution, akin to a request for marriage and divorce at the same time.

In the logic of federalism, sovereignty association is read as separation and separation is like a divorce. Divorce is painful and to be avoided at all costs. While divorce is central to the argumentative strategy, and is implicitly heterosexual, federalist accounts of such a relationship try not to gender the two partners in these claims because of the persistent feminization of Quebec. In Diane Francis's article, Quebec is simply named as the "spouse who wants to leave." There is a disavowal of any suggestion, in the words of one writer, that "federalism is a pig."[30]

While some federalist supporters equate the position of the wife with that of a victim, the tendency in media accounts of this conflict is to feminize Quebec as the wife who wants to leave the husband, abandon her children, and split

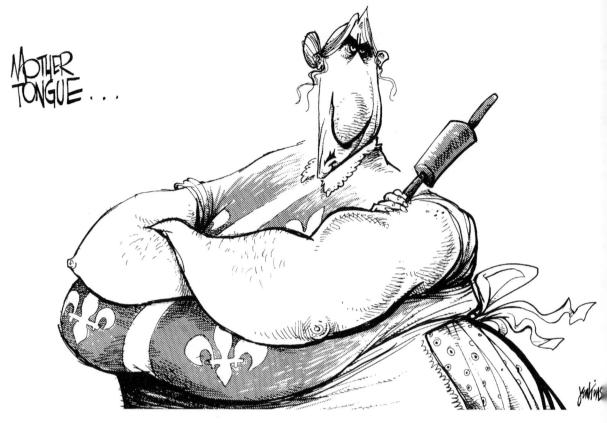

MOTHER TONGUE . . .

Figure 4. "Mother Tongue," by Anthony Jenkins.
Reprinted from the *Globe and Mail*, August 17, 1996.

up the household. In some instances, such as an October 1995 broadcast of Arthur Black's Saturday morning national radio show, this translates into sympathy for the "battered woman."[31] However, in an editorial cartoon, taken from the *Globe and Mail*, Quebec returns as an overweight peasant woman, "Mother Tongue," who threatens to clobber Anglophones in the province into submission by the institution of language laws (fig. 4).[32]

When supporters of Quebec independence use the marriage metaphor, the history of this marriage is given a different origin. Montreal writer Yves Beauchemin dates this bad marriage back to 1759, arguing that it is outdated to think that any couple must stay together at all costs. In Beauchemin's analysis, the current situation is untenable because one of the partners has been asked to abdicate her "personality" for the sake of the couple.[33] The marriage typically is gendered so that Canada is figured as male, Quebec as female. In these discourses federalism is pictured as the authoritarian, patriarchal husband who will not let "la belle province" go. From a Quebec nationalist perspective, a bad marriage is not worth saving. It is only after the partners have been divorced that they can come back together as friends and negotiate a settlement on equal terms.

Personal and Collective Narratives of Pain

> **... to have suffered together, enjoyed together and hoped together, this is worth more than any agreement on customs regulations or strategic borders. These are the things that everyone can understand, despite differences in race or language. A moment ago I said "having suffered together"; yes, grief binds people together more surely than joy. On occasions of national remembrance, sorrows count for more than triumphs, for they entail duties.**
>
> Ernest Renan
> "Discours et conférence"

Philosophers and clinicians have considered how the experience of pain can bring the human subject to the very threshold of language. In Canadian and Quebec politics there is no escaping the centrality of language, a cardinal point within debates on politics, culture, and identity. My dilemma here and my constant doubling of descriptions and terms indicate the impossibility of writing with any kind of neutrality or external position about this subject precisely because terms must be chosen: *sovereignty* or *separation*; *independence* or *amputation*; *cooperation* or *colonization*. Current provincial discussions about bilingualism and signs as exemplified and regulated in Bill 101 are only the contemporary evidence of a trauma that has been around since 1760. There are two predominant narratives that tell the story of how the damage came to pass.

In one narrative, the French colonial regime peacefully transferred administrative power over Upper Canada to the British. In the other retelling of this story, the British subjugated and colonized les habitants. In the words of Pierre Falardeau, Quebec nationalist film director and writer:

Me too, I am sick. It's 35 years that I have been sick, it's 223 years that I have been sick. I have been sick since the Referendum, since October 1970, since conscription, since 1867, since 1837, since 1760. Since 1760, since the beginning of the world. It's there, my pain.[34]

Falardeau's list underscores the cultural specificity of narratives of suffering and belonging that are distinct to a sensibility and recollection of the past in Quebec.[35] In Falardeau's case this recalling of betrayal, suffering, and conquest displays the profound differences in our rememberings and forgettings. This list may also include the signing of the Proclamation of 1763; the rebellions in Upper Canada of 1837 and 1847; the Durham Report of 1839; and extend right up to the October Crisis of

1970, the 1980 referendum, and the present. Within these historical narratives, the bodies of individuals and their pathologies may be understood as parallel to the story of a nation that is sick. Each of these dates refers to a specific moment in Canada-Quebec relations that most Quebecois would be familiar with, but that most Anglophones find mystifying. If, as Ernest Renan has said, nations are founded on sorrow and grief, and not just on constitutions, then our sufferings and our memories of historical injustice and wounding have not been the same.[36]

This chasm between the stories and felt historical experiences of these two nations is akin to some of the ontological dimensions of pain, or the gap between the experience of pain and the rendering of this experience into language. This occurs in three identifiable ways. First, the urgent presence of the sensation of pain, as lived by the person who is suffering, makes communicating pain to another difficult. Extreme pain may bring us to a preverbal state of communication and prohibit any utterance but a sob, a whimper, a cry, or a scream. These sounds and the gestures that accompany them, such as grimacing, shaking, or sweating, communicate, but this communication is not conventionally known as speech. It is difficult to incorporate into textual forms of analysis, although it may be describable in retrospect, after the fact.

Second, this incapacity to feel and thus fully apprehend someone else's pain, our inability to live in each other's skins, may call forth our empathy, as we remember our own past traumas, or pity. But it may have the opposite effect and result in an incomprehension and a denial of the extent of the other person's pain. For the person in pain, as Elaine Scarry notes, there is an absolute certainty of its existence.[37] For even the most empathetic observer of someone in pain, there is an irremediable gap between oneself and the person suffering. In this case, seeing and hearing a story of pain, particularly a tale of chronic pain, may inaugurate or widen the ontological gap between self and other.

Third, this disbelief inspires a search for physical evidence: a cut, a scrape, some tangible sign of that trauma. But as pain researchers Ronald Melzack and Patrick Wall note, the "puzzle of pain" is the absence of a necessary link between pain and injury. While in most instances, hitting one's finger with a hammer may produce a painful sensation, twenty percent of those who have surgery feel no pain for days or hours after the injury or incision, while seventy percent of those with chronic lower back pain may have no apparent injury.[38] Medical technologies are marshaled to the cause of providing certainty through attempts to image the source of pain. Yet pain is not necessarily localizable in the body in any kind of clear way, indicating that the body itself is not merely a fixed substance with clearly demarcated boundaries and neurological pathways. We construct stories around our pain, give it recognizable somatic form, name external referents, draw images of the source of the hurt to make sense of the intangible.

Here I would like to draw a homology between expressions of pain and expressions of national identity. The individual experience of pain and the collective feeling that one belongs to a nation or a culture share some characteristics. First, just as one cannot see pain directly, one cannot see the nation. Although pain may leave traces of its presence in various physical and material testaments, such as blood or open wounds, these referents are not indexical signs that can actually point to a singular location. The relationship between the site of trauma and felt pain is much less immediate.[39] Still, we construct referents. In a homologous way, a people concretize the nation-state in maps, museums, monuments, and buildings which signify the presence of political power. Second, just as to the person in pain there is absolute certainty of pain's existence, for the observer there may be doubt. A similar incredulity exists on the political level. To the person who feels a sense of belonging to a nation-state, this sense of belonging may be insistent, and very real. To the non-believer, this sense of belonging remains irrevocably intangible.

Images and words can nurture the affective identification of the citizenry with the state by materializing the body politic. As Hélène Pedneault wrote in *La Presse*, just two days before the referendum:

Moving towards autonomy isn't a political act, there is nothing political here. I know this in my body and in my soul. Politics is nothing but the result of my choice. The choice for independence is a choice to live. It is necessary so my blood can circulate better. Independence is food for the molecules, it's oxygen for our lungs, it's calcium for our bones, it's what nurtures our soul. Contrary to the dominant discourses, to choose "no" is to choose temporary survival. It is just enough to maintain us at the threshold of life before choking us slowly.
To say "yes" is to choose life.[40]

Pedneault wrote to the Francophone federalist paper in an attempt to reach and sway Francophone women voters, whose support for the sovereignty movement is statistically lower than other demographic groups. Pedneault's plea is akin to Falardeau's history of pain. Both collapse their bodies with that of the nation state and make the health of the individual dependent on the health of the collective.

This visceral political language has a "constitutive function," to borrow from Maurice Charland's interpretation of Kenneth Burke. It creates an affinity for the citizen with the body politic. Charland's reading of the construction of a "peuple Québecois" argues that there are no transcendental subjects to be mediated outside of discourse. According to Charland, mediation is not a process that impinges on a subject from a position of alterity. Citizens are not only persuaded to do this or that, but they are identified, and in their identification they embody discourses.[41] I would add that citizens do not only embody discourses, but that their discourses are in themselves embodied. This process of incorporating the citizen into the embrace of the nation-state is part of visual and verbal speech and is expressed in corporeal rituals, such as draping oneself in the nation's flag at parades and in the habit of painting the face and/or the body with the nation's colors and emblems at parades and demonstrations.

This collapsing of the individual and collective body becomes acute within times of crisis. Narratives of pain materialize an abstract entity like the nation-state to its citizenry, transforming it into a body that is symbiotically connected to that of the individual. A healthy nation, one without pain, promises to enfold the denizens of the nation in the embrace of a unifying state structure that will resolve all contradictions and heal all wounds. However, the frequency and intensity of the pain-filled language and the historical persistence of conflicts over sovereignty indicate that the wounds are spread throughout the body politic, that they are chronic injuries, and that they cannot be zipped shut quite so readily.

Conclusion

The vocabulary associated with the political body in pain illuminates the rhetorical strategies of avowedly federalist and sovereignist spokespersons. Chronicling this grief, as I have attempted to do here, is an exploratory venture into the wounds of our history that offers no solution outside of this impasse, but does explain some of our mutually exclusive, deeply rooted political assumptions. It is a necessarily incomplete process. The ambiguous results of the last referendum pose the possibility of a third try. The Canadian supreme court is trying to establish the legality of a future referendum on sovereignty, but the preceding analysis teaches that the issue of sovereignty is not only a legal issue to be decided in the courts. It is a political issue that implies very different conceptions of the body politic.

Within a federalist framework the nation is a body in crisis threatened from within by one of its own. It is about to be dismembered. This change is not liberation, it is separation. But even more, this separation is really a divorce that will destroy the family. Within this diagnosis the nation, like a house, should not be divided. Instead, the two sides should cohabit, side by side, peacefully within the same basic (federal) structure. The strategy is to remind the inhabitants—a family—that such grave political change will increase the pain, not alleviate it.

From the position of Quebec nationalism, the nation is a body, but the body is not being allowed to grow and develop normally. This body takes the form of a wife or a woman's body and "she" is not being allowed to leave home. Political change in this scenario is called independence and independence means survival, a new partnership so the two entities can grow together, side by side but distinct, different but equal in separate homes. While wounds from the past must be recalled to legitimate the desire to leave, on this side of the debate, the strategy is to minimize discussions of future pain in the event of change, to create a sense of optimism and hope. This transformation is not separation, it is sovereignty.

Notes

My sincere gratitude to Caroline Martel, who worked with dedication as a research assistant on this project. Her insightful questions profoundly transformed my own thinking.

1. Allan R. Gregg, "Can Canada Survive?" *Maclean's Special Report* (December 25, 1995/January 1, 1996), 14-15.

2. The sovereignty movement found support among a variety of groups across the political spectrum. In the English language media, this popular support for independence has been deemphasized and is generally discussed only under the rubric of a coalition of white males: Lucien Bouchard, Jacques Parizeau, and Mario Dumont, a former member of the liberal youth wing.

3. The Bloc Québecois is a federal party committed to serving Quebec's interests in the House of Parliament. Bouchard's status as a Quebec hero began when he crossed the floor of the House of Commons to form the Bloc Québecois (BQ) after the defeat of the Meech Lake Accord in 1990. Bouchard secured this status with his miraculous recovery from the "flesh-eating" disease that resulted in the amputation of one of his legs. The television cameras repeatedly feature Bouchard in a long shot limping into a room with his cane, reminding viewers of this struggle.

4. Miro Cernetig, "Alberta, British Columbia in No Mood for Conciliatory Approaches to Separatism," *Globe and Mail*, October 27, 1995, A1. These comments were made by Leo Boileau, a former resident of Quebec.

5. Quoted in Mario Fontaine, "Le démembrement du Canada serait 'une tragedie,' selon Bob Rae," *La Presse*, October 12, 1995, B1.

6. Editorial, *Montreal Gazette*, February 21, 1995, B2.

7. Jerry Lagan, telephone conversation with the author, Montreal-Oakville, August 10, 1996. When I interviewed him, Mr. Lagan stated that he would have preferred to feature the heads of Daniel Johnson and Jacques Parizeau on the publicity. His advertising agency advised against it.

8. Elaine Scarry, *The Body in Pain* (Oxford: Oxford University Press, 1985), 14.

9. Tony Wilden, *The Imaginary Canadian: An Examination for Discovery* (Vancouver: Pulp Press, 1984).

10. The ostensible source of the conflict is whether the constitution should include a "distinct society" clause that recognizes Quebec's difference from The Rest of Canada, know as TROC in the Francophone presses. See Kenneth McRoberts and Patrick Monahan, eds., *The Charlottetown Accord, the Referendum, and the Future of Canada* (Toronto: University of Toronto Press, 1993).

11. Selections for entry into the archive were initially made from the time of the PQ's election until the present. A list of words in English and French associated with pain served as an initial guide and means of finding headlines and articles.

12. Jacques Parizeau, "Quebec Is Canada's Constant Toothache Until It Leaves," *Canadian Speeches: Issues of the Day* (December 1994).

13. This position was resurrected in Parizeau's final virulent speech upon losing the referendum. In this nationally broadcast speech on the night of October 25, he blamed "money and the ethnic vote" for the loss.

14. Jacques Parizeau, "Quebec Is Canada's Constant Toothache Until It Leaves," 11.

15. Francine Lalonde, "Avenir du Québec: Il faut d'abord donner un coup de couer!" *La Presse*, October 6, 1995, B3.

16. Ken Dean and Brian Massumi, *First and Last Emperors* (New York: Autonomedia/Semiotexte, 1994), 138.

17. For a useful summary and analysis of the referendum, see Denis Monière and Jean H. Guy, *La Bataille du Québec: Troisième Episode: 30 jours qui ébranlèrent le Canada* (Montreal: Editions Fides, 1996).

18. Marcel Coté, "Cost of Separation So Great It Won't Happen," *Canadian Speeches: Issues of the Day* (March 1995), 52.

19. Federalists emphasize the responsiblity and reasonableness of the federalist position as opposed to the irrational, emotive separatist solution. See for example, Patrick Monahan, "Cooler Heads Shall Prevail," *The Referendum Papers* (Toronto: C.D. Howe Institute, 1995). This corresponds to the general characterization of Quebec as the heart of the country. As Trudeau commented on August 2, 1969, in a speech at St. George de Beauce, Quebec, "Without Quebec, Canada wouldn't have any heart and Canadian life would cease." Pierre Elliot Trudeau, *The Best of Trudeau: A Compendium of Whimsical Wit and Querulous Quip by Canada's Putative Prince* (Toronto: Modern Canadian Library, 1972), 21.

20. Dubuc is editor-in-chief of *La Presse*, a newspaper owned by Paul Desmarais, a longtime Francophone federalist. Despite the avowedly federalist position of the paper an incredible amount of space was devoted to "Oui" supporters, although it was mostly confined to the opinion section of the paper.

21. This position is similar to that of Conrad Black, owner of the Southam Press, who argued that "one cannot build a country" on social programs. Conrad Black, "Hope for a No, But See the Opportunities in a Yes," *Globe and Mail*, October 27, 1995, A19.

22. Both quotes from Landry and Johnson are taken from "Anglo Angst Is Real," *Montreal Gazette*, March 27, 1996, 1, 3.

23. John Hartley, *Understanding News* (London: Methuen, 1982), 116.

24. See, for example, Richard Mackie, "Johnson Warns of Huge Quebec Job Loss: Thousands of Federal Positions at Stake in Separatist Hotbed, No Leader Says," *Globe and Mail*, October 10, 1995, A1.

25. Thomas Hobbes, *Leviathan* (Harmondsworth, Penguin, 1968), 81-82.

26. Trudeau, *The Best of Trudeau*, 56.

27. Dean and Massumi, *First and Last Emperors*, 138

28. Moira Gatens, *Imagined Bodies: Ethics, Power and Corporeality* (London: Routledge, 1996).

29. Diane Francis, "It's High Time for a National Refer-end-it," *Maclean's*, September 16, 1996, 13.

30. *Globe and Mail*, August 10, 1995.

31. *Basic Black*, CBC Radio, October 28, 1995.

32. Within Quebec, Anglophones are a "linguistic minority," composing about 15 percent of the total population in the province, with higher numbers in the Montreal area.

33. Yves Beauchemin, "Séparer ce qui a été mal uni n'est pas une bien grande séparation," *La Presse*, October 24, 1995, B3.

34. Pierre Falardeau, *La liberté n'est pas une marque de yogourt: lettres, articles, projets* (Montreal: Stanké, 1995), 25.

35. See, for example, Jean Hamelin and Pierre Provencher, *Brève Histoire du Québec* (Montreal: Boréal, 1987); also Fernand Dumont, *Genèse de la Société Québecoise* (Montreal: Boréal, 1993).

36. A full-page advertorial, excerpted in the epigraph to this section, was composed of a long quote from Renan's 1887 text "Discours et Conference." A longer excerpt appeared in the *Globe and Mail*, October 28, 1995, in French and English. It was paid for by Morris and MacKenzie Insurance Brokers, Inc. For a similar reconstruction of this narrative, see Denis Moniére, Guy Bouthillier, Maurice Champagne, Pierre de Bellefeuille, Gaston Miron and H. Pelletier Baillargeon, "La Soveraineté pour notre unité, notre liberté et notre identité," *La Presse*, October 3, 1995, B3.

37. Elaine Scarry, *The Body in Pain*.

38. Ronald Melzack and Patrick Wall, *The Challenge of Pain* (New York: Basic Books, 1973), 15.

39. Benedict Anderson, *Imagined Communities: Reflections on the Origin and Spread of Nationalism* (London: Verso, 1983), 163.

40. Hélène Pedneault, "Au NON des femmes," *La Presse*, October 26, 1996, B3.

41. Maurice Charland, "Constitutive rhetoric: the case of *les peuple québecois*," *Quarterly Journal of Speech* (Fall 1987).

Theodore Wan

Bridine Scrub for General Surgery

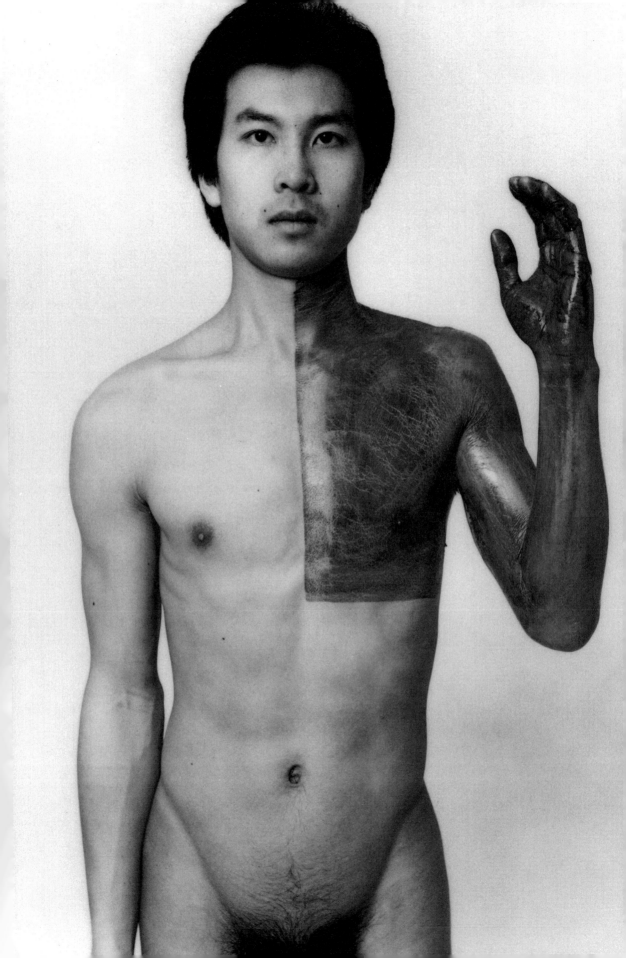

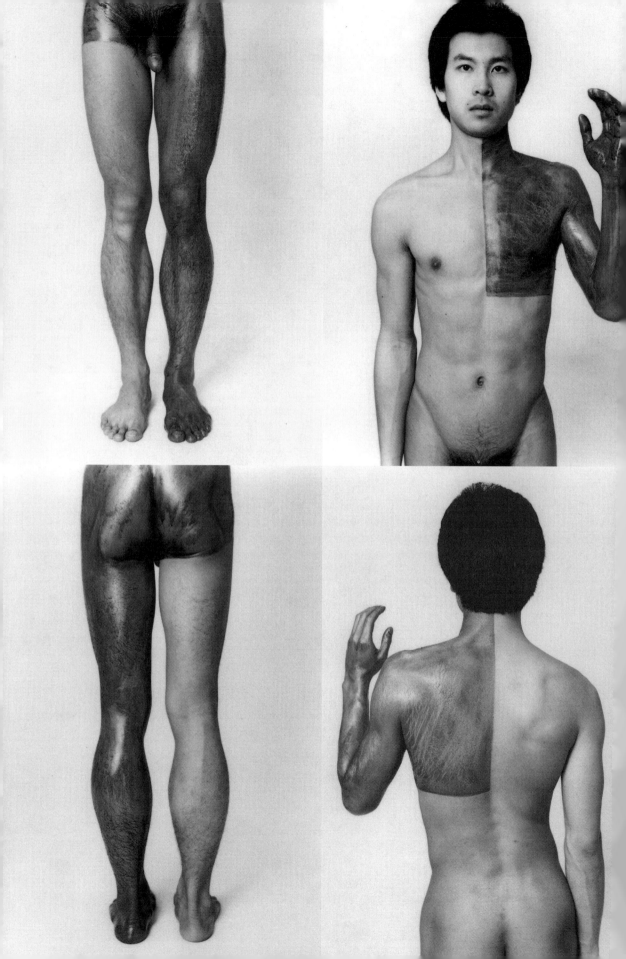

Johanne Sloan

Spectacles of Virtuous Pain

CATHOLIC ART of the late sixteenth and seventeenth centuries represented bodily suffering in relentless detail, creating a visual archive of pain unparalleled at any other moment in the history of Occidental art. Earlier ideals of religious serenity were superseded by a reconceptualization of Christian faith as an inner fever or a physical affliction, destabilizing the individual's attachment to the phenomenological world. Images of torture and martyrdom became normative signifiers of this exemplary passion. As attributes of Christian pain were brought to the foreground of representation in accordance with Counter-Reformation religious practices, a new spiritual and aesthetic rhetoric was set in motion, with the imperative that the spectator "see the martyrs' blood flow ... be witness to their painful agony."[1] There was now a discourse that reframed human pain in terms of divine grace coming into abrasive contact with the profane, temporal world; in the world of visual representation, gestures and expressions of pain marked this boundary. During this epoch of civil wars and social turmoil, however, it was more than ever demanded that works of art serve the needs of the church, and if the body in extremis became more intelligible, it is because each corporeal spasm could register the sentience of the body politic.

During the violent upheavals of the church's schism, then, the ideal form of (Christian) subjectivity implied a willingness to insert one's body, in the most explicit way, into the ideological conflict; it was increasingly the responsibility of individual men and women to monitor the desires and sensations of their own bodies for the common good. But the spectacularization of bodily pain had specific connotations for women, who since antiquity had been deemed constitutively more "enfleshed" and less spiritual than men. Counter-Reformation art's new pantheon of women martyrs and ecstatics presented heroic examples by virtue of the physical abuse they seemed to endure, yet their brand of pain and heroism necessarily appeared in a discursive context quite distinct from that of their male counterparts. For a revitalized Catholic regime, the transient effects of pain and pleasure on female bodies were not only deserving of close scrutiny; there developed as well an aesthetic code with particularly feminine properties.

Questions of gender are perhaps not immediately evident in studying this period, for sixteenth-century religious dissenters throughout Europe assailed the corruption of the Papacy and the clergy, the sale of indulgences, and the excessive idolatry of the saints. It was in reaction to the threat of dissolution posed by such reformers that the centralized power of the Papacy set out to defend the moral foundations of its various institutions, including many forms of representational practices. Challenges to ecclesiastical authority were uniformly categorized under the rubric of heresy, and this of course included the distant threats of Islam and other "pagan" cultures, as well as the nascent creeds of Protestantism. But more than ever before, there was a concerted effort to identify and eradicate contaminants present within the church's borders—witches' and heretics' transgressive quests for knowledge and experience outside the dominion of the established faith.[2] It was around the figure of the witch—a feared, malignant, and damned female body—that the crises in faith and femininity converge.

In relation to the repertoire of imagery under consideration here, it is significant that the violently oppressive solutions of the Inquisition and witch-hunts were instituted concurrently with the church's productive evangelism, which laid a new emphasis on the individual subject's accountability for her or his own faith. Christian identity was beleaguered, and it could come perilously close to dissolution, but it would be reconstructed so as to revitalize and strengthen ecclesiastical power. This project required, however, new practices whereby the particularities of each devotee's sinning body and soul could be rendered intelligible. Every individual's interior monologue would henceforth become a constituent part of a Christian metalanguage. Michel Foucault has discussed the emergence of the confessional mode of discourse in the seventeenth century, how "for every good Christian . . . an imperative was established: Not only will you confess to acts contravening the law, but you will seek to transform your desire, your every desire, into discourse."[3] In Foucault's view, the "invention" of individual conscience at this historical moment would have critical repercussions for modern conceptions of subjectivity and sexuality.

These normative techniques of autogenous prayer, leading to admissions of guilt and so to penance, had to be learned by the uninitiated. Prior to this epoch, the clergy had been positioned as intermediaries between the laic population and the divinity. Even reading the Bible was a privilege of the clerical elite: "The idea that individuals were responsible for their own salvation transformed the belief structure."[4] Documents such as Saint Ignatius of Loyola's "Spiritual Exercises," written in 1522 and disseminated widely thereafter, served as models for the self-scrutinizing, self-censuring practices advocated by Counter-Reformation authorities. As the title of his work suggests, the spiritual faculties had to be exercised; the individual was encouraged to experience faith as a perpetual struggle against sin, and this was accomplished by imaginatively repulsing assaults to the corporeal body. Saint Ignatius enumerated the distinct sense-by-sense impressions the exercitant should invoke while contemplating martyrdom, death, or in this case, hell: "By my sense of smell I will perceive the smoke, the sulpher . . . , by my sense of taste I will experience the bitter flavours of hell: tears, sadness . . . , by my sense of touch, I will feel how the flames touch the souls and burn them."[5] With the almost synesthetic stimuli provided by these practices, every manifestation of physical discomfort or pain is welcomed, as an opportunity to test the limits of the quotidian sensory world against the immutable reality of divine right.

The spectacle of bodily pain in Counter-Reformation art promised to render visible the imbrication of psychic and somatic realities, in such a way that viewers would barely distinguish between the mimetic and the aesthetic. Baroque churches are still replete with paintings of saints enduring gruesome flagellations, decapitations, and dismemberments, but for seventeenth-century adherents to the faith there was no question of averting one's gaze from the horror (as contemporary cinema viewers often do, for instance). For it was by looking long and intently that viewers could interiorize the fiction and make it come to life again on the surface of their bodies, under the gaze of the divinity. Artworks were thus to be actively deployed in the religious war, so that "the people are instructed, and strengthened in remembering, and continually reflecting on the articles of faith."[6] For the Jesuits, who were important patrons of this art, as well as for other missionary orders, representations of martyrdom were used, quite explicitly, to encourage the brothers heading for Japan, Africa, or America to prepare for their forthcoming glorious deaths at the hands of "pagans." On the domestic front, these representations functioned somewhat differently, instituting a visual equivalent to the narratives of self-realization being promulgated by orthodox theologians, and to the body-and-soul dialogues that had been a literary genre since the Middle Ages. This dualistic matrix had traditionally implicated body and soul in divergent teleologies; in general terms the *body* was debased and damned while the *soul* or *spirit* was considered a transcendent term. Yet the status of the body (and of nature, the temporal world encasing the body) continued to be disputed in both Protestant and Catholic camps. The imaginative concept of body and soul as "warring entities" in seventeenth-century literature, as discussed by Rosalie Osmond, was inevitably enacted by adversarial allegorical figures.[7]

In the visual arts this conflict could be rendered visible on individual human figures, and if any reconciliation of the body-mind schism was possible, it would be concretized in the canonical lives and bodies of the saints, both male and female. Artworks illustrated accounts of the extraordinary bodies of saints: bodies that withstood the ravages of torture and disease; that produced miraculous stigmata; that resisted decomposition, remaining warm and fragrant after death. In her study of such practices among medieval women, Caroline Walker Bynum has suggested that while women's association with the body carried a burden of malignant connotations, this could also be interpreted positively, as a proximity to the fact of Christ's bodily incarnation. Counter-Reformation representations correspond with this compensatory reading of the debased body, where "body is not so much hindrance to the soul's ascent as the opportunity for it. Body is the instrument upon which the mystic rings changes of pain and delight."[8] But it is significant that the epoch's religious crisis—the church's will to triumph over the forces of paganism, nature, and the body—intersects with the development of a new scientific paradigm in the seventeenth century, which construed nature as the irrational and feminine raw material that must be subdued and dominated by male reason. Evelyn Fox Keller has observed that "the real impact of the scientific revolution was . . . to take God out of woman and out of material nature."[9] Therefore, at a time when the nature of femininity and the femininity of nature are unstable categories throughout the belief structure, the religious art of the Counter-Reformation in a certain sense was able to provide a venue for the articulation of this tension.

The idea that Christian women and men should be anxious to discover the limits of their own embodiment, that spiritual potency could thus be put to empirical trial, was epitomized in graphic representations of saints being tortured. Often, their faces are transfigured by smiles of divine contentment. The pleasure-pain threshold successfully crossed by saints—that which the ordinary devout could only strive for—was the corroborative evidence of their virtue. On the one hand, therefore, such representations of a spiritual elite reinforced the hierarchic structure of the religious institution. And yet, on the other hand, the public persecution and torture of witches served a similar role, for the discourse around diabolism, depraved female sexuality, and anamorphic bodies was an inversion of the understanding of sanctified bodies.[10] Christina Larner has described the social consequences of this identification: "The execution of a witch . . . redefined the boundaries of normality to secure the safety of the virtuous community."[11] However, in both extremes of feminine identification—the behavior and appearance deemed either witchlike or saintlike—we find bodies that are similiarly sites of paranormal metamorphoses, through, for instance, the capacity to cause or cure illnesses in other people. How to distinguish between them? If the bodies of evil women (witches) were manifestly different from those of virtuous women, it was necessary to interpret and categorize a range of physical symptoms and articulations. And so the most extreme conditions of pain and pleasure could become gendered texts, subject to exegesis only by the church's most learned men.

Distinguishing between diabolical possession and (correct) mystical transport was to be a crucial, if contested, procedure for Counter-Reformation authorities, especially in the case of women. Even a famously devout woman like Teresa of Avila, who was sanctified and achieved cult status throughout Europe shortly after her death, was interrogated by the Inquisition and her experiences repudiated by some church doctors as "nothing more than erotic, diabolical possession."[12] If women were associated with "body, lust, weakness and irrationality, [and] men with spirit or reason or strength," then it followed logically that malevolent forces would be rampant in their occupation of women's bodies.[13] The expulsion of such evils from women's bodies, through torture, constituted a particular kind of moral victory: it was a triumph of patriarchal order over the perceived chaos and corruptibility of feminized nature. In her analysis of the political attributes of torture, Elaine Scarry has written of "the translation of all the objectified elements of pain into the insignia of power, the conversion of the enlarged map of human suffering into an emblem of the regime's strength."[14] The visible evidence of assaults on women's bodies coincided with the production of a double archive of testimonials relating to female identity, made accessible to the ecclesiastical authorities through physical suffering; confessions of transgression and conspiracy torn from

Figure 1. *Ecstasy of Saint Teresa*, by Gian Lorenzo Bernini (1645).
Reprinted with permission from the Bibliotheca Hertziana, Rome.

women through acts of torture; or, confessional accounts of victorious self-realization and conformity, resulting from torments either imposed or self-induced.

The mangled bodies of "witches" displayed in public spaces throughout Europe were clearly an imprimatur of the regime's omnipotence, providing "proof" of the victory over a degenerate (female) nature. Counter-Reformation art's saintly heroines provided an alternate performance for doubtful spectators, in their ability to transcend the worldly pain inflicted by their oppressors, achieving states of extraterrestrial bliss: Saint Barbara, executed by her heathen father; Saint Agatha with breasts severed from her body; Saint Lucia, whose eyes were gouged out. These are only a few who were represented again and again. While such violent assaults were no more cruel than the decapitations and flayings inflicted on male saints, the lone women being attacked by a group of men were usually defending their virginity and youthful beauty as much as their faith. In the simulacral realm of religious art, the plasticity of the human body knows no bounds. Reborn out of bloodshed and violence, the female body achieves another register of beauty, in contrast to the provisional, seductive attractiveness of mere earthly bodies. The discourse superscribed on, alternately, evil or virtuous women underlined the relevancy of self-disclosure for the population at large; if feminine subjectivity was an inherently problematic category, women's beauty, sexuality, and faith had to be discursively circumscribed.

The case of Saint Teresa of Avila is somewhat anomalous within the epoch's rostrum of favored feminine identities because, unlike Saint Barbara or Saint Agatha, she was not a quasi-mythic figure from the early days of Christianity. She died at the end of the sixteenth century, when the Counter-Reformation was in full operation, so it is possible to trace the rapid transformation of her life story into official discursive territory, and into a privileged position in the visual arts. She was not martyred, and yet the ecology of pain instituted by the Catholic regime necessitated an arduous struggle toward full Christian subjecthood, and so as proof of her fidelity she induced her own access to an emancipatory realm of pain. Teresa was a prolific author of theological texts and founder of several convents, but these prosaic accomplishments were secondary to her reputation for communion with the divine. In one of her mystical episodes, which became the subject of numerous paintings, Teresa was spiritually betrothed to Jesus Christ, a union symbolized by his giving her, not the usual ring, but one of the nails from his crucifixion.[15] Receiving this privileged signifier of pain was a guarantee of Teresa's empowerment as an individual, allowing her to exceed the dictates of nature, including the "obstacle" of her femininity. Gian Lorenzo Bernini's sculpture of 1645, known as *Ecstasy of Saint*

Teresa or the *Transverberation*, also interprets a passage from Teresa's writings, where she described how an angel "plunged [the great golden arrow] into my heart several times so it penetrated to my entrails ... The sweetness caused by this pain is so extreme that one cannot possibly wish it to cease" (fig. 1).[16] Similarly to other representations of women martyrs and mystics, this work presents the spectacle of a body in torment, and simultaneously in bliss, which also displays a youthful, sexualized body.[17] With regard to the effects of both nail and arrow on Teresa's body, Teresa's pain is not local or specific to any particular limb or organ, nor is it even specific to her body. Rather, the mystic enters into a universe of pain that does not respect the boundaries of individual bodies. Bernini's sculpture depicts a woman with her head thrown back, parted lips, and almost trembling limbs, yet the body is veiled by an enormous wave-like drapery and so does not contravene the prohibition on nudity in religious imagery. While on one level this portrayal seems to bespeak a woman's absolute surrender, her masochistic loss of self, it is also possible to regard this phenomenon differently. Alison Weber has argued that "Teresa's rhetoric of feminine subordination ... produced the desired perlocutionary effect. Her words were taken as an ingenuous act: 'This woman is not a deceiver.' "[18] Women were obliged to appear enthralled by and in thrall to the divinely patriarchal order, but the institution of this relationship also allowed women a discursive space within which to study, write, and speak. Teresa was ultimately judged to be an authentic Christian because, unlike the "deceiving" heretics and witches, her personal testimony, in appropriate Counter-Reformation fashion, convinced its readers that the myriad pains and pleasures of her body were righteous sensations and desires. Teresa's "divine sickness" announces the health of the Christian regime. The extreme sensuality of Teresa's text and of many contemporaneous artworks—considered erotic in contemporary terms—was not censored by the seventeenth-century church, and thus representations of women's (self-induced) pleasure entered into religious discourse. Other images, such as the *La Madeleine* paintings of Michelangelo da Caravaggio (fig. 2), also portrayed a "possessed" woman, back arched and gesturing skyward. But if these bodies are ostensibly "sights" presented to a divinely omniscient male gaze, they are also, paradoxically, women oblivious to all gazes, completely engrossed by their own thoughts and desires. It is important once again to consider the pathological sexuality that was contemporaneously ascribed to witches, heretics, Jews, and various other infidels. While witches' purported acts of fornication with the devil were threatening to social and psychic order, Teresa's anguished, quasi-sexual encounter with a specter could be recuperated by the ecclesiastical authorities, and even enhanced in works of art.

Figure 2. *La Madeleine*, by Michelangelo da Caravaggio (1606).
Reprinted with permission from the Musée des Beaux-Arts, Marseille.

If Counter-Reformation practices promised that the soul's victory could elevate the status of the body, women's successful attainment of such utopic harmony was still deemed a particularly miraculous occurrence. Even within officially sanctioned mystical practices, women's bodies would continue to be an unstable category, productive of an excess libidinal energy that could not be described or subdued within existing institutional parameters. Foucault writes that "the phenomena of possession and ecstasy, which were quite frequent in the Catholicism of the Counter Reformation, were undoubtedly effects that had got outside the control of the erotic technique immanent in this subtle science of the flesh."[19] A social space, however restrictive, was created that allowed the "problem" of women's embodied experiences to be articulated, but the particularities of women's pains and pleasures would require more and more discursive territory, in the nascent secular disciplines of medicine, psychiatry, and jurisprudence.

Notes

1. Emile Male, *L'art religieux après le Concile de Trent* (Paris: Armand Colin, 1932), 147.

2. The persecution, torture, and execution of such enemies of the state was common to both Catholic and Protestant camps, reaching a crescendo during the latter part of the sixteenth century and continuing throughout Europe for the next hundred years. See Christina Larner, *Witchcraft and Religion: The Politics of Popular Belief* (Oxford: Basil Blackwell, 1984) and Norman Cohn, *Europe's Inner Demons* (London: Oxford University Press, 1975).

3. Michel Foucault, *The History of Sexuality, Volume One* (New York: Vintage Books, 1978), 21.

4. Larner, *Witchcraft and Religion*, 65.

5. Ignatius of Loyola, *The Spiritual Exercise and Selected Works*, ed. G. Ganss (New York: Paulist Press, 1991), 141.

6. From the "The Canons and Decrees of the Council of Trent," quoted in Jonathan Brown, *Images and Ideas in Seventeenth-Century Spanish Painting* (Princeton, N. J.: Princeton University Press, 1978), 57.

7. Rosalie Osmond, *Mutual Accusation: Seventeenth-Century Body and Soul Dialogues in Their Literary and Theological Context* (Toronto: University of Toronto Press, 1991), 20.

8. Caroline Walker Bynum, *Fragmentation and Redemption: Essays on Gender and the Human Body in Medieval Religion* (New York: Zone Books, 1992), 194.

9. Evelyn Fox Keller, *Reflections on Gender and Science* (New Haven, Conn.: Yale University Press, 1985), 54.

10. *The Malleus Maleficarum* (The Hammer of Witches), published in 1486 by the Dominicans Sprenger and Institor, was a papally endorsed text that described the alleged sexual practices, social behavior, and physical attributes of demonically inspired women and was still considered a definitive text in the seventeenth century.

11. Larner, *Witchcraft and Religion*, 45

12. Alison Weber, *Teresa of Avila and the Rhetoric of Femininity* (Princeton, N. J.: Princeton University Press, 1990), 160.

13. Bynum, *Fragmentation and Redemption*, 202

14. Elaine Scarry, *The Body in Pain: The Making and Unmaking of the World* (New York: Oxford University Press, 1985), 56.

15. Male, *L'art religieux*, 163.

16. From the "Life of St. Teresa," quoted in Howard Hibbard, *Bernini* (Harmondsworth: Penguin Books, 1965), 137.

17. "[Teresa] is sometimes depicted as a large woman with heavy, almost coarse features, after the authentic portraits that exist; but more usually, especially in Italian painting, her appearance is much idealized." James Hall, *Dictionary of Symbols and Subjects in Art* (London: John Murray, 1974), 298.

18. Weber, *Teresa of Avila*, 159.

19. Foucault, *The History of Sexuality*, 70.

Theodore Wan

Bound by Everyday Necessities I and II

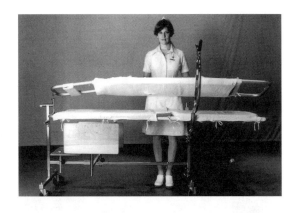
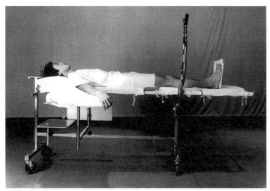
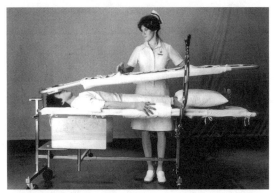
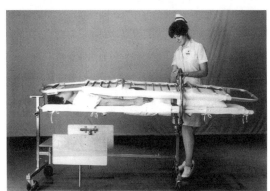
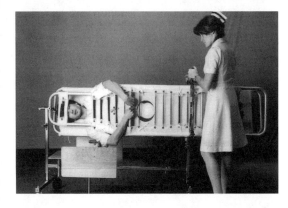
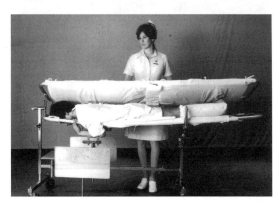
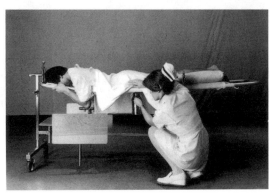

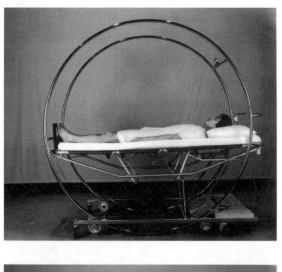 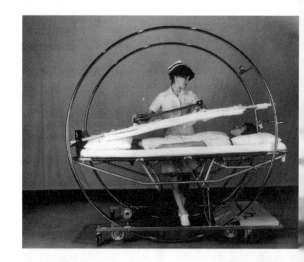

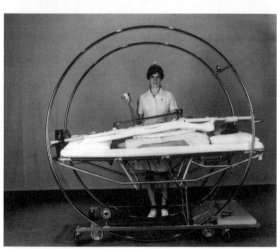 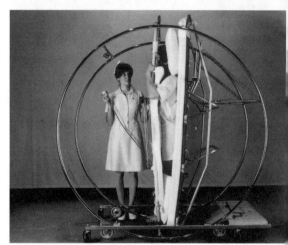

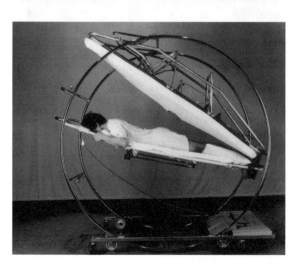 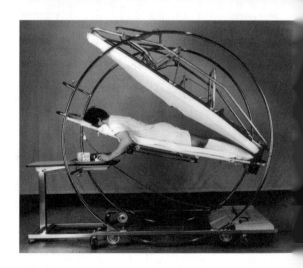

Gregory Whitehead

Display Wounds:

Ruminations of a

Vulnerologist

[*In the operating room: cutting through flesh, the metallic clink of surgical equipment.*]

Uhh . . . it's a nasty cut. OK . . . let's see. Give me the number seven probe . . .
Yes. Something . . . have to get . . . underneath the bone there. Good . . . OK.
The clamp . . . The skin is . . . it's kind of wrapped around the muscle there.
Get me a sponge?

And . . . I'll need a little piece of that tape there.
It is *not a pretty cut* . . .
But we'll get it.
The scissors . . . And . . . let's see if we can clean it up here around the edges.
OK.

We're losing . . . we're losing a lot of blood.
Could you . . . yeah, that's right.
Just hook it up. Thank you.
The problem is there's a *bone* back here that . . .
refuses to cooperate with us.

[*Begin bandoneon: slow tango*]

And, uh . . . OK. Now let's see if we can get . . . I'll get that.
Yeah, it's coming . . . got to get all that *stuff* out of there . . .
and we'll be able to close it up and no one will ever tell the difference.

[*Music rises to full volume. Cuts abruptly, change of room tone, more of an office environment*]

No wound ever speaks for itself. The only thing that you will find emerging spontaneously from a wound is blood. If you're interested in the deeper significance, then wounds have to be *read*. They have to be *interpreted* and *deciphered*. Vulnerology, or the science of wounds, is the activity of this interpretation.

What you saw earlier was simply stopping the bleeding, and stopping the bleeding has really nothing to do with treating the wound. Treating the wound is an *interpretive* process. Attempting to understand and decipher what the wound *is*.

cutting sound/the "voice" of the wound

We are a society that prides itself on the invention of new, faster, more powerful, more dynamic technological innovations. We do not want to have to grapple with the fact that every technological innovation carries with it a contribution to what I call the *woundscape*.

People frequently comment that I have a way of speaking that is unusually slow. Well, this is not simply a way to avoid wounding my larynx; it's a way of making a *personal* contribution toward the deceleration of a highly lethal woundscape founded on *speed*.

cut/voice/wound

It's interesting that you introduce the comparison to language because my approach as a vulnerologist is to think of the wound as a sign between the individual body and the technological landscape. The wound is an inscription that's left on the surface of the flesh by—

Gregory Whitehead

cut/voice/wound

[*Bandoneon, full volume, continuing lower as vulnerologist begins*]

It's impossible to think of a specific technology in separation
from the damage that it can do. And, in this sense, I think of a whole . . .
handwriting, a whole . . . *handwriting*, in this sense, I think . . .

it's a handwriting that is based on the potential within that culture to . . .
hurt . . . itself.

[*Full volume tango, fading as vulnerologist continues*]

There are a lot of problems, there are a lot of problems of interpretation
that one confronts in deciphering this peculiar kind of handwriting. That's because
wounds will always play the fool. Wounds are *compulsive liars*.
The way the wound appears on the surface is rarely an accurate identification of the
full dimensions of the wound.

Stopping the bleeding has really nothing to do with treating the wound. Treating
the wound is an *interpretive* process. I don't feel that the wound has really been
treated until it has been given a voice, until it has been empowered to *speak*.

No wound ever speaks for itself. The goal of the vulnerological interpretive activity,
then, is to construct a voice for the wound.

The first thing that we do is we make an abstraction of the wound. We try to construct a representation—through fiber optics, and fractal geometry, we construct
the image of the wound. What we discovered is that most wounds, biomechanically,
have a strong resemblance to the human larynx.
So the next step was to find ways to get . . . the wounds . . . to *speak*.

cut/voice/wound

[*Slide projector runs; first "slide" sequence begins*]

This next series shows multiple blood trauma wounds suffered by a female subject during a train collision and subsequent derailment.

[*Click*] You can see from this first projection that the surface of the body is pretty much untouched. [*Click*] It's simply impossible to conceive of this degree of internal wound prior to a certain stage of technological development. [*Click*] And I think this series demonstrates pretty well the connection between the technological environment and the woundscape. [*Click*] It's hard to know where to begin descriptively with blood trauma; the wounds are so . . . massive and widespread. [*Click*] But in this projection you can see that almost all of the organs have been displaced, and there's generalized occlusion. [*Click*]

[*Female tango singing begins full volume, continues, lower, through speech. Singing begins during "lecture" and continues throughout*]

It was over the course of analyzing this particular sequence that we began to understand the complexity of the language of contemporary wounds. [*Click*] The voice appears to center around the abscess in the lower left corner of this shot there. [*Click*] This is a magnification. [*Click*] And now we see it from a rather different perspective, from underneath. [*Click*]

[*Female singing ends. Tango music begins quietly and continues through vulnerologist*]

Obviously, if you're analyzing a wound resulting from a collision of bullet trains or a crash of a supersonic jet or an . . . automobile collision, the literal meaning of the wound frequently cannot be translated. The practice of the vulnerologist is oriented more toward getting the *feel* of the wound.

Sensing its *emotion*. Sensing its *quality*. Getting the *feel* of the wound.
Sensing its emotion. Sensing the deeper nature of its experience.
Sensing the implications of the *kinds of wounds* that can be expected.

The danger is that the woundscape will produce a society of monsters.

[*Tango swells and ends*]

Gregory Whitehead

[*Slide projector turned on; second slide sequence*]

[*Click*] This is a projected simulation of a head wound, taken from our historical archives. [*Click*] It was originally suffered by a German foot soldier, on the first day of the Battle of Verdun, during the First World War.
[*Click*] A battle, which, incidentally, played a critical role in the formation of the contemporary woundscape. [*Click*] And in this magnified fractal tomograph, you can see the thoroughly dispersed endusium grisium. [*Click*]

[*German singing—World War I funeral march—begins faintly*]

That foggy mass in the lower right would seem to indicate that the subject suffered a retrograde conduction avalanche deep inside the hypothalamus. [*Click*] If you follow the residual wound tract through the crushed tween-brain ganglion, you can see what we think is the wound's voice. [*Click*]

[*Singing is full volume. Click. End of singing; then bandoneon tango begins again low, continues through below*]

It's interesting that you introduce the comparison to language because in Western tradition there's a very deep relationship between word and wound.
If you think, for example, of the five wounds in the body of Christ— Well, theologically, each one of those wounds represents an authentic verification, in blood, of the essential humanity of Christ.

Each wound is an *opening* into the word of God, and the body of Christ on the cross is then a living materialization of scripture.

The theater of wounds is a memory theater.

Somehow the vocabulary of the spirit and the vocabulary of the flesh intersect in this image.

[*Bandoneon/tango music full volume, ends. Slide projector runs third slide sequence*]

[*Click*] This last series illustrates the third category of wounds. Wounds that are

visible, not physiologically, but genetically. [*Click*] This is the chromosomal structure of an infant born to parents who suffered prolonged exposure to radioactive
waste. [*Click*] With the assistance of a computer, what we've done is simulate five
successive generations in the language of this wound. [*Click*]

[*the wound speaks: five generations of screeching, each higher pitched than the one before.
Tango music, full volume*]

It's impossible to think of a specific technology in separation from the damage that
it can do. And, in this sense, I think of a whole . . . *handwriting*, a whole . . . *handwriting*, in this sense, I think . . . it's a handwriting that is based on the potential
within that culture to . . . hurt . . . itself.

[*Tango music, full volume, dies out in next rumination*]

There are a lot of problems . . . there are a lot of problems of interpretation that
one confronts in deciphering this . . . peculiar kind of handwriting. Wounds do not
speak a language that is readily accessible. The wound is an inscription that's left on
the surface of the flesh by this other body, which is a technological body.

Treating the wound is an *interpretive* process. Attempting to understand and decipher what the wound *is*. Staring into the dark *hole* of the wound. The *abyss* of the
wound. Looking backward—obsessively, fixated on the wound: which *gave blood*.

cut/voice/wound

Working as a vulnerologist carries the same kind of stigma as a mortician—wounds,
after all, represent dead subjective experience, dead experience that most people
would prefer to suppress or forget. Wounds are the physical repositories for the
memory of experience that most people would prefer to suppress or forget.

The experience of receiving a wound is a shock, and the connection between shock
and amnesia is pretty well known. There's simply a massive individual and cultural
resistance to recognizing the significance of wounds. The theater of wounds is a
memory theater, which most people would prefer to suppress or forget.

Gregory Whitehead

So why do we do it? That's a difficult question. Wounds cannot speak for themselves. And yet wounds are the evidence of stories that are of profound importance. If they are neglected, ignored, simply stitched up and forgotten, then we will get to the point where we can't look at ourselves. The wounds become deeper, less apparent, more *structural*, if you will, even *genetic*. Wounds that become apparent only in the second or third generation.

The theater of wounds is a *memory* theater. Our failure to look at wounds *now*, and interpret them *now*, may lead us to give birth to a society of monsters.

[*Return to the sounds of the operating room*]

It is *not a pretty cut* . . . But we'll get it. The scissors . . .

And . . . let's see if we can clean it up here around the edges. OK. We're losing . . . we're losing a lot of blood. Could you . . . yeah, that's right.
Just hook it up. Thank you.

And, uh . . . OK. Now let's see if we can get under that . . . yeah, it's coming . . . got to get all that *stuff* out of there . . . and we'll be able to close it up and no one will ever tell the difference.

cut/voice/wound

[*Bandoneon begins, continues through vulnerologist*]

Wounds are lost individually. They're ignored, they're suppressed, they're forgotten. They scab over and they're gone. My hope is that I can join them together in a chorus. And perhaps that . . . chorus . . . will be heard.

[*Music ends. Broadcast ends*]

Barbara McGill Balfour

Senile Uterus / Macerated Liver (from *Dermatographia,* 1992)

Senile Uterus.

longitudinal section of smooth muscle

' cross-section of smooth muscle.

All pains last longer

Drawings illustrate atrophy of muscle due to senility

than the stimulation causing them.

E.H. Weber On the sense of Touch and Common Sensibility
1846

Macerated Liver

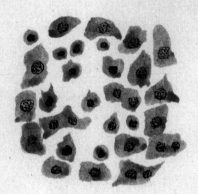

showing blood islands.
composed of nucleated reds.

I bruise so easily.

J.D.Balfour

Take a Pill

Stephen Busby

Taking Control: How I Learned to Live with AIDS

My Health History: Pain

I HAVE been living with AIDS for more than two years now. Pain of one kind or another is a fairly constant companion: physical pain caused by various illnesses and medications, compounded by fear and anxiety from the uncertain course of the disease, the inability of medical science to provide a cure for it, and the stigma associated with it. The active management of my health has become my full-time job, reading and talking to others about their experiences.

Unfortunately, many people with AIDS do not have the same opportunities and advantages that I have. They may feel isolated without the support I receive from family, friends, health professionals, and the community. In many cases, AIDS quickly reduces people to poverty. I hope to provide some insight into the reality of living with this terminal illness, to show how I have come to terms with it, and to suggest to others some possible ways to regain control of one's life. An integral part of this process has been the recognition of cultural myths, their acceptance by me and by others, the often negative effects they can exert by increasing the stigma and shame people experience.

My health began to decline in the fall of 1990 until, several months later, I was no longer able to walk upstairs without stopping, sometimes more than once, to catch my breath. I had known for several years that I was HIV-positive but I somehow thought that if I took my AZT every day I'd never get sick. I was diagnosed with pneumonia in February 1991. It was devastating to realize that I had now "crossed the line," that I met the official criteria for AIDS.

The conditions required for an AIDS diagnosis are set by the Centers for Disease Control (CDC), an American government agency that tracks epidemics. Their definition, which has been updated several times, is widely accepted. It creates a huge perceived gap between those who are HIV-positive but asymptomatic and those who have had a life-threatening opportunistic infection and are therefore said to have AIDS. It is becoming more common to refer to the entire course of illness as HIV disease, eliminating the artificial distinction between those who are HIV-positive and those with "full-blown" AIDS. This may encourage those who are asymptomatic to accept that their immune function is declining, even though they have no symptoms.

Pneumocystis carinii pneumonia (PCP) completely drained my energy. Even when I was lying still, my breathing was shallow and labored and the least exertion left me gasping for air. I became so tired I did not want to get out of bed in the morning. At night I would sweat so much that I would often wake up freezing and have to change the sheets. The standard treatment for pneumonia is Septra, a sulfa drug. Several days after treatment began, I realized that I was allergic to it. The top half of my body turned bright red and I had a high fever. The combination of fatigue and fever left me completely disoriented.

At the same time I noticed a large purplish patch of Kaposi's sarcoma (KS) on my leg. My doctor also found two more patches on the roof of my mouth. Kaposi's sarcoma used to be a rare cancer of the capillaries until AIDS appeared. It may remain confined to a few spots and not cause problems, but it may infect internal organs or the bottom of the feet, where it can make walking unbearable. Candidiasis (a yeast infection commonly known as thrush) also spread from my throat down my esophagus, making me throw up all the time. Often I would throw up my breakfast and then leave for work. Having all these problems at once was overwhelming. Everything centered on surviving one day at a time.

In the midst of all these infections and a bad drug reaction, I felt I had to break the news to those closest to me and deal with their responses. Although my parents knew I was HIV-positive, none of my family or friends had any idea of the seriousness of my condition. I thought that I could remain healthy indefinitely with the help of medication and by taking good care of myself. I did not want to be treated as a patient, dependent on others.

When I returned to work after having been off almost a month, my coworkers were aware that there was something quite wrong with my health. I had lost more than twenty-five pounds in two months and wasn't looking at all well. It was difficult to deal with their comments, however well meaning they were. I didn't know how my bosses would react if they knew about my condition, so I told them as little as possible. As a consultant on contract, my position was somewhat precarious. A consulting company would rather lose an employee than risk losing a client. I had only started this job the previous autumn. I thought the client might guess my status and tell my employers that they no longer wanted me. The excuse for letting me go would be the amount of time I had taken off, which had put my part of the project a month behind schedule.

Under the terms of our long-term-disability-insurance policy I had to work another seven months or lose all benefits. I felt that financial pressures would mount in the future, and I made the decision to stick it out at work for the rest of the year if I possibly could. Having AIDS can be expensive if you end up requiring private nursing or attendant care. I am luckier than the many people who have no drug or disability benefits and few savings.

Those few months were a blur of working, eating, and sleeping. Often I would come home from work exhausted and just flop into bed. My only goal was to make it to October. I was expected to work faithfully all day, to attend meetings and produce papers no matter how badly I felt. Not being able to produce to capacity is seen as a personal problem rather than a shortcoming of the workplace structure. Finally, the last day of work arrived and I experienced a welcome relief from the hectic schedule of the past months. My health seemed to stabilize, and I established a comfortable routine.

At regular weekly appointments, my doctor would ask me about my vision and whether I noticed any "floaters." I wasn't sure what floaters were, but I hadn't noticed any changes in my vision. Then, one Saturday morning I was shopping and had just put the groceries in the back of the car. As I got in, I looked at the sky and it was covered with small black spots. I knew immediately it was cytomegalovirus (CMV), a viral infection that can attack various organs but most commonly causes retinitis. If untreated, blindness results within several weeks, something I had always been terrified of. I saw the ophthalmologist two days later, and the presence of CMV was confirmed.

Everything happened so fast that day. I was taught how to do an intravenous infusion myself, a three-hour procedure that has to be done every day to prevent blindness. The infusion often really tires me out, and I have learned not to eat during it or risk diarrhea. It is only painful if I accidently do it too fast, the first indication being numbness in my lips and face.

At first, the drug was given in my arm, but an operation was immediately scheduled to implant a catheter directly into a vein close to my heart. Six days a week, I have a tube dangling from my chest to attach the IV tubing. I feel disfigured and am no longer comfortable taking my shirt off in public because I feel others would be revolted by it.

Health and fitness are important to most gay men, and I was always very conscious of keeping fit. A positive body image was an important component of my self-image. AIDS often marks its sufferers with lesions or a general look of ill health due to wasting; many people lose so much weight that their clothes hang loosely on them. On the days I look tired and worn, I don't want to be seen, especially by other gays, as I feel they will recognize my condition and either condemn me or pity me.

The face is accorded more importance than any other part of the body. It is thought to mirror the inner self and determines to a large extent how people react to us. When KS lesions appear on the face, as they often do, people react with revulsion to them. The word *aids* has been inscribed on the face as punishment for deviant behavior,[1] and it is no longer possible to pretend that you are suffering from some other ailment. The marks on the face of a leper, syphilitic, or person with AIDS can be seen as signs of a progressive mutation, a decomposition. More important than the amount of disfigurement is that it reflects underlying, ongoing changes, the dissolution of the person.[2] Deviance, or nature's presumed punishment for it, is revealed as a visible, physical "deformity."[3]

The mainstream media ignore people with AIDS who don't look sick and searches out the most visibly ill.[4] Simon Watney labels this the "spectacle of AIDS" featuring the "AIDS victim," usually hospitalized and physically debilitated. The faces and bodies of these individuals clearly disclose the stigmata of their guilt.[5] Any possibility of positive sympathetic identification with actual people with AIDS is entirely expunged from the field of vision.

I have a viral infection that has covered parts of my face with small warts. It is most noticeable around my eyes. There is no real cure, but they can be somewhat controlled for cosmetic reasons. This involves freezing them every couple of weeks. They then blister up and leave my face covered with red blotches for about a week before they heal. Although they are not life-threatening and are really only a minor annoyance, their visibility has meant that some people close to me are more concerned about them than they are about more serious health problems.

Stephen Busby

One of these problems is cryptosporidium, a parasite that invades the digestive tract. It is a common cause of traveler's diarrhea, which many people contract in Mexico or the Caribbean. Crypto causes uncontrollable, watery diarrhea, to the extent that you can be literally on the toilet all day. You lose all desire to eat. People with healthy immune systems usually recover quickly, with or without medication. However, people with AIDS have no immunity against it. I lost fifteen pounds in the first three weeks. Although treatments are still experimental and may have side effects, they have been effective for some people.

I also suffer from many general and unexplained complaints, fevers, chills, fatigue, lack of energy, and muscle soreness. Sometimes I throw up for no apparent reason. I also have small, itchy spots over my chest and back and partway down my arms, which can be controlled but not eliminated. Symptoms such as these could indicate any number of health problems. Western medicine does best when it can identify and name an illness. In the absence of a diagnosis, treatment can still occur but only at the level of symptom control. Alternative and Eastern practitioners emphasize maintaining good health and are often adept at treating ailments that baffle Western doctors.

Every day I take thirty-two pills to keep a variety of infections under control. Just about every drug I take can cause diarrhea, and it usually does for me. Other medications cause peripheral neuropathy—painful sensations in the hands and feet, aggravated by heat and cold—which often doesn't respond well to pain killers. Every week a nurse visits to change my tubing and to check my vital signs, and a lab technician takes my blood to ensure that my kidneys are still working. Most people take their health for granted. I never know if I'll wake up full of energy or if I'll spend the day in bed. Sometimes in the middle of the day I suddenly feel so worn out that I simply have to be down.

The Emotional Impact of AIDS: Shame

Denial is the most common initial reaction to the diagnosis of a life-threatening illness. HIV infection can take months or years to progress to AIDS, and when nothing seems to be going wrong, it becomes easy to deny that you will ever become sick. Furthermore, it was unclear at the start of the epidemic whether everyone infected would progress to full-blown AIDS. Many of us thought we would be spared.

As the reality of the situation sinks in, a whole range of painful emotional responses ensues. Elisabeth Kübler-Ross has documented the stages of acceptance of death and dying as denial and isolation, anger, bargaining, depression, and acceptance. I think that Kübler-Ross's theories are often simplified and misunderstood. In my experience they have provided a good paradigm for under-standing the reactions to a terminal illness. It is important to realize that one can go through the stages in any order and may cycle through them repeatedly.[6]

AIDS is often seen as a calamity one brings on oneself,[7] and gay people often blame themselves for not having foreseen the consequences of their be-havior. Anger is directed at the doctors who diagnosed you but who can't cure you; at society, which condemns you; at the injustice of the situation and your inability to al-ter it. I find that I have less patience with both people and things and am more easily frustrated. Some people, however, are so consumed with anger that it dominates every aspect of their lives.

At first, like most people, I constructed an explanation of how I became infected, although it is impossible to know. After a time, I stopped wondering just when I was infected and started to worry about how many people I might have passed the disease to.

AIDS is regarded as shameful because it is linked to sexual indul-gence, perversity, and illegal drugs. Although it can be contracted through any blood contact, AIDS is often considered a venereal disease.[8] AIDS reveals you as part of a "risk group," a community of pariahs.[9] The concept of risk groups gives the impres-sion that one gets AIDS because of membership in the group rather than as the result of certain behavior.

The source of many of these standards of morality and of other Western myths remains the Bible, whether one is a practicing Christian or not. Throughout the Old Testament, God is shown to use disease and plague to punish individuals and societies. For example, Moses tells the people of Israel:

If you do not obey faithfully all God's teachings that are written in this book and if you do not honour the wonderful and awesome name of the Lord your God, he will send on you and on your descendants incurable diseases and horrible epidemics that can never be stopped. He will bring on you once again all the dreadful diseases you experienced in Egypt, and you will never recover. He will also send all kinds of diseases and epidemics that are not mentioned in this book of God's laws and teachings, and you will be destroyed.[10]

Job, who is covered with sores as part of the testing of his faith, declares, "I am skin and bones and people take that as proof of my guilt."[11]

Stories of Jesus healing the sick conflate illness and deformity with sin. Jesus heals the lepers, the "unclean," with the words, "Your faith has made you well."[12] Historically, leprosy was characterized as a breakdown of moral values, divine punish-ment for sexual transgression.[13] A modern expression of this belief is Jerry Falwell's declaration that AIDS is "God's judgment on a society that does not live by His rules." The secular version is the view that people are just getting what they deserve.

Blaming the victims of an epidemic disease is much easier when they can be conceived of as "different," and when a distance can be established between the self and the "other." This is accomplished by excluding from the "general population" homosexuals and IV drug users, members of society who are already isolated and stigmatized. Mikhail Elbaz and Ruth Murbach discuss the physical exclusion and symbolic exclusion of the other during historical epidemics of plague, leprosy, syphilis, tuberculosis, and cholera. The body of the victim is seen as the "signature of evil," a living incarnation of sin.[14]

The burden of shame and the homophobia attached to AIDS because of its identification with gay men and promiscuity make it difficult for people with AIDS to share their pain. In my case, I resisted telling certain people, especially those closest to me, about my diagnosis because of my concern about their reactions. I now have fewer but more intense relationships with people who know my situation. Some writers in the gay press suggest that a split has developed in the gay community between HIV-positive and HIV-negative individuals. Certainly, there is a profound difference in lifestyle and values between the two groups. Younger gays in particular often view AIDS as a problem of older gays who were not careful and are now paying the price. On the other hand, people who have lost many friends often feel tremendous loss and survivor guilt.

I broke up with my last lover about two years ago. Although the breakup was not directly due to my illness, the stress involved with having AIDS had a lot to do with it. My sexual desire is low when I feel well and nonexistent when I don't. Although I get lonely at times living by myself, developing an intimate relationship seems unlikely since I lack self-confidence and don't get out to meet people.

I sometimes feel so old at thirty-nine, retired and without the energy to enjoy the things I used to. Working out at the gym used to be an important part of my daily routine, but I haven't been for more than two years now. People invite me out to dinner, and I always wonder if I'll have the energy to go and if I'll be able to eat anything. Often I am too weak and nauseated to eat at all.

I had conventional middle-class goals for my life: success and recognition in my career, financial security, and personal development. My choices are now much more limited. The growing realization that I would never work again was a big adjustment. My life has become more focused and my values have changed, knowing that my time is limited. I am thankful for small things, just waking up every morning and still being able to function.

A great deal of my time and energy is now spent trying to maintain my health. Just about every day I have an appointment with a health specialist or I have to pick up medications. I spend a lot of time reading about experimental treatments and their evaluation by medical and pharmaceutical professionals. Over time I have learned to deal with the health bureaucracy and have developed partnerships where my opinions are listened to and respected. Although in a sense looking after my health is now a "job," it really doesn't provide many positive rewards. If I don't get sick, I'm succeeding at it, but I often feel that my health is in a gradual decline. I feel that I have lost control over the direction of my life.

I lost my first friend to AIDS in 1985, although at the time he told everyone he had cancer. I have since lost count of the number of my friends and acquaintances who have died. For the gay community, death has become a regular occurrence. Dennis Altman writes that in the Western world in the past half-century, the loss of so many friends and lovers has been confined to old age and war. The only precedents for the loss of so many young people in peacetime are the great epidemics of history: smallpox, cholera, influenza.[15]

I have already arranged my funeral and have chosen a spot in the cemetery for my ashes. It's a rather eerie feeling to look at my gravestone, set in place with my name already engraved on it. Death seems an ever-present reality.

It was only this past spring that I actually watched a friend die. After his admission to the hospital, his energy slipped away and he became weaker and weaker, confined to bed and no longer having the strength to sit up or to feed himself, until finally he could no longer breathe without oxygen and required suctioning several times a day to remove the buildup of mucus. Due to the nature of his infection, he had had numerous seizures, was disoriented, and often did not recognize family or friends. It was difficult to sit with him in silence, not knowing if he realized you were there. When his kidneys failed, he could no longer tolerate any of his medications and we knew the end was near. There was a heroic quality in his fight against inevitable death.

After my last visit, I sat in the park across the street from the hospital and cried. It was a beautiful summer day and the park was full of people going about their daily lives. I thought how life would go on in much the same way, even though he would no longer be a part of it. I thought about my own death and wondered how much impact any of us really have.

It was difficult watching a friend succumb to the disease, but it was also a terrifying preview of my last days. Will I suffer as he had? How long will it be before I can no longer care for myself? Will I be confined to bed or a wheelchair?

Will I lose my grip on reality and no longer recognize family and friends? How will they react to this? Is this how they will remember me?

I find my emotional well-being depends to a great extent on my physical well-being. It is easy to be optimistic when things are going well, but not in times of illness. Even the strongest person can be overwhelmed by hopelessness, anxiety, and depression. A friend of mine committed suicide rather than face the gradual loss of his health. At the time, I felt it was a cowardly response, especially since he was still in relatively good health. I understand now what led him to the decision to take control of his death.

Learning to Survive: Hope

Factors acknowledged to alter the perception of pain include fear, anxiety, anger, loneliness, depression, isolation, and loss of control. As my own experience indicates, there is no shortage of these negative and conflicting emotions with AIDS. A person's tolerance to pain, the duration and intensity that can be endured, varies from day to day depending on one's psychological state and overall well-being. The ability to deal with pain is affected by cultural background, previous experiences, and the expected duration of pain. Everyone experiences and copes with pain differently. One's psychological stability and ability to cope with painful situations in the past provide a good indicator of the ability to deal with the pain of illness. The question remains: How can we improve our ability to deal with the pain of AIDS?

I began reading from a wide variety of sources to discover the facts about AIDS. I soon became aware that much of what is presented as fact is actually conjecture and that the "facts" are in flux. In order to make sense of the new reality of AIDS, information has been interpreted in terms of existing beliefs and standards. The medical and pharmaceutical establishments, alternative health practitioners, established religions, the media, and governments have each developed stories to serve their own purposes and bolster their worldviews.

These interpretations can be harmful when they serve groups whose interests do not coincide with those of the person with AIDS (PWA). People with AIDS need to realize this since they are affected by others' views on a daily basis. People make decisions based on what they believe to be true, decisions that may adversely affect me and other PWAs. It is important to realize this and be ready to confront these views.

Although the official definition of AIDS by the CDC has frequently changed, AIDS is always considered ultimately fatal.[16] This implication of a "death sentence" leads people to feel they are doomed from the moment they are found to be HIV-antibody-positive.[17] Many doctors reinforce this feeling by telling patients they can expect to survive for only a short period.

Others have been harmed or killed by prejudices and ignorance. The emphasis on risk groups convinced many physicians that women don't get AIDS, and gynecological problems caused by AIDS have only recently been recognized. Although the risk of infection is now known to be small, irrational fears persist among health care workers, and there is widespread resistance to treating PWAs.[18] The desire for avoidance and exclusion often leads to the unnecessary use of masks, gloves, and gowns. Between one quarter and one half of nurses believe they should have the right to refuse care to persons with AIDS. Much of this seems to be due to homophobia, an unrealistic assessment of risk, and feelings of powerlessness and loss of control.[19]

Infectious diseases to which sexual fault is attached have always inspired fears of easy contagion and bizarre fantasies of transmission. People have been stigmatized and destroyed as much by the "idea" of AIDS as by its actual effects on the body.[20]

The media have misinterpreted and misrepresented much of the information flowing from the medical world, deliberately or not. Mass-media stories of findings originally reported in medical journals automatically have high credibility. Risk groups and CDC classifications—useful tools for epidemiologists tracking the spread of the epidemic—have been assigned "meanings" by the media and the public that were never intended.[21]

The media alternately scares us and assures us there is nothing to worry about.[22] The division of people with AIDS into guilty and innocent victims allows the sympathetic portrayal and identification with certain people while others are condemned for spreading the infection. Network television has not played a big role in disseminating useful information or advancing the debate, a role that would require open debate about homosexuality, anal sex, and safe sex.[23] Instead, it picks up stories of celebrities dying, "general population" breakthroughs, and people with AIDS who "should not" have been at risk and ignores the fact that the vast majority of people with AIDS in Canada are gay men.[24] When this is reported the media blames the gay community for the disease instead of recognizing them as the ones hardest hit with it.

The media also conflates AIDS with other dreaded illnesses such as plague, cholera, and tuberculosis. Each of these carries with it an image of the nature of the infection, the nature of its victims, and an "explanation" of why they were infected. These explanations are overwhelmingly negative.[25] We need to examine

Figure 1. Portrait of David Chickadel, AIDS patient. *People*, August 3, 1987.
Photo by Peter Serling.

both the objective meaning and the connotations of terms such as *invasion, pollution, crisis,* and *epidemic* or *plague*.[26] For example, by definition a crisis has a relatively short duration and a definite turning point.[27] There is no sign that this is so in the case of AIDS: the idea of an "AIDS crisis" mainly invokes images of panic.

The media are constantly interpreting new situations in terms of those already analyzed and interpreted for us and therefore "understood." The most common metaphors for disease generally are military, so we often speak of fighting a cold, of winning the war on cancer, of germs invading the body. It is important to examine and analyze these images since they have become so common that we rarely consider their origins. Many people feel that military metaphors are particularly harmful. The implied hostility of these images may easily become directed at the victim rather than the disease. Death is viewed as the ultimate defeat and not as a natural part of life. With AIDS, the media have used the military metaphor to talk about the invasion of outsiders (the marginal groups hardest hit) into the mythical mainstream of innocent bystanders (the general population).

On a personal level, individuals interpret new situations in terms of their own history, personality, and beliefs. This includes the myths and metaphors they understand and feel comfortable with. For example, I find the military concept of not accepting one's fate but "mobilizing" all one's resources to "fight back" is an empowering one. As time goes on, we form whole systems of belief about particular subjects. It is important to evaluate images we personally create as well as those we internalize from the media, since when we are later confronted with new situations, especially those containing incomplete, misunderstood, or incorrect information, we may interpret the situation in ways that are inappropriate but that fit our belief system. Internalization of negative images is particularly common in periods of low self-esteem and when the message is from a highly credible source. In this way, myths and metaphors may not be helpful in evaluating new situations but may get in the way of seeing reality clearly.

A common media image places the AIDS "sufferer" by a window, alone and helpless, the shadow of the blinds forming bars across the face, watching the world go by. This image is readily accepted because many people believe that it represents reality. In fact, people with AIDS are often engaged and defiant and not at all "victims."

An awareness of the myth-making process was the first step in my examination and evaluation of my own beliefs. Reading and reflecting on the history of illness and the reactions of society to epidemics in the past put the current discourse in a different perspective. By taking control of how we think about and talk about AIDS, people with AIDS can become conscious of negative images, of who creates and circulates them, and who benefits.

The stigma and shame of AIDS can make it difficult to admit one's situation and may inhibit people from seeking treatment early enough or from making a greater effort to get competent treatment. Many people have completely lost faith in traditional medicine, and many have turned to remedies with no proven usefulness. It is important not to judge treatment on the basis of images created by others but to consider any treatment that might be effective. However, desperate sufferers may fall prey to those promising easy cures. Unbalanced diets, unproven new drugs and treatments, and books and lectures promising to heal one's life by banishing negative thoughts may not only be ineffective, but actually harmful and often expensive. For instance, some people talk of AZT as poison and refuse to take it, even though many studies have shown that it prolongs life and decreases the risk of HIV-related dementia.

Louise Hay, a popular author of self-care books, moves the cause of illness from an external agent such as a virus to the patient's negative view of self or an inability to forgive the self or others. Hay attributes AIDS to "denial of the self. Sexual guilt. A strong belief in not being 'good enough.' " She says, "We create every so-called 'illness' in our body." This is not only naive, but it makes the patient responsible for his or her health. Hay maintains that if your health is declining, it's your own fault.[28]

Part of the reason for the rejection of traditional medicine is the way that doctors and other health professionals present themselves as the experts who

Figure 2. Portrait of Ron Farha, AIDS patient.
The Gazette, Montreal, September 13, 1992. Photo by Peter Martin.

should be left in charge. The conception of AIDS as a strictly biomedical problem ignores its behavioral and social dimensions and leaves out much of our actual experience of AIDS.[29] Medical science has been unable to produce a cure or even a control for HIV infection. The best protection we have is prevention, especially safer sex, which has been promoted, for the most part, by community organizations. Medical science has also tended to ignore other implications of AIDS as linked to gay men: issues of homophobia, confidentiality, possible alienation from the family and society, and problems with self-image and self-acceptance. The fact is that the medical establishment initially ignored AIDS and it was community organizations who first responded.

Pharmaceutical companies would have us believe that drugs are the sole answer to disease. They set the research agenda, driven by the profit motive. The role of diet and vitamin therapies and the use of already existing drugs are often not aggressively investigated because there is little money to be made. On the other hand, drugs are now available for the treatment and prevention of many opportunistic infections, although they are often still experimental and almost all have side effects. The development of these treatments may be slow, but their efficacy has been proven through research and testing. The average life expectancy after diagnosis with AIDS has increased from five months in 1985 to twenty-seven months in 1992.[30] Yet small breakthroughs and gradual improvements in treatment are seldom considered newsworthy enough for mainstream media.

As more knowledge is obtained, myths may or may not be abandoned, depending on who they serve. Discovery of the mechanism of HIV transmission seemed to lead to even more myths. Theories postulated the existence of rugged

Figure 3. Portrait of David Snoddy, AIDS patient.
The Toronto Star Syndicate, February 7, 1993. Photo by Peter Cheney.

vaginas and fragile anuses as a "scientific" argument against anal sex. AIDS was seen as a general body breakdown from too much sex, a "scientific" argument against promiscuity.[31] The medical and scientific establishment tends to accept only the information that fits its already existing belief system. It often finds it difficult to question new data, even while claiming to make decisions in a rational, scientific way that avoids myth and deals only with "reality."

I have been lucky to find doctors who are caring, knowledgeable, attentive, and open to discussion about treatment. Although the overall course of infection is much better understood, it is impossible to know when the next infection will appear or how serious it may be. It is important to recognize symptoms quickly and to get proper treatment as soon as possible. I have followed my doctors' advice quite closely, although I have investigated alternative therapies and do not rule them out as methods of treatment.

I love to get massages, either my feet or my whole body. I find I can often dull my pain by pressing quite hard on my temples or abdomen just under the ribcage. Breathing slowly and consciously while imagining a relaxing scene can also lessen the intensity of pain.

Many of us have adopted long-term survivors as role models. From them we have learned the importance of maintaining a strong will to live, and of staying active and stimulating both the body and the mind in accordance with our energy levels. These survivors often incorporate nontraditional therapies but make sure they always feel comfortable with the treatment options they have chosen. Helping others through volunteering or political action may provide them with a sense of purpose and a focus outside the self, especially if they are no longer working.

I am fortunate to be in a position to be able to influence the quality of my care. Many people do not understand the options or are not capable of making complex medical decisions. A patient advocate—either a family member, friend, volunteer, a social worker, or nurse—can ensure that you get the best possible care. It is important to identify caregivers who will act according to your wishes before a crisis occurs. AIDS is so overwhelming that in order to come to terms with it, most people find they need someone to confide in. Admitting the need for help requires making yourself vulnerable. Family members and friends may find it even more difficult to get the assistance they need.

I try to maintain a positive attitude, not perpetually cheerful, but able to evaluate my situation clearly. I am able to make decisions that will improve my condition because I am still in fairly good health; I live in a large urban center with access to information that I am able to understand and act on; I am assertive and am able to deal with the health care bureaucracy. Therapy has also helped me to deal with the fear and uncertainty and to prepare mentally for whatever may happen.

The future will undoubtedly bring increasing amounts of pain as infections continue to gradually destroy my body, and there is little I can do to influence the course of events. Becoming aware of the emotions involved and the social construction of the disease has helped me to face the situation realistically and with less fear. At some point I will have to recognize that I can go on no longer, that I can only try to manage my pain—and that in the end I will be released from it.

Epilogue: Love

A year has now passed since I wrote this article about my illness. Over the past few months, my health has deteriorated significantly. My cryptosporidium is completely out of control and I have constant diarrhea, although I have tried every known remedy. I have spent almost the whole summer in the hospital as a result of blood infections. I am being fed intravenously since my digestive system can no longer handle food by mouth. I spend about fourteen hours a day on these infusions, although much of this is overnight. The alternative would be a gradual wasting away until I was too weak to fight off infection.

My family and friends have become increasingly anxious about my health. The support I have received from them has been incredible. I could not have survived this long without it. At the same time, they are trying to deal with my illness and impending death themselves. At first I was angry when they did not react in ways I thought they should. I had to realize that we all are dealing with the situation as well as we can and that we're all struggling to invent ways to cope as we go. It has been difficult for me to realize that I had to allow each person space to come to terms with my condition in their own way.

I have found it increasingly difficult to deal with the limits on my independence that each decline in my health leads to. I feel I am losing the control I have fought so hard to maintain. On the other hand, AIDS has had many positive effects on my life. It has changed my opinions of what is really important and shown me how much we all depend on each other. The fact that my time is limited made each day important and made me thankful for each one. My relationships are deeper than before, more honest and caring. The ultimate lesson of AIDS may be that all we have in the end are those who are close to us so it is vitally important to care for and love each other.

Notes

1. See Franz Kafka, "In the Penal Colony," *The Metamorphosis, The Penal Colony and Other Stories* (New York: Schocken, 1948), for the origin of the inscription metaphor.

2. Susan Sontag, *aids and Its Metaphors*, originally published by Farrar, Straus and Giroux, 1989. Page references are to *Illness as Metaphor and aids and Its Metaphors* (New York: Doubleday, 1990), 129.

3. Martha Gever, "Pictures of Sickness: Stuart Marshall's *Bright Eyes*," in *aids: Cultural Analysis, Cultural Activism*, ed. Douglas Crimp (Cambridge, Mass.: MIT Press, 1988), 115–16.

4. A notable example is the case of Kenny Ramasaur, subject of Stuart Marshall's film *Bright Eyes*. Kenny suffered from an unusual and ghastly disfiguration. One headline, "What the Gay Plague Did to Handsome Kenny," is typical. See Gever, "Pictures of Sickness," 115–16; and Jan Zita Grover, "Visible Lesions: Images of the PWA in America," *Fluid Exchanges: Artists and Critics in the aids Crisis*, ed. James Miller (Toronto: University of Toronto, 1992), 32.

5. Simon Watney, "The Spectacle of AIDS," in *aids: Cultural Analysis, Cultural Activism*, 78.

6. Elisabeth Kübler-Ross, *On Death and Dying* (New York: Macmillan, 1969).

7. Sontag, *Illness as Metaphor*, 114.

8. Sander Gilman discusses how AIDS was first characterized as a sexually transmitted disease. See Sander Gilman, "AIDS and Syphilis: The Iconography of Disease," in *aids: Cultural Analysis, Cultural Activism*.

9. Sontag, *Illness as Metaphor*, 112–13.

10. Deut. 28:58–61.

11. Job 16:8. See also Job 2:7, 6:4, 7:5.

12. Luke 17:11–19. See also Matthew 9:1–7, Matt. 8:16, Mark 1:40–42, 10:50–52.

13. Mikhail Elbaz and Ruth Murbach, "Fear of the Other, Condemned and Damned: AIDS, Epidemics and Excursions," in *A Leap in the Dark: aids, Art, and Contemporary Cultures*, ed. Allan Klusacek and Ken Morrison (Montreal: Véhicule, 1992), 3.

14. Ibid., 2–8.

15. Dennis Altman, *aids and the New Puritanism* (London: Plato, 1986).

16. The latest proposal changes the definition of AIDS to include everyone with CD4 counts less than 200. This will significantly increase the number of people considered to have AIDS and is a major change in the way AIDS is conceptualized by the CDC.

17. Sontag, *Illness as Metaphor*, 108–9, 116–21.

18. Ibid., 115, 161–62.

19. Ruth Gallop et al., "Fear of Contagion and AIDS: Nurses' Perception of Risk," *aids Care* 4, no. 1 (1992).

20. Gilman, "AIDS and Syphilis," 88.

21. Originally, the four groups considered at highest risk were homosexuals, hemophiliacs, IV drug users, and Haitians. These groups have been set up in the media as opposed to the "general population." The CDC classifies those who are ill in four main groups and a number of subgroups depending on how advanced their illness is, one of which is those with "full-blown" AIDS.

22. Paula Treichler, "Seduced and Terrorized: AIDS and Network Television," in *A Leap in the Dark*, 136.

23. Ibid., 145.

24. For example 86.5 percent of cases in Ontario are gay men. "AIDS in Ontario," Ontario Ministry of Health, March 31, 1992.

25. Gilman, "AIDS and Syphilis," 98–99. AIDS is often compared to syphilis, the gay male functioning as both the male sufferer and female source of pollution depicted in traditional representations. Traditionally, the woman (usually a prostitute) was seen as a "carrier" of syphilis, infecting "innocent" men who were unfortunate victims. The current representation allows for alternate condemnation of the source of disease and sympathy for the victim of it, depending on how the media want to present the story.

26. Sontag, *Illness as Metaphor*, 105; and Kenneth Keniston, "Introduction to the Issue," in *Living with aids*, ed. Stephen R. Graubard (Cambridge, Mass.: MIT Press, 1990), xxx–xxxii. Invasion is a common metaphor for cancer, as pollution is for syphilis.

27. Keniston, "Introduction to the Issue," xxxi.

28. Louise L. Hay, *You Can Heal Your Life* (Carson, Calif.: Hay House, 1994), 5, 151.

29. Keniston, "Introduction to the Issue," xxxii–xxxiii.

30. These figures were presented at the conference "HIV/AIDS: Practical Approaches for Health Care Professionals," held in Toronto on December 4, 1992.

31. Paula Treichler, "AIDS, Homophobia, and Biomedical Discourse: An Epidemic of Signification," in *aids: Cultural Analysis, Cultural Activism*, 37–39, 47–49.

Bob Flanagan

Pain Journal

January

BACK IN New York, the Gramercy Park Hotel. Back in bed. Forget what time it is—I mean, who cares? It's been an awful Christmas and an even worse birthday. Me, my whiny, wheezy, grumbling self, scaring the shit out of everyone, acting like I'm going to die at any moment. Still depressed. All I want to do is die—I mean cry—I meant to write *cry* and I wrote *die*. How Freudian can you get?

Birthday party over—thank God. Success from the looks of it. People. Presents. Cake. But me? Where the hell was I? Laid out naked on the Gurney of Nails, big marzipan penis on my stomach, candles blazing. Everybody impressed at the sight of me, I guess—but I wasn't *really* on the nails—not all of me—too chicken-shit to let go. Couldn't breathe. My idiot's lament. Terrified at the sight of Sheree with her big knife, slicing into the marzipan penis—afraid she'd go too far—afraid of accidents, always afraid, so can't get into it, like I can't get into anything these days. Always on the periphery. Always terrified, exhausted, annoyed, pissed, anxious, out of it—out of the loop, out of my mind, out of time.

Horrible stomachaches and nausea. Heavy little shits. Is it the new antidepressant, the Wellbutrin? Don't know if I'm sick or crazy. Short of breath everywhere I go. Making like I'm dying. Am I exaggerating? Why would I? Who am I trying to impress? All the time thinking I'm going to die, talking myself into a frenzy of phlegm and fatigue. Maybe I'm getting better. Maybe I'm not. Now they say I should exercise. First they say use the wheelchair and conserve your energy. Now they say "exercise." Exercise, wheelchair. Exercise, wheelchair. Hard to know what to do or who I am in it all. And while I'm dwelling on death—Preston, twenty-three-year-old from cystic fibrosis (CF) summer camp, died a couple of days ago. Funeral tomorrow but I'm not going. Should have called him last week, but what would I have done, wished him luck?

Depressed. In the hospital. Taking big red Wellbutrin pills but still depressed. Mom and Dad's forty-fifth anniversary—I make the call—no, I didn't—they called me 'cause I'm the sick one in the hospital. Their sick child. Their dying boy. When my mother calls and tells me I sound like I'm getting better, I tell her no, not really, not yet. I'm almost rude to her about it. No, I'm not. I'm not better. I'm not ready to be better, so stop making me better already. And of course I spend the whole day feeling guilty about cutting her off because she was feeling so good that I might be feeling better, but I'll make it up to her tomorrow. I will be better, even thought I just now spit up a big wad of blood—I'll still be better, just you wait and see.

February

Again the dim light of the television, dim Bob whines as Sheree snores, but I can't hear the TV 'cause I don't want to hear Sheree so I've got earplugs in, which is frustrating because I'd like to hear bald Dennis Hopper talking to Tom Snyder, but I can't stand the sound of Sheree's snoring—I mean I *really* can't stand it. It unnerves me. I'm the worst snorer in the world, but she doesn't know it 'cause she's out and I'm up—always up. A nervous wreck. Antidepressants. Antianxiety. Vicodin. Steroids. Feel like crying all the time. I don't want to go on this trip to Boston and Berlin. Gave every last ounce of energy to "Visiting Hours" in New York. Can't give any more. But I'm doing it. I'm hating it, and I'm doing it. I took the earplugs out—so I could hear the TV with one ear, but all I can hear is Sheree—I love her, I want to be with her, but that sound! Argh! It makes me want to scream.

I don't know when the last time was that we had sex. I say that because I'm watching two people fuck on TV. Sheree and I are close, yeah—closer than ever, in some ways—but physically we don't know where to start. Antidepressants? Maybe. Good excuse. But I still can't shake my depression. This time Sheree's doing great and I'm the one wallowing in darkness—now *that's* true role reversal. I stopped taking Paxil because I couldn't come. Now I can come, but I don't care. Lately, I don't even get hard. I come, but I don't get hard. No help from Sheree. She's dead asleep. And when she does try to help, I run. Last night I snapped her head off because she wanted me to hold her. What kind of jerk am I becoming? Mr. Artist. We get news today of Art Matters grants. $2,000 for me and $1,500 each for Sheree and Kirby. But it doesn't lighten my mental load—I'm still full of shit.

March

My irritability and depression are amok. I feel like crying all the time. My computer keeps crashing, which is exactly how I feel. I've been off antidepressants since Christmas. Time to go back? I guess. Will it help? Is all this oxygen related? I've got it up to three liters. Too much? Not enough? Who knows. The TV is on but I can't hear it because I've got earplugs in my ears to block out Sheree's snoring. I want to run upstairs and fiddle with the computer to get it working again so at least something's back on track, but it's too late (4 A.M.). I was asleep but woke up an hour ago with an awful stomachache and the usual heartache. Don't know what to do with myself. Took a couple of antianxiety pills. Oxazepams, but they only make me sleepy, so now I'm sleepy *and* anxious. I guess I'm really into the pills now. The age-old quest for happy pills. But there ain't none. My body throbs with unhappiness. It's like a big weight, a giant distraction all the time. So I'm always annoyed by it, antagonized from the minute I wake up, till the time I finally go to sleep—doesn't leave room for much of anything else.

Up again at 3 A.M.—what gives? Sound asleep since 11. Up at 3, no matter what. Thought I'd escape writing tonight, but found myself mulling over why it is I don't like pain anymore. I have this performance to do on April 1, and I'm shying away from doing or having S/M stuff done to me because pain and the thought of pain mostly just irritate and annoy me rather than turn me on. But I miss my masochistic self. I hate this person I've become. And what about my reputation? Everything I say to people is all a lie, or at least two years too late—what the . . . ? It's not 3 a.m. It's only 1:30. Can't even tell time. I knew it had to be earlier because the TV shows were all wrong.

Bob Flanagan

April

Hotel performance done. The audience gathered together in one hotel room and peered through telescopes and binoculars while I performed supposedly autoerotic activities in my own room across the courtyard all alone. Don't know who saw what or what anyone thought, or what it all meant. I'm just glad it's over. Wine enema, butt plug, alligator clips, ball whacking, piss drinking, masturbating bondage—they wanted a show, I gave them a show. Felt disoriented and depressed through most of it, as I feel disoriented and depressed through most of everything these days.

The hospital—finally. Seems like I've been talking about coming here ever since the last time I left. Haven't been breathing or feeling well the whole time and will probably never breathe well or feel well again. I'm not being pessimistic when I say it's only going to get worse. That's the reality. My blood gases are much worse: PO_2 81, PCO_2 57. Don't know if that's forever, but it's fucked.

Here I am tippy-de-typing on the couch 'cause I'm still on drugs, nothing interesting, just antibiotics. Lately, I've been longing for Demerol. Flashbacks to those days of postop—sinus surgery, pericarditis, pneumothorax—when I got it when I wanted it and I liked it—perhaps a little too much. But, ho hum, nothing tonight but Tobramycin, Piperacillin, and Ceftazidime in my veins and a couple of Vicodin in my mouth, but that doesn't do much anymore beyond dulling the headache, which is fine I suppose. Sheree's here on the couch, too. Not sleeping 'cause she slept till noon today. She's out on stress leave so she has no schedule. She's waving her naked legs in the air. She's reading about gardening, her new hobby. I want her to put dozens of alligator clips on my dick and balls, but I don't know if I'd freak her out or not. I can put a couple on myself. It hurts like hell but most of the time I can hold on until the pain subsides and I get kind of a rush. But can I take it when she's in control? The ultimate question.

Getting hard to breathe again. Thought I was doing much better, but it never lasts. My mood has been improving, though. And I've got a renewed interest in sex, mostly fantasizing about this alligator clip thing, and trying it out a little bit with a couple of clips here and there, those jagged little teeth biting into my tender spots as I grab hold of something like the bed rail and squeeze until the pain floats off a little, turns sweet almost, until it's time for another clip. It's almost like eating hot chili peppers, except that the taste buds for this delicacy are in my balls, not my mouth.

May

I had a great hard-on, but now it's gone, and now that I'm writing and not masturbating, it's coming back. That fucker. I was sound asleep, several times. Sheree and I went to bed early, tuckered out after Mother's Day lunch at Barney's in Beverly Hills. A worm crawling along the rim of my plate after an incredible dish of sturgeon got everyone grossed out and me a free lunch. Came home and fell asleep watching *X-Files* with Sheree, but woke up just in time to catch her videotaping me as I lay naked and snoring. I made my penis talk for the camera. Drunken bar penis: "All right, all right, I'm comin' goddamn you, you prick." Then it was sleep, cough, wake up; sleep, cough, wake up, until now, where it's 2:30 A.M. Sheree's snoring and I can't stop her, even if I shake her, even if I pinch her nose. So it's earplugs in, which makes it impossible to hear *Perry Mason* on TV. Before Sheree plunged into the sawmill, earlier on, after my little penis show, she wanted me to suck her nipple while she masturbated with the vibrator. Not that I didn't want to, but I was still tired and ready to go back to sleep, and it usually takes her such a long time to come (we Paxil pals), that I just didn't want to get involved, but it would have been awful to deny her, so I went forth and commenced my sucking. I felt just like I did earlier this afternoon when I went out to the car to wait for her while she shopped at Barney's after lunch. I was too out of breath to walk around to shop with her, so I sat in the car listening to the radio and waited for her to finish, knowing full well it could take forever. But lo and behold she came out relatively quickly, and what do you know, she came fast, too, here in bed, with a nice little shudder of completion, and before we knew it were both fast asleep, until now, for me anyway. Some weird dream I just had, too. I had a pet parakeet, maybe two of them. I kept trying to play with it in its cage: giving it food, toys, playing with it with my hand. But somehow I was fucking it up. Suddenly, the cage was a plastic bag, and I tried to shift the bird around so it could breathe. At some point the cage was like an oven, and I could see the parakeet getting singed and burned, but it was too hot to put my hand in. Finally, I managed to coax him out. He was alive still, but kind of crispy. One of his feet was melted. When I put him back in his cage, I could see that he wasn't going to live. He was tiny but stiff. I felt guilty. I thought, since this was the second bird in one day that I had killed, did I do it on purpose, under the guise of "play"? Then I woke up and wrote all this stuff. Now it's back to sleep, and maybe a hard-on if I'm lucky. And look, another *Perry Mason* episode that I won't be able to hear.

Saw Dr. Riker today. He said I looked good. "Must be the haircut," he said. I tried to tell him that I was slowly starting downhill again. Feeling like shit whenever I try to do anything but there's not much to do about it. It's CF. I've got several strains of pseudomonas, but what am I going to do about it unless I want to go back into the hospital and start the IVs again. Not ready for that. Too much to do, or try to do, on the outside. Sheree's depressed again, first time in a long time, mostly about art. I tell her it's not unusual to have doubts about your work, it's part of the process. I think something else is going on. Menopause. She's all sweaty and clammy and tossing and turning in bed all night. Whining and moaning. I like squeezing her big butt. I should go down on her or something. But any kind of sex is too much of an effort, especially where I have to lie down and go down and not come up for air. I panic when I think of it. It's not sex I'm afraid of, it's breathing. I think of sex the way I think of walking up the stairs: I go out of my way to avoid it. Except that I don't miss walking up the stairs.

June

Fun and frustration with the computer. First, I added some photographs to the January journal, which I just finished transcribing last night. But mostly the computer's given me nothing but trouble today. I was trying to do more scanning and cropping, but the damn thing kept bombing and freezing and crashing. There are a few things I can try tomorrow, but I'm not sure what's going on. We're taking it in to the shop anyway to add a couple of gigabites, so maybe Les can fix whatever's wrong. I sound like a real computer geek, I know, but all my projects are on it now. I'd rather be in front of the computer than anywhere else. Something to do with getting my life in order. My command post. A place where I can get a lot done without doing a lot (physically). I get depressed when it starts giving me trouble. The waste of time. The confusion, the disarray. My life, which is all computerized and digitized by now, feels like it's crashing around me when the system dies. A little melodramatic, yeah, but I'm only human.

After all the complaining, of course I'm in the hospital again. Headaches, chest aches, phlegm, and all the rest of the shit, the boring shit, my mean mantra. Can I get some other kind of pain relievers maybe, like Demerol or morphine? Don't know if I really need something that heavy, the pain's not excruciating, it's just constant and annoying, to say the least. But why shouldn't I be able to zone out a little? Where am I going? What else do I have to do?

Vicodin kicking in. Not much of a kick anymore. More like a tap on the shoulder. And when I turn around there ain't nobody there. And then the headache's back.

Who's this nurse I've got tonight? Never saw a porta cath before? I hate new nurses that don't know me at night. I want *them* taking care of *me*, not me them. What a whiner. Looks like I'll be here till next Monday. Sheree's none too happy 'bout that, but that's the way it goes. Maybe I'll actually use the time wisely and do some serious writing while I'm here, now that I've got this new laptop computer. Almost finished transcribing the handwritten part of this year's journal, up to the point where I started using this here laptop with a lip. I call it a laptop with a lip because it has this software that lets it talk back to me. It reads my stuff in this real sad disembodied voice that I find quite compelling. This is nuts, but it reminds me of when I was a kid and used to have puppets with me to keep me company in the hospital. Now instead of making a puppet talk I can make this machine my alter ego. I think my Vicodin wave has passed. I prayed for Demerol, not because I needed it, but because my body keeps flashing on it, how fucking good it felt, for a few minutes anyway. But there's no real justification for it now. I keep looking for one, but no. I'm feeling better and breathing better, but I'm not doing anything but sitting here in bed. I'm remarkably well adjusted to being here. Sheree wants me home, though. She sounded very lonely on the phone. It's harder on her than it is on me. It always will be. I'm the center of attention, even at the worst of it. But for her, she'll always be alone. I just called her back and had the computer say, "I forgot to tell you I love you." And I do.

Tonight's notes, before I slip off into my pharmaceutical soup: more aches and pains from the aches and pains department. No Demerol. Some Vicodin. The names of these drugs are capitalized as if they were gods. Saint Vicodin. Lord Demerol. Our Lady of Cephtazidime. Let's not forget the great and powerful Zoloft, son of Prozac. And now we're trying Percocet to melt the headaches—which are all real, make no mistake about it. I'm not just looking for a cheap buzz. I want relief. The Percocet works a bit, I s'pose, but the "buzz" aspects of Demerol are sorely missed. I was supposed to try this stupid bipap thing again tonight. It's a respirator designed for snorers that was supposed to give me relief during the night and maybe alleviate the headaches and chest pain the next day. But it only made the headaches worse, which is too bad because I was looking forward to incorporating the stupid-looking face mask into a leather hood, so at least the humiliation of it all would have a more erotic component, and I wouldn't look so much like a geek wearing a jock strap on his head all night.

July

What's with my siblings? Is it survivor's guilt? They hate me for all the attention I've gotten over the years due to the CF, and they feel guilty for that and for being the healthy ones, the bad ones, the survivors. But fuck it, it's time to grow up. Time is running out. If they want survivor's guilt, I'll give them a whole shitload of survivor's guilt real soon. A lot sooner than they realize. As far as details of the day and the life go: I'm dirty, need a shower and a shave. Finally brushed my teeth. I think they're rotting, but I don't want to do anything about it. Carl was here cleaning up while the painters and roofers were patching up and I was spitting up, as usual. Congested. Bad bad, dizzying headache this morning, but better now, thanks to Mr. P. No real buzz anymore, but it still quells the spells. And speaking of pain, I again promised Cathy Busby an article on pain for her book. That was last Friday, and still no article. All I am is a pain in the ass with my false promises and procrastination. I took the '95 journal references to pain and wove them into an eleven-passage massive tumor. Now I've got to operate on it to see if it's benign or cancerous. And the final detail of the day is I got commissioned by someone at MGM to write ad copy for a film about a guy dying of AIDS who throws himself one last going-away party. Am I the right guy for this job or what?

I wuz asleep. But now I'm not. Drugged. Groggy. Headache. Sweats. The Prednisone. The Percocet. The Oxazepam. Distracted as I write because I'm watching Jack Nicholson in *Wolf* on TV. Strangely flat and compelling, possibly completely stupid, but queer as hell. Good TV, nonetheless, for 5 in the morning. As I said, I wuz asleep after returning home exhausted from Dana Duff's birthday party in Culver City. Exhausted from dealing with Sheree, stoned and creative and panicking over her "reading" at some leather lesbian soiree. I got real exasperated, fucking nasty with her. The Prednisone. Spent the whole day in Photoshop putting a birthday cake into a 10-year-old photo of Dana and me, then smack-dab in the middle of the cake is my big dick (what else) with a candle in it. I think I'm obsessed with these cyber penises of mine because sex in the real world is so much more difficult these days. We did manage to fuck this morning, if that's what you call it. I tweaked a hard-on for the camera and Sheree stuffed it in and rode it a while as she choked me and snapped a few photos for Aura Rosenberg's book of men's faces in the throes of orgasm, but there was no orgasm here, thanks to the almighty Zoloft. Afterward Sheree did get off with the assistance of the vibrator on her clit and my teeth on her tit. But later that day it was my fangs in her jugular while trying to help edit her damn lesbian piss tape while she raved and yammered and drove me nuts. I didn't want to be mean. Didn't want to say "Shut up!" But I'm just as out of it on my drugs (Prednisone) as she is on hers (pot). It all just made me feel shittier and more anxious, so I took more pills, Oxazepam. Sheree's pretty understanding about the whole thing, or so stoned she doesn't give a shit. So all's right with the world. The sun's coming up. The headache's subsiding (Percocet). And we're watching *Wolf*. The new day awaits. Grrrrrrr

We thought we could sit forever in the fun, but our chances really were a million to one. Home from the last night of CF summer camp, the last campfire, the last roundup for me, and somehow I pulled it off. I sang at the campfire, I went around to the cabins and sang good-night songs to the kids and I sang dirty improvs at the counselor meeting afterward. Considering all I could do during the day was lie around wondering how it was I was going to do anything ever again, it's a miracle I dragged my ass down there and slipped into the groove again, singing the old songs like I'd never been gone. I'm amazed I had any reserve left at all. Suddenly, I could not only breathe, but I could shape that breathing into some decent singing, not like it used to be, but what I now lack in physical ability, I make up with experience and a sense of showmanship that I've picked up along the way. If I wanted to, I could really do something with the singing even now, even with the oxygen. I'd be unique, that's for sure. Who wouldn't give the pathetic oxygen boy a chance? Not that it wasn't work for me, it was. It took every ounce of oxygen to get those songs out, but I did it and I did it well. I even introduced my "Supermasochistic Bob" song and they loved it, both the clean version and the real version. I feel kind of weird about the last "Jenny" improv and the "Suck My Jesus" song that I sang for the counselor meeting. A little over the top perhaps, but that's what they asked for. After a long week of hard work, and the sadness of the last campfire where the kids remember all their dead friends, I perform a kind of a service by singing these ridiculous over-the-top songs. I relieve the tension of the week. I'm as close as they get to getting drunk and tearing the place apart. But I still feel kind of weird about it. But fuck it, I'm home. Obligations done. Naked now. TV. My own work. Fucking Sheree. My life and what's left of it.

August

New month, same old body, feeling older than it is or will ever have the chance to be. I'm afraid my heart's starting to give out. My ankles have been swelling up since last week when I was Mr. Troubadour at camp. In contrast to the great burst of energy I had "way" back then, today I can barely move without being severely short of breath and can barely stay awake when I'm not moving. While trying to help Sheree with the Pee Boy fountain this morning, I couldn't help stepping outside myself to catch the irony of me huffing and puffing trying to get our naked white nasty dick-holding boy to pee in the bowl properly, working up a sweat trying to get the pump connected the right way, frustrated as hell 'cause my own pump felt so fucked, my connections all kinked and haywire, and even my dick not much good or much use to anyone. Feeling sorry for myself I guess. But if not me, then who? What bothers me most is that it's so hard to do work. I just want to lie around all day and watch TV. I have twenty or thirty different projects or commitments to work on, not to mention the IV antibiotics, the breathing treatments, the physical therapist, pharmacies, doctors' appointments—how can I resist just curling up on the couch, watching the O.J. trial, and saying, "Fuck it"?

Ants are crawling in and out of my teeth and around my eye sockets and my nostrils. The moisture is draining out of me and I'm starting to shrivel up. My little applehead effigy looks great, almost as good as the real thing, the real thing being me, when I'm dead, buried with a videocamera to document my ongoing "deconstruction," but Sheree's having second thoughts. Now she wants me cremated so she can keep my ashes. Of course, Kirby's rooting for Plan A, the video burial as a ready-made ending to his "Bobumentary." So to placate Kirby and to sell Sheree, I came up with this applehead prototype. Who knows, maybe I'll be able to interest a collector or two. I also did a pretty good drawing today for the "Bobumentary": it's a drawing montage of "me" with a big hard-on, standing at a dark room enlarger to which I've attached a needle, something I did twenty years ago because I couldn't get up the nerve to stick a needle in my dick without automating it this way. Now, at Kirby's request, I'm in the process of illustrating this and other autoerotic "torture" machines I've designed over the years. And they're working out real well, despite the fact that the computer kept giving me hell. Sheree had to take the external drive for repairs. It's OK and so is my stuff. Not only is the computer fucking up (Photoshop was also a real bitch today, too), but my body is still on the fritz, even though I'm feeling better and doing more. I'm all filled up with fluids, from my right armpit to my ankles, with a large protruding abdomen in between. Looks like I'm pregnant. Feels like I've had an enema. More to worry about. But now I've got to go to sleep.

I feel like Superman, Underdog, Popeye—not the macho heroes, the bloated Thanksgiving Day balloons. I feel like I'm walking on the moon. One small step for man, one giant leap closer to the grave. I'm the Pillsbury Doughboy, overdone, crumbling. *Nothing says lovin' like somethin in a coffin.* Heh, heh! I'm really feeling the pressure of having to get my life in order before my body gives out entirely. The dying part will be easy (for me), but the constant interruptions, the drives down to the doctor's in Long Beach (even Kirby's had it with that), the drug deliveries that don't come, the oxygen that runs out in the middle of a movie, assuming I have enough energy to drag my ass out of the house to go to a movie, the true humiliation of having to watch Sheree work like a dog to take care of me, who used to get so hot being her slave, sickness or no sickness, what a whining wimp I've become. "No" is the first word out of my mouth, it's part of my breathing, *no . . . no . . . no . . .* I see it like a knife in Sheree's back every time she hears it, and she's getting tired of it, too, but I'm doing the best I can, that's my mantra these days, but so what? It doesn't take the sadness away, and maybe I'm not always doing the best I can. I ain't no superhero, that's for sure, and this is no fucking holiday.

Reflections on Pain Journal
Sheree Rose

It's difficult for me to realize that Bob has been dead for two years. I think about him almost every day, and still miss his physical presence, no matter in what condition. His voice is strong within me, and when I read his words, written during his last, agonizing year, the power of his personality is staggering—I am transported back to those months when the death-watch began in earnest.

It was painful to watch his slow deterioration, and to know that his days were numbered, and there was nothing all the medicine, all the doctors, all the pills, all the respiratory therapists, all the high-tech IVs, all the king's men, could do to put him together again. His death was inevitable, but his dying was tragic. He wasn't ready to die, he was filled with plans and ideas for future projects. In fact, while in the hospital that last year, he applied for a Guggenheim grant. I gathered the necessary material, put together a project package—all the activity supervised by Bob from his bed. Ironically, he was awarded a Guggenheim grant in January 1996, just days after his death. When the committee found out that he had died, they rescinded the grant because of a policy of no posthumous awards. Talk about bad timing! I believe that if Bob had been alive when he found out he had received the Guggenheim, he probably would have willed himself another year of life in order to honor his commitment and realize his ambition to complete his final work—the Death Trilogy.

What amazes me most was Bob's uncanny ability to wrest humor and art from the macabre and sad events of his last months on earth. He never lost his touch for turning a phrase so precisely, or for expressing his turmoil, anger, and sarcasm so eloquently. Even the most degrading bodily functions and intimate personal feelings were transformed into poetic language in which exotically named drugs become gods to be worshipped and adored.

Ultimately, Bob was only human: neither the superheroes he tried so hard to emulate nor his mistress whom he truly loved and attempted to obey were able to save him from a fate that was sealed from the moment of his conception. But through his heart-breaking humanness along with his breath-taking honesty, the rest of us are enabled to understand, empathize, and mourn the loss of this super-ordinary man.

February 2, 1998
Culver City, California

Bill Burns

Analgesia

PILL MINE has been called a state-of-the-art post-industrial unit. But seeing is believing, and those who stop by are going home with faith in a lot more than the curative potential of pills. Once dead and acrid tailing ponds now teem with fish and mollusks; former slag heaps have been reclaimed as boreal adventure forests where large mammals such as antelope and white-tailed deer can be spotted. Workers spend much of their free time involved in environmentally friendly activities, be it composting waste at the vegetarian diner, listening to digitally recorded sounds of nature in the *Bufferin Audio Library*, or simply swimming with the sturgeon and turtles at the *Advil Aqua Park*. Staff, visitors, guests, and children at the twenty-four-hour daycare center are treated to nutritious snacks prepared from local minerals and indigenous herbs and greens, some of which were, until recently, endangered species. Happily, now that Pill Mine has established the *Tylenol Biodome* not only are local plant and animal populations secure but numerous genetically engineered species have been introduced locally with great success! It's little wonder people are starting to say that Pill Mine and Painkiller Factory have put the *e* back into *pharm-e-cology*.

Painkiller Factory is a composite facility where pill ore is processed and eventually tested on volunteers. Dirty pills arrive in trucks powered on methane gas, generated by an in-house night-soil extraction system. Impurities are removed from the ore with high-pressure biodegradable solvents in the "wet room." This pill-cleaning process is known as sluicing. Clean pills are formed into ingots, then carbon-dated and classified by weight, color, texture, and brand name. The pill ingots are now considered product. Animal testing is out of the question; samples of product are scientifically tested for acidity, taste, efficacy, and possible nonanalgesic properties before being allowed into the Inert Halcyon Sector (IHS). The IHS is often called the first line of defense against chronic pain. Many volunteers, who are considered guests, come to the IHS seeking relief from stubborn somatic maladies such as migraine and back pain. All treatments are free, confidential, and medically super-vised. While registered at the luxurious *Wellcome House* guests share the Committee for a Pain-Free Body's recreation and pain-management center with workers. Not

Bill Burns

surprisingly, reservations are a must for workers, guests, and their families wishing to sojourn at the IHS.

Although the two facilities have a health and safety record second to none, work at both the mine and the factory can be difficult and sometimes dangerous. Some of the occupational hazards of both Pill Mine and Painkiller Factory include "pink lung," caused by Valium dust, and "white finger," caused by the constant rattling of power machinery. Regrettably, many miners and factory workers never fully recover from their ailments, but with proper pain management they can continue to be productive contributors. Besides swimming and wave pools and a gymnasium, the recreation and pain-management complex provides conventional physiotherapy, shiatsu, reflexology, yoga, hot and cold water therapies, and the latest in virtual reality therapy and training, the *Simulatorium*. Widely viewed as the next generation in high-performance virtual systems, the *Simulatorium* allows trainees and injured workers to simulate all aspects of their job with absolutely no risk of

injury or hazard. What's more, disabled workers have been instrumental in changing work habits and working conditions to provide for a safer and healthier workplace.

When it comes to human resources, there are no simple answers but there are smart choices. Job-safety particulars are voted on fortnightly. Although worker unanimity is required on the perceived safety of all work orders, they are seldom rejected thanks to proactive industrial communications; those that are rejected are submitted to the Committee for a Pain-Free Body for revisions and recommendations. Many workplaces experiment with democracy; at Pill Mine and Painkiller Factory, it is a way of life.

In spite of the recession, work has been steady at Pill Mine and Painkiller Factory. As a matter of fact there is every reason to believe that the two facilities will be expanding in the very near future. Industry experts are optimistic that the payroll-reduction program and a continued commitment to research and development will enable the company to maintain its position on top of the global high-tech heap. In celebration, the gigantic Monument to Analgesia, the largest pain reliever ever built on the planet, is now entering its final phase of construction. Its featherweight teflon panels will form a space-age skin over the superstructure. With the exception of the platinum-encrusted communications tower, the entire structure will be made of recycled material. It is no secret that parts of the original Skylab mission craft are being reused on this project. At Pill Mine and Painkiller Factory, where the environment is concerned, action is in, reaction is out. Plenty of room has been made for the three *R*'s: re-cycle, re-use, and re-duce. Let's make room for one more: re-think.

Elsie Petch

Reclaiming Responsibility: Seniors, Medication, and Health Promotion in South Riverdale

ANALGESICS, OR PAINKILLERS as they are commonly known, are among the most frequently prescribed medications for seniors. Moreover, over-the-counter (OTC) analgesics are the most popular of all medications bought for self-care.[1] Misuse of these and other medications reflects larger individual and structural barriers to their efficacious use. Canadian public health insurance provides universal coverage, but it is still a top-down health care system largely oriented to provision of services by professionals. This system does not deal well with the complex needs of older people, or the management of chronic illness. It does not promote health in a holistic manner. Seniors, like other users of the system, are encouraged to play a passive role as consumers. Appropriate information to help seniors participate in their care and make decisions about their health is limited.

Seniors receive an unfair share of the blame for the inappropriate and costly use of our health system. Discussions about the need for health care reform invariably include demographic and fiscal projections accompanied by grim forebodings about our aging society. An aging population does not necessarily mean an increase in cost. Rather, one of the major problems in our health care system is the overuse—indeed overmedication—of seniors, which increases costs and, most important, places the health of seniors in jeopardy. Various studies show that approximately 20 percent of all hospitalization of people age sixty-five and older, is due to medication misuse.[2]

This tendency to overmedicate seniors is supported by a drug industry that spends enormous amounts of money on research, manufacturing, and aggressive marketing to physicians and the public to ensure that doctors will continue to prescribe, pharmacists will continue to distribute, and that patients will continue to buy medications. Despite the money spent at the end of this process, it has been estimated that approximately 50 percent of all medications are taken incorrectly.[3] To cite another example, a recent examination of older women found that 24.6 percent failed to have one or more prescriptions filled after a visit to the doctor.[4] Despite these statistics, the costs, and resulting ineffectiveness, little research has been done to explore why people do not take their medications appropriately. Even more rarely are older people consulted and encouraged to come up with practical, cost-effective, healthy solutions to medication misuse.

This is the story of the South Riverdale Community Health Center (SRCHC), a community health center that uses health promotion strategies that focus on community development, education, and advocacy to promote safe medication use among seniors. The center, located in East Toronto, serves approximately sixty-five thousand people from a wide range of socioeconomic, linguistic, and racial backgrounds. It is one of fifty community health centers funded by the Ontario Ministry of Health and governed by a community board. At the center, individual services are provided by salaried doctors, nurse practitioners, chiropodists, social workers, and a nutritionist. Health promoters work with community members to address broader issues related to health such as air quality, food access, and literacy. This model of a publicly funded constituency-run health center allows for flexibility and creative strategies that can respond to locally identified needs.

Our work with seniors and medications began in 1988, when the South Riverdale Community Health Center began programming to enable seniors to remain living independently for as long as feasible. Early in the programming, community residents and professionals working directly with seniors were asked to identify health issues. Everyone named medication misuse as a major area of concern, but their visions of the problem differed according to their place in the system. Physicians identified noncompliance, overmedication, self-medication and doctor hopping. Front-line workers, like nurses and social workers, talked of difficulties with packaging and labeling, saving medications, sharing medications, combined medication and alcohol use, and limited consumer access to information about medications. The real learning occurred when seniors spoke out, sharing their experiences and insights on their treatment by health professionals. As a result of these testimonies, consultation has become an integral part of the information gathering and educational programming used to promote safe medication use.

Seniors Speak Out

In 1989 we began educational programming. A video, *The Wise Use of Drugs*, was shown in a subsidized seniors' residence building. The film, which features seniors, encourages older consumers to take charge of their medications by becoming more informed about them and by participating actively in their health care. During the presentation, a pharmacy deliveryman laden with prescriptions for the seniors, joined the group. Subsequent discussion revealed that the physician who visited the building twice a week frequently changed his prescriptions from one visit to another. Further, the prescriptions ordered by the physician by phone were dispensed at a pharmacy located several miles away rather than at a pharmacy located two blocks away. This arrangement did not encourage seniors to ask questions and seek clarification about their medications from their pharmacist. Ontario provides a Drug Benefit Plan to pay for any medication listed in their formulary and the dispensing fee for people age sixty-five and older. The plan came under review because its cost increased from 2 percent of the total health care budget in 1979 to 5 percent of the budget in 1992. The residents in the group expressed concern about the health risks, the cost to the system, and the waste involved in frequent medication changes.

Desiring more information than the video could provide, the seniors organized a series of talks that focused on learning about their medications, as well as complementary modalities to pills such as proper eating, exercise, therapeutic massage, and stress reduction.[5] Recognizing the value of the film, the deliveryman asked if it could be shown in other seniors' buildings where he made his deliveries. Over the following year the majority of the original group found new physicians and transferred their business to the local pharmacist.

The unexpected success of this first talk initiated a new process: seniors themselves identifying their specific issues of concern and making suggestions to improve the system. The programming that we shaped was developed over a two-year period of consultation and mutual education. This work culminated in a series of four two-hour presentations published in a manual titled *Wise Use of Medications: A Health Promotion Approach to Community Programming for Safe Medication*

Use with and for Seniors. The program features participatory learning, allowing seniors rather than "experts" to inform each other.

When it is presented in its entirety, the four-part program spans about a month. This allows time for new learning to be reflected on and reinforced. It also provides opportunities for seniors to develop support networks to become more connected contributing community members. Although there are stated objectives and a presentation format supplied by the manual, each group tailors the presentations to suit their own needs. The program educates not only seniors. Pharmacists, physicians, nurses, a nutritionist, a librarian, and social workers are invited to present and to learn from seniors.

Each presenter raises a range of issues and community resources. Local pharmacists, for example, often discuss the role of their profession. Seniors may not realize that the pharmacist can be a source of information about both prescription and over-the-counter drugs. Sessions revealed that most seniors did not know that pharmacists also can provide easy-to-open containers and large-print labels. Pharmacists, in turn, learned about the need for more information and improved communication.

Physicians are concerned about noncompliance by seniors. Compliance suggests a passive role, that is, the doctor orders and the patient follows orders. The standard answer is that noncompliance is due to a mistrust of medicine and medical practitioners, poor communication, sensory and memory changes in seniors, confusion due to multiple medications, or a lack of knowledge and understanding about specific medication. However, I hypothesize that some noncompliance is due to a desire by seniors to remain independent and healthy. According to our experience at the center, backed by various studies, seniors themselves are far more concerned about independence and health than death.

Adherence to medication and other treatment regimes improves markedly with good communication between patient and physician. The relationship between seniors and physicians is key to the wise use of medications. Many seniors state at the beginning of the program that they don't worry about their medications, as "the doctor looks after it." During the lifetime of these seniors, they are encouraged to view doctors as "omnipotent authorities achieving wonders with new technologies and medications which were literally life-saving."[6] Doctors may not be aware of the total numbers of medications being consumed. This is borne out by a 1992 Angus Reid poll that found 92 percent of a group of seniors who were taking medications prescribed by two or more doctors thought each of the doctors was aware of all the prescribed and OTC medications they were taking.[7]

In reality, the current system does not encourage coordination of care, and this can increase health problems. Shortly after our programming sessions began in 1989, we heard the story of an older man who was unable to sleep nights. On further questioning, he reported he had to get up frequently during the night to urinate. The physician at the presentation checked his drugs and found he was taking three diuretics: one ordered by his doctor, the second by a specialist, and the third when he was in the hospital. Each medication had a different name, shape, and color and was filled in three different pharmacies. This man did not know what each pill was for. Therefore, he did not know he was taking three similar medications.

A lack of centralized information is not the only reason that incidents like this happen. Seniors involved in the programming often identify feeling rushed during their visits to their doctor. They often say that they are not comfortable asking questions or seeking clarification. This is not only a psychological problem embedded in the doctor-patient relationship. It is also a structural and economic issue. One study of community health centers that pay physicians on salary shows that drug costs are reduced by up to 21 percent compared to fee-for-service doctors.[8] This involves two issues: time and money. First, it takes a physician longer to explain why a medication is not needed than it does to order one. A salaried doctor is likely to take this additional time. Second, drugs often are prescribed to provide quick-fix solutions for psychosocial problems such as caregiver stress, isolation, and poverty.[9]

As a result of these oral presentations, health care workers learn that seniors do not intend to abuse the system. They learn that a fragmented system that relies heavily on medications may be making seniors sick. Seniors learn that it is necessary for them to become informed and to take more responsibility for their health care.

Health and Literacy

As the presentations continued, the participants identified a need for clear, accessible information. The center is located in an area where literacy levels are a concern. Literacy and health are closely linked.[10] People who read will have greater access to print information and have more opportunities to make informed decisions about their health. In the senior population, 64 percent of older Canadians experience some degree of trouble reading printed materials.[11] People who design consumer information related to health rarely consult a range of people the information is intended to reach.

In order to reach more people in the community the project included development of clearly written materials. If materials are written in clear language, they will reach an additional 29 percent of seniors who are able to read at a level that is not too complex.[12] Design, print size, style of type, and color contrast improve readability for those with eyesight changes. Seniors were involved in all phases of the development of the print resources. The result was three educational pamphlets. One of the pamphlets, requested by the community, contained information about pain pills, warnings, and alternatives. Self-care and pain pills were frequent topics introduced by seniors during the group sessions. Confusion about prescribed analgesics and other medications sometimes resulted in, for example, anti-inflammatories and muscle relaxants being taken mistakenly in larger doses in response to pain. A recent study of women age sixty-five and older showed that 30 percent of the women misused OTC medications due to wrong understanding or lack of understanding and that analgesics containing aspirins or aspirin itself were the most likely to produce adverse effects.[13]

The development of clear language materials at SRCHC also produced a Safe Medication Record Card. This process involved collaboration with more than one hundred seniors. The design, color, and content of the record card were decided on by seniors themselves. The card, which allows seniors and consumers of all ages to keep track of their medications, is useful in everyday situations and serves as a means of communication with health professionals. People are encouraged to have all their medication, including over-the-counter drugs, reviewed regularly by their doctor, nurse, and/or pharmacist. A separate section for OTC medications asks people to record how often, and why, the medication is taken. This helps the professional to identify if the medication is being taken correctly. The review often results in medications being eliminated, thereby reducing side effects, interactions, and confusion about organizing medication-taking regimens.

The card is also used in emergency situations. The senior owns and controls the use of the card. It is this *control* that has been most appealing to seniors. It is this card that has proven to be the most effective product of our programming. The card has been reproduced in tens of thousands by various agencies and institutions. Some rather unlikely partners have emerged including the Canadian Auto Workers Union, which has incorporated the card, as well as the program and pamphlets, into its peer educator model. Former workers in the plant return to the workplace to discuss medication use and abuse. Literacy learning program tutors in the downtown area have helped their students fill out their medication cards. Following such a session, one young man, living on the street, came into the learning program after the weekend most excited because, following an epileptic seizure, he woke up in a hospital emergency room rather than the "drunk tank," as he had on several previous occasions. The police had found the card, realized he had a seizure, and took him to the hospital where he received care and a review of his medication regimen.

Seniors in the community are most enthusiastic about sharing the card with others. More than two thousand have been distributed locally, directly by seniors who developed the card, to other seniors and health care providers. The seniors delight in telling about the cards, which they have also mailed to relatives in rural areas and given to friends who travel. They have also related several stories about how the card has improved communication with professionals and has been credited with saving lives in emergency situations. The seniors have learned to modestly take credit for the success of the program and now provide consultation to health care professionals on how to develop clear, relevant health messages.

This model, which emphasizes process and beginning with specific needs, has resulted in materials developed in consultation with communities barred from the safe use of medication because of cultural or linguistic differences. The Francophone community has arranged for the program manual to be translated and has redeveloped the materials with and for French-speaking seniors. A similar grassroots process involving seniors was used to reach the Chinese communities that comprise up to 25 percent of the population in some areas of South Riverdale. The Chinese version of the medication card, which is written in both Chinese and English, is designed to enhance communication with an English-speaking health care system.

Conclusion

Between 1992 and 1994 the province of Ontario, through the Drug Reform Secretariat, examined how it could reform the Drug Benefit Plan to cut costs and extend benefits equitably to other consumers while not compromising the health of seniors. The process permitted South Riverdale and other community agencies and seniors to advocate and present recommendations for reform, which include opportunities for seniors to have more control for the use of their medications. A report published in January 1993 for the Canadian Public Health Association (CPHA) stated in its first recommendation that the CPHA work with consumers' associations and professional associations to develop effective strategies to educate people in benefits, risk, and cost-management issues on a broad level.[14] The response from the Drug Reform Secretariat to date has been to largely make decisions and fund approaches that do not involve consumers, education, or control.

The World Health Organization defines health promotion as a process of enabling people to have more control over their lives in order to improve their health. As a concept, health promotion encourages people to look at individuals in the context of larger structural issues that affect the health of everyone. Medication misuse does not occur suddenly in later years. Rather, it is an outcome of a system that encourages individualized, quick-fix medical responses to a range of issues and that promotes a passive role for consumers of services.

Many representatives of the bureaucracy, the pharmaceutical industry, and various professional groups remain skeptical of the benefits of consumer education and control. This is expressed in statements such as, "We can't give people pages out of the CPS" (*Compendium of Pharmaceuticals and Specialties*) and "We don't know what education is." Senior consumers are becoming more educated through the media about their need for more proactive approaches. Two recent public forums on medication issues have brought out several hundreds of seniors who are angry and who are challenging the health care system. As economic pressures create the need to examine the established mode of delivery of health care services, it is likely that some consumers, including motivated, demanding seniors, will get more attention from health care funders and providers. Long since denied a role in their health care decisions, older consumers increasingly are becoming a force to be reckoned with.

Seniors have long been seen as sources of many problems related to the delivery of health care. The experience of South Riverdale Community Health Center demonstrates the wisdom, resourcefulness, and ability of senior consumers to work with health professionals toward creative, proactive, grassroots solutions.

Notes

1. Lan T. Gien, *Health Education and the Use of Over-the-Counter Products in Self-Treatment of Common Minor Ailments in Elderly Women: A Randomized Controlled Study*, Proceedings of the First International Conference on Nursing Research, Adelaide, South Australia (1991), 81.

2. Joel Lexchin, "Adverse Drug Reaction: Review of the Canadian Literature," *Canadian Family Physician* 37 (January 1991): 109–19.

3. Dorothy L. Smith, *Understanding Canadian Prescription Drugs: A Consumer's Guide to Correct Use* (Toronto: Key Porter Books, 1989), 1.

4. L. T. Gien and J. A. D. Anderson, "The Impact of Health Education on the Use of Medications in Elderly Women," in *Aging and Health: Linking Research and Public Policy*, *Michigan U.S.A.*, ed. S. Lewis (Lewis Publishers, 1989), 110–20.

5. The expression *complementary modality* has replaced the term *alternative* in the health care field. Alternative implies that therapies, such as massage, exercise, and so on, are at odds with "mainstream medical practice," whereas complementary implies that one form of treatment can enhance the other.

6. Ronald Bayne, *Medication Use and the Elderly: Problems and Challenges*, Proceedings of the British Columbia Invitational Workshop, Medication Use and Elderly People (1989), 9.

7. *Survey on Medication Use: Seniors Info Exchange*, Seniors Secretariat, Health and Welfare Canada, Spring 1993, 9.

8. Douglas E. Angus and Pran Manga, *Co-op/Consumer Sponsored Health Care Delivery Effectiveness*, (Canadian Cooperative Association, 1990), 10.

9. William A. McKim and Brian L. Mishara, *Drugs and Aging* (Toronto and Vancouver: Butterworth, 1987), 22.

10. *Literacy and Health: Making the World Healthier and Safer for People Who Can't Read* (Toronto: Ontario Health Association and Frontier College, 1989).

11. *Learning: That's Life—Literacy and Older Canadians*, Conference Proceedings (1990).

12. Ibid., 8.

13. Gien, *Health Education*, 81.

14. *Benefit, Risk and Cost Management of Drugs*, Report of the CPHA National Advisory Panel on Risk/Benefit Management of Drugs, Canadian Public Health Association (1993), ix.

Fred Tomaselli

Self-Portrait

SELF PORTRAIT   JUNE 8, 1956   JULY 26, 1996

PERCODAN
ACETAMINOPEN
METHAMPHETAMINE
DIPHENHYDRAMINE
CODEINE
ALCOHOL
HEROIN
XANEX
L.S.D.
QUININE   P.C.P.
MESCALINE
IBUPROFEN
EPHEDRINE   CAFFEINE
EPTO BISMAL
LIBRIUM   OPIUM
NITROUS OXIDE
CANNABIS
MPICILLIN
ASPIRIN
QUAALUDE
ANTACID
BENZPHETAMINE
CHOCOLATE
HYDRERGINE
ENTOBARBITOL
PEYOTE
MORPHINE
COCAINE
SECOBARBITAL   DIAZEPAM
NAPROXEN   AMPHETAMINE
CORTISONE   DARVON
PENICILL
ALKA SELTZER
PSILOCYBIN
DEXTROAMPHETAMINE
PSEUDOEPHEDRINE
AMYL NITRITE   NOVOCAINE

Charles R. Acland

Take Two: Post-Fordist Discourses of the Corporate and Corporeal

AT FIRST glance, pills appear uniformly smooth. The corporate logos, colors, and shapes may vary. Some are dry and chalky, while others are enveloped in a soft, semipermeable material. But without exception, pills are smooth, without sharp edges, and continuously enclosed.

And yet, in fact, they are marked, deeply and permanently. They hold invisible ridges that comprise their social geometry. These ridges are *striations* of the social, a term used by Gilles Deleuze and Félix Guattari to describe those forces that act to establish stratas, systems of order, and hierarchies.[1] All pills spring from a mixture of smooth space and striated space. Deleuze and Guattari submit that this involves the blending of the nomad and the sedentary, of the war machine and the State apparatus.[2]

Captured in the smooth forms of pills is a complex apparatus of contemporary social knowledge. It follows that one can conceive of pharmaceutical drugs as a precise location in which certain social powers are enacted. Drugs are a site of *micro-power*; they condense and reproduce exacting relations of power among the fields of industry, medicine, and bodies. As a space between the war machine and the

State, they concern movements and hierarchies, tactics and deflections. In general, particular knowledges about the body, pain, scientific discovery and authority, health, and capital resonate through all practices of modern medicine. The smooth and striated space of prescription and non-prescription drugs is a nexus for the effectivity of medical discourse, in addition to being a product of the same. In this way, the banal objects that are pills testify to those epistemological constructs, and their attendant stratas and systems of order. The smooth and the striated aspects of pharmaceutical drugs form the vectors along which certain social powers are distributed. In what follows, I wish to explore the sense in which the products of the pharmaceutical industry are both the power and site of the application of power at the foundation of post-Fordist medicine, and to point to some of the implications for the human condition of illness. The final issue, and ultimately the only one that really matters, though it is often obscured and forgotten, is the location of the body in pain in the post-Fordist medical machine.

There is no better nomadic entity than the post-Fordist corporation.[3] This is because rather than investing in the continuity of a particular mode of production—for instance, the spatial anchored assembly line—the post-Fordist company invests in its own fluidity.[4] If Fordism was about a social hegemony of efficiency management, division of labor and time-motion analysis, then post-Fordism is about the efficient movement of labor and capital, and the circulation of finance, all on a global scale. As companies grow to dwarf many nations in terms of economic influence, they maintain a certain mobility. This includes flexibility in the services or products offered, in the production process, in the labor force, and in the location of operation. One now witnesses an increasing speed of the transfer of global economic resources. This velocity extends one of the axioms of capitalism to an extreme: that once capital stops moving and stops reconstituting itself, it dies, a relation that Marshall Berman describes as a dialectic between construction and destruction.[5] Post-Fordism, one might say, is the state of the developed industrial world having learned that lesson, perhaps too well. Importantly, as with Fordism, a complex set of social relations develops around these changing forces. The concomitant developments involve shifting structures of work, consumption, and politics.

National governments have been actively facilitating the emergence of the post-Fordist world. Free-trade pacts, the selective reduction of trade barriers, and the changing structures of government subsidy programs are all avenues pursued by national governments on the international scene to expedite the flow of capital and goods across their borders. Individual industries benefit differently from these tendencies. But certainly, pharmaceutical companies are among the largest and most flexible of multinationals today. As one of the few industries left untouched by the recession of the early 1990s, they are striking exemplars, and beneficiaries, of the logic of post-Fordism.[6]

To begin with, two key dimensions are at work in the distribution of power and social activity among the post-Fordist pharmaceutical industry. The first involves the cultural history of medical research and scientific discourse. The human body itself, despite its aggravatingly material presence, is far from a "natural" or essential entity. Its cultural construction, buttressed by the terms *illness* and *health*, are at the heart of the particularities of medical practice, which has always made strategic and historically specific moves to recognize certain symptoms and qualities over others. This is an uneasy presence, for the hand of culture is supposed to be kept silent; medicine, with the massive history of Western science hoisting it up, is to be universally valid and objectively determined by the scientific mind, isolated from the muddying annoyances of culture. Consequently, a critique that reveals the influences of culture and history on medical practice provides a window to the forces that establish the ideologies of science. In particular, feminist critiques of science have complexly demonstrated the manner in which so-called neutral science has operated with culturally predetermined assumptions and biases.[7] The result, as this research has soundly documented, has been a set of structured absences and blind spots in science, operating to deploy and secure notions of gender, class, and racial difference. The work on the cultural construction of the body has served as an important touchstone for examinations of the politics of medical practice. For example, some of the most powerful work on AIDS, including that by Paula Treichler and by John Erni, examines the consequences of biomedical discourses for gay subjectivity and their implications in the context of a medical crisis.[8] Within structures of knowledge about both homosexuality and illness, in Erni's words, "a technoethical consciousness about AIDS treatment has emerged, through which the politics of the control of the medicalized body is shaped."[9]

Here, science as a language of truth is investigated and challenged in order to expose its ideological foundations. Many such critiques, for all of their differences, fold back on what Anne Balsamo characterizes as "a deceptively simple question: how is the body, as a 'thing of nature,' transformed into a 'sign of culture'?"[10] Or, speaking to the concerns at hand, this question can be restated as follows: if culture necessarily "invades" biology, then what do the forces of post-Fordism inject *specifically* into that influence?

The second key aspect concerns what we take for granted as the industrial structure of medical research, development, and marketing. With few exceptions, contemporary medicine is brought into being through a system of corporatist capitalism, an exemplar of which is the pharmaceutical industry. Here, one must think of product differentiation more than any myth of Hippocrates. Pharmaceutical firms vie for position against one another in order to capture a piece of the multibillion-dollar annual market. In Canada alone, prescription drugs are a $4 billion industry, making it the seventh largest market in the world.[11] Internationally, American Home Products produces Advil, Upjohn produces Motrin IB, Schering-Plough produces Drixol, and Bristol-Myers Squibb produces Nuprin. These painkillers are the commodity personifications of corporate entities. As drug companies find their niche through a form of symbolic territorialization, they equally compete for symptoms, they organize pains, and they combine ailments. In so doing, they produce forms of knowledge through which consumers understand their own bodily sensations.

Quite distant from the model of free-market competition, a series of barriers to entry into the industry protects and limits the number of major participants and beneficiaries. The most notable barrier is the massive cost of capital investment and the extended period of time it takes to develop and test a new medical commodity before it can be put on the market. The primary players in this process are the State, research facilities, and corporate structure. With the complex institutional interdependency of these entities and their interests, as well as immense economies of scale, there are increasingly fewer actors in the medical industrial establishment. Mergers abound, the result of which has been an increased centralization of the structure, including both vertical and horizontal integration.

An advertisement in the *Globe and Mail* supplies an ideal snapshot of this situation (see fig. 1).[12] It boasts a half-page image consisting of two giant pills, each bearing a corporate name. This is not unusual in and of itself; we expect the mark of corporate capital on every facet of contemporary existence, including pills of various kinds. The advertisement, however, is not selling the pills; it is announcing a merger of two pharmaceutical giants, Bristol-Myers and Squibb, reported to have cost $12 billion. Though this was the largest, in fact there have been of a number of takeovers and mergers of medical corporations over the last decade.[13] These actions by multinational corporations increase the mobility of their capital; they become more abstracted and less beholden to any one regulatory agency. The direction of medical research, and ultimately the production and policing of certain forms of medical knowledge, is drawn further away from any particular state apparatus. We witness the concentration of the world market share of the pharmaceutical industry into fewer hands; the logic of post-Fordist capitalism seems to spin

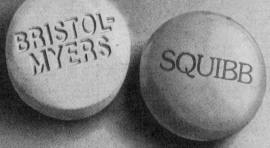

Take Two superlative groups of researchers, who have joined forces to form one of the world's pre-eminent research and development organizations with a research budget of over $900 million to invest in therapies for heart disease, cancer, AIDS and other major illnesses...

Take Two companies dedicated to the enhancement of life worldwide, who have merged to form one diversified pharmaceutical company, uniquely positioned for the 1990s and beyond, and...

You have Canadian research history in the making, with Bristol-Myers Squibb announcing one of the largest research funding agreements ever concluded in Canada by a pharmaceutical company for basic biomedical science research...

You have $5.75 million awarded by Bristol-Myers Squibb to the Samuel Lunenfeld Research Institute of Toronto's Mount Sinai Hospital. The award will allow researchers to study how genes control the development of different cell types and how changes in the genetic blueprint play a role in diseases as diverse as cancer and mental illness.

The ceremony was held at Toronto's Mount Sinai Hospital and brought together from left to right: Dr. Alan Bernstein, Associate Director of the Samuel Lunenfeld Research Institute, Mr. Gerald Turner, General Manager, Mount Sinai Hospital and Mr. Timothy Meakin, President of Bristol-Myers Squibb.

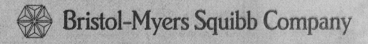

Figure 1. "Take Two . . ." August 14, 1990.

wildly out of control. Yet as the merger advertisement suggests, the body remains one important site at which these corporate battles are played out.

"Take two . . . " reads the copy. Here, the corporate merger transpires at the moment of ingestion, thus conjuring a rather vivid image of corporeal intrusion. The immediate suggestion is that there is both an ailment and an easy cure available, and that this has to do with the medical industry. In this home-remedy depiction, one is recommended to "take two superlative groups of researchers" and to "take two companies dedicated to the enhancement of life worldwide." It seems, given the rhetoric of the advertisement, that untapped research possibilities will be taken advantage of by this new megafirm. But what exactly is the nature of the "recovery" promised?

The "enhancement of life worldwide" is a general pledge of all pharmaceutical corporations. But what form of "enhancement" is being discussed? How is it measured? And in the context of the imperfect world we inhabit, which segments of "worldwide life" are catered to first? The same sentence, in its attempt to direct responses, reveals an important clue. It says that these two dedicated companies have "merged to form one diversified pharmaceutical company, uniquely positioned for the 1990's and beyond." The phrase "uniquely positioned" refers to market share and industrial competition. Thus, the sentence offers insight into the founding duality of modern medicine: the ethical drive (enhancement of life) checked by the logic of the market (uniquely positioned). The presumption is that ethical decisions are turned over to the "impartial" judgment of the market. And the dispassionate market is held in check by an imagined certainty of moral virtue. This has been a dangerous exchange, however, one that has repeatedly left "unprofitable" drugs unavailable to those who need them. For instance, research funds are virtually unavailable for thalassemia and sickle-cell anemia, despite the fact that each disease affects approximately 180 million people. This is because these diseases are concentrated in so-called Third World nations, making them, in the terms of the medical industry, an unattractive target market. Research efforts are guided toward ailments that demonstrate some profit potential, often regardless of human suffering at stake.

The commonsense slide of the advertisement is that the post-Fordist corporation leads to an improved quality of life for the globe. The logic suggests a form of trickle-down theory of health benefits, where the ultimate gains of multinational corporate and industrial structure filter back to improve the human condition, eventually. And as all good multinationals must do, they tie their global ambitions to national economics: take two such nationless companies, and "you have

Canadian research history in the making." Even a specific, and immediately re-warded, amount is announced. With the merger, "you have $5.75 million awarded by Bristol-Myers Squibb to the Samuel Lunenfeld Research Institute of Toronto's Mount Sinai Hospital." The funds are intended for a current hot-ticket medical research item, genetic research. With this support of domestic research, the reference to a worldwide enhancement of life actually indicates a potential export market. However, despite this sort of posturing, there is little allegiance to nationhood, nor can there be, given the internationalist nature of the post-Fordist company. Characteristically maintaining an eye on its own flexibility and mobility, the contemporary multinational is a fickle creature, one that remains fluid enough to dash at a moment's notice. National governments live under this gun, and often with remarkable complicity: if they no longer provide the necessary friendly environment to the corporation (in the form of patent protection, tax breaks, labor laws, etc.), then the corporation simply relocates.

This has become particularly pronounced in Canada with the debate over drug-patent-protection laws. In February 1993, Bill C-91 was passed into law, with a review to take place in 1997. It extended patent protection on pharmaceutical products to twenty years. This is intended to encourage additional research and development from brand-name drug corporations by protecting them from the immediate appearance of generic drug versions. Until 1987, Canada was understood internationally to be a haven for generic drug manufacturers. In 1969, the Canadian patent law was amended so that any drug company could get immediate license to manufacture any drug, having only to return a 4 percent royalty. As a result, with the most significant barrier to entry knocked over, Canadian generic drug companies, the largest of which are Toronto-based Novopharm and Apotex, had the room to grow and become fixtures in the industrial scene domestically. This meant that new drugs were rather rapidly available at an affordable cost. This circumvention of intellectual property, however, was taken as a reluctance on Canada's part to play the post-Fordist game. As Michael Hodin, a brand-name lobbyist working for Pfizer International, writes, "Canada's sorry history of public policy restrictions on the research-based pharmaceutical industry . . . [has put] . . . short term cost savings over longer-term quality of health care and other legitimate national economic objectives associated with technological progress."[14] Generic drug companies are seen as parasitical, feeding on the "healthy" economic potentials produced by brand-name company research. By the mid-1980s, many brand-name pharmaceutical companies agreed with then–Trade Minister John Crosbie's assessment that, in terms of protection of drug patents, "We're being put in the same camp as Third World countries." One industry commentator described the Canadian laws as "industrial genocide" for the brand-name pharmaceuticals.[15]

In 1987, Bill C-22 extended patent protection to ten years. In exchange, the Pharmaceutical Manufacturers Association of Canada, representing the brand-name companies, agreed to increase research substantially. While there has been some evidence of a slight increase in research, the cost of drugs to consumers indisputably doubled between 1988 and 1991. With a slight drop in the price of brand-name drugs in 1994, the cost of drugs in Canada remains 55 percent above world prices.[16] As Joel Lexchin's research has demonstrated, "the price spread between the least expensive and most expensive versions of a drug depends not only on the overall number of companies selling the drug but also on the degree of generic drug competition at any level of overall competition."[17]

In many respects, this bill was actually a stepping stone to the pending free-trade agreement with the United States. In 1991, this policy came under review, and with Bill C-91, it was recommended that the protection be increased further. As the argument went, research did not increase substantially because the length of patent protection was insufficient. The bill was retroactive to December 1991, which means that any investment on the part of generic drug companies since then was lost. This was expected to affect twenty-nine drugs then in development.[18] The bill also limits the export of generic drugs during the same period of patent protection. Not only will the generic drug industry be hurt, the increased cost to consumers varies from Ottawa's official estimate of $129 million over five years to projections of $7 billion over the next fifteen years.[19]

Pharmaceutical companies, both brand-name and generic drug producers, shifted their corporate advertising to address this issue alone. Looking at Upjohn's notice, the company again invokes the general trope of the medical industry (see fig. 2): "enhancing the quality of life worldwide." The subtext of this pronouncement is that it takes a "worldwide" company to offer such possibilities. The smaller, more locally bound generic companies become self-interested entities—short-term cost reduction instead of long-term benefits. But as is inevitable for a huge multinational firm like Upjohn, it must return to a version of nationalist rhetoric; after all, though the brand-name companies complain vociferously about protectionist policies for the generic firms, they are lobbying, for themselves, for what amounts to a protectionist law, enforced by the Canadian state. In their contradictory appeal, again an example of trickle-down benefits, "enhancing the quality of life worldwide" becomes dovetailed with Upjohn's objective of "improving the quality of life for all Canadians." Bill C-91 thus acts as that which papers over this contradiction.

Enhancing
The Quality of Life
Worldwide

Upjohn is a company with a century-old commitment to
enhancing the quality of life throughout the world.
We believe that the discovery and development of innovative
new products is the way to achieve that goal. With the passage
of Bill C-91, extended patent protection will bring more
discoveries and more investment in Canada, therefore
improving the quality of life for all Canadians.

Upjohn

Upjohn supports Bill C-91.

Figure 2. "Enhancing the Quality of Life Worldwide."

Brand-name drugs trade on sign value; although they are identical to more affordable generic versions, brand-name drugs rely on the additional appeal of their image. In the debate around Bill C-91, there was a linkage between two essentially separate issues of international reach and the sign value of medical commodities. Here, multinational corporations and brand-name giants are taken as the same entities, just as national companies and generic drug firms are condensed into one. This arrangement of equivalency for Canadian economic policy makers sets up a choice between the two as a package deal. The current dominant argument, the one manifested in Bill C-91, suggests that if you choose to side with the generic firm, you sacrifice international competitiveness. The sign value, in other words, is the most important aspect of the medical industry for the State because it permits the connotations of export and research opportunities. For all of the abstraction of post-Fordist economic debates, and the struggles between key industrial players in the reconfiguration of globally integrated markets and laws, the very idea of the suffering body recedes until it cannot seriously enter the discourse. In fact, *the body in pain is caught in a discourse that only wants to make it disappear*. Yet, there is a profound irony to the situation, one that many nations, particularly smaller international economic players, are facing with increasing frequency. This is the post-Fordist sacrifice of the domestic economy in the name of some distant promise of future international competitiveness. It is taken for granted that in order to have a strong national medical establishment, research must be encouraged. This means, in the present context, support for international companies, which, in the end, can give little guarantee of their commitment to the domestic scene.

If we return to the Bristol-Myers Squibb merger announcement, the small photograph of "the ceremony" is particularly interesting, if only because it seems so amateurish next to the slickness of the rest of the advertisement (see fig. 3). It represents the research monies awarded to Mount Sinai Hospital, and not the announcement of the merger, as one might mistakenly believe, after a brief glance at the advertisement. The caption tells of the ceremony's location, but with the anonymous closed setting, this scene could be taking place anywhere. And, in fact, similar scenes are probably being played out repeatedly in a variety of places. The central aspect of the ceremony is three smiling suited men exchanging something. The plaque—literally, an award—is clearly a sign for the research funds *and* for the agreement itself. The exchange includes a panoply of structured arrangements between the multinational corporation, the national government, the individual hospital, and the research team. As six hands crowd around the plaque, carefully and respectfully not touching one another, there is no direction to the transfer,

Figure 3. The ceremony from "Take Two."

thus conveying a sense of equitability, perhaps even moral virtue. The three faces are plainly happy, although the two hospital representatives beam broadly while the president of Bristol-Myers Squibb, on the right, displays an affect of paternal pride. As the men stand before three flags, this ceremony—this spectacle—encourages a complicity in the post-Fordist fiction that medicine and capital know no border or limits to their generosity.

The advertisement contains a clear narrative structure. It begins with the presumption of ill health and, deploying its doctor-like authority, recommends the metaphoric consumption of two corporate entities. This leads down the page to the "healthy" consequence of support for local research initiatives. Further, there is a circularity implied, for the ultimate direction of medical research is the production of new forms of medical commodities. Take two of these, and two of these, and so on. With this narrative, what are we invited to swallow? Simply another placebo for post-Fordist capitalism.

Having addressed the level of corporate discourse and its embodiment of new structures of fluid capital, let me now turn to a simultaneously more local and more dispersed site: the body in pain. What does the post-Fordist medical discourse say of the consumer, the ill? The key question concerning the specificities of medical discourse can be formulated as follows: what happens when the experiential (pain) is transformed into a knowable entity (causes, physiological determinants, treatments, etc.) in and through postindustrial capitalism? How does the corporeal experience of suffering fit into the corporatist scheme? What, then, is the political and ideological dimension of the arrangement of physical bodies for strategic conquest?

Such military metaphors are apt; the medical industry, like other massive corporations, is an instance of Paul Virilio's "logistics of military perception."[20] He argues that in fact the most important organ of destruction is the eye. Vision is what allows for a constructed relation between weapon and target. Virilio traces the parallel history of technologies of warfare and technologies of expanded visual orientation. He points to the first use of the searchlight in battle in 1904, the use of aerial and satellite photography, and other mechanisms that permit the eye to see far beyond the horizon. To see, argues Virilio, is to construct something as a target; seeing informs strategies of conquest and destruction. And of central importance is Virilio's argument that this has suffused the logic of everyday existence. The "logistics of military perception" are a view to the world that has pervaded contemporary existence to the point of being a mode and structure of experience and knowledge. It is precisely in this manner that *target* marketing functions.

Markets are more that just aggregations of individuals and needs. Demographic and psychographic configurations are written through conceptions of an abstracted and generalizable human form and condition: male, female, child, adult, disposable income, residence, and education. In medical discourse, bodies are defined according to the specificity of ailments and socially constructed notions of the "healthy body": back pain, headache, menstrual cramp, pain caused by cancer and disease, noise, stress, or simply the dull throb of existence. As such, bodies are arranged to be within the strategic reach of modern medicine as standardized and interchangeable. With pharmaceutical drugs, or the very image of corporate medication, then, travels a whole array of discursive practices. They are host to and juncture of the "coming into being" of the body, sectioned and available for medical manipulation and the marketer's masculinist dreams of penetration; this is exactly a "coming into being" in the corporate social, a moment of self-definition under the giant shadow of a multinational medical establishment.

Since the nineteenth century, production and distribution of medicine have been available to large populations through an industrialized structure. As indicated above, medicine is the contentious hybrid of science and commerce, "contentious" because the latter term, *commerce*, with its guiding hand of the profit motive, is supposed to be a silent and hidden influence. Only *science*, and the accompanying ethical discourse, is to act as the measure and criteria of what is researched, how, and for whom. But science is not blind, nor is it random. Problems, discoveries, solutions are not stumbled on or divinely revealed. There is an assortment of assumptions informing how decisions are made and acted on, how results are to be understood and evaluated, and how that knowledge is selectively deployed. Those instances in which accident has led to a fortuitous revelation are immediately mythologized, not to discredit the influence of the scientific mind, but to attest to the "neutrality" of the procedure.

More than servicing the greater social good and the utopia of medical universality ("enhancement of life worldwide"), the manner in which medical judgments are made guides and shapes the responses. In fact, this has been surrendered to the market through the medium of state control. The result has been a powerful and at times profoundly amoral medical industrial establishment, one in which the question of medical ethics has been subsumed by that of supply and demand. And while the traditional economic model may be disrupted by the additional influences of the State—usually in the form of subsidized research grants or joint ventures like the National Research Council of Canada—the medical industry still operates under the auspice of that model. Hence, all the consequences of those procedures, those discourses of corporate capitalism, can be expected to surface in a multitude of locations, like pharmaceutical commodities.

Beyond the crass motivation of profit potential, there are other consequences of the marriage of industrial capitalism and medicine. Segmentation, as part of the "logistics of military perception," is also a fundamental aspect of industrial capitalism. This involves various techniques of designation and fragmentation of labor, of products, and of markets, all in the interest of efficiency, predictability, and reproducibility. This operation is woven into the habitual activities of industry. Each pill in a bottle of two hundred, each bottle in two thousand, must be identical, within accepted degrees of variation. The often frustrating task of guaranteeing an exceptional level of consistency is part of the impetus for the medical industry's massive investments in the U.S. space program, providing yet another link between the

State, the military, and medicine. The vacuum of space will provide the ideal atmosphere for pharmaceutical production in which no contaminating elements will enter. Until then, we must be content with the imperfect, though neatly concealed, practices of standards control.

The danger of segmentation is that some possible arrangements are lost. For instance, lost is the ever-more abstracted hand of labor, pushed aside in an increasingly automated production process, and absent from the product. Drugs must appear immaculately conceived. The automobile industry, for example, has consistently romanticized the proud, male (and more recently female) assembly line worker, ideologically building car and national (i.e., corporate) wealth simultaneously. By contrast, the advertising of pharmaceuticals eliminates the possibility of human involvement in their production. Assembly line images of pills dropping into bottles are never presented; instead, actors in white laboratory coats toss reports into a pile for the camera. Pills appear to descend from pristine sources, from the ether or from the grid-work imaginary of computer space.

Equally lost is the ever-present trap of nature and culture. Pills are the ideal statement of Claude Lévi-Strauss's the raw and the cooked; the elements are transformed magically in order to resolve essential problems of bodily discomfort.[21] This is alchemy assisted by the contours of civilization. Moreover, pharmaceuticals embody the dream of perfect influence, calculated and strategic, over nature. This is, in part, influence over the frustrating corporeal aspect of our existence. Drugs, then, are the symbolic performance of the drama of Culture winning over Nature. Or, at least, this is the conceit.

The cultural imbrication of our bodies and their treatment is firm and uncompromising, touching virtually every facet of life. For example, in Ontario, police escorts are required to transport heroin requested by dying cancer patients. This makes availability extremely restricted and rarely convenient. Even as a painkiller, heroin still carries the connotations of the demon recreational drug. The comfort and interests of the individual (the paying consumer) in pain are sacrificed to the moral agendas of the day. The logistics of military perception assert themselves in this tie between State surveillance, cultural and medical understandings of a painkiller, and the body in pain.

The pharmaceutical commodity travels. It travels in several directions, not randomly, but dispersed. It is the force of the social; it is the dream of the scientist; it is the reassurance of the laborer; it is the revenue of the capitalist; it is the object of aesthetic contemplation; it is the symbolic utopia to be sold by marketers. It carries the shape of state regulations on research, the expertise of researchers, and the accumulation of a society's medical knowledge. Its presence, its cost, its availability, or, conversely, its relative unavailability, speak of a particular ethics concerning public health, the role of the State, the mediating activity of the market, and the entrepreneurship of corporate capital. All this is acted in, on, and through the body in pain. In other words, with pharmaceuticals travels a system of bodily realization in the social; and the body, as it is segmented and sectioned, wends its way as the most abstracted and the most consequential element of the medical system.

If the medical industry has succeeded in one thing over the past two centuries, it is in democratizing hypochondria. To varying degrees, we are all hypochondriacs; this endless sense of ill-being, of low-level sickness, is a prevalent mode of contemporary existence. We are involved in a process of self-evaluation, or self-incrimination, within the broad apparatus of the health and medical industries. We are aware of the discourses of knowledge about our bodies, our pains and discomforts, though we do not all have the resources to do something about them. Still, the discourses of bodily complaint are shared and frequently form the topic of quotidian talk and concern. Every day promises to be yet another unhealthy day, or at least a day in which our ever elusive maximum healthy body has slipped away again. And, of course, there usually are good reasons for complaint and discomfort; the imaging of pain through corporatist medical discourse does not make the pain imaginary.

Notes

1. Gilles Deleuze and Félix Guattari, *A Thousand Plateaus: Capitalism and Schizophrenia*, trans. Brian Massumi (Minneapolis: University of Minnesota Press, 1987).

2. Ibid., 474–75.

3. I take *post-Fordism* to imply that we continue to live with the remnants of Fordism rather than to suggest the absolute death of that earlier organization of social and productive forces. Some prefer the term *neo-Fordism*.

4. The literature on post-Fordism is expanding at a phenomenal rate. What began as a marginal critique of traditional economic theory is now influencing a variety of disciplines and approaches. Two reasonably accessible overviews are Scott Lash and John Urry, *The End of Organized Capitalism* (Madison: University of Wisconsin, 1987); and David Harvey, *The Condition of Postmodernity* (Oxford: Blackwell, 1989). Other intriguing commentaries include Donna Haraway, "A Manifesto for Cyborgs: Science, Technology and Socialist Feminism for the 1980's," *Socialist Review* 80.2 (1985): 65–108; and Mike Davis, *City of Quartz* (New York: Verso, 1990).

5. Marshall Berman, *All That Is Solid Melts into Air* (New York: Verso, 1983).

6. While the recession saw a 4 percent decrease in earning for all U.S. industry, the drug companies saw a 34 percent increase: see Robert Neff, "Drugmakers: Prescribing for the Hangover to Come," *Business Weekly*, July 15, 1991, 54–55.

7. Some exemplary work includes Mary Jacobus, Evelyn Fox Keller, and Sally Shuttleworth, *Body/Politics: Women and the Discourses of Science* (New York: Routledge, 1990); Sandra Harding, *The Science Question in Feminism* (Ithaca, N.Y.: Cornell University Press, 1986); and Evelyn Fox Keller, *Reflections on Gender and Science* (New Haven, Conn.: Yale University, 1984).

8. Paula Treichler, "AIDS, Homophobia, and Biomedical Discourse: An Epidemic of Signification," *October* 43 (1987): 31–70.

9. John Nguyet Erni, *Unstable Frontiers: Technomedicine and the Cultural Politics of "Curing" aids* (Minneapolis: University of Minnesota Press, 1994), xii.

10. Anne Balsamo, *Technologies of the Gendered Body: Reading Cyborg Women* (Durham, N.C.: Duke University Press, 1996), 3.

11. Gilles Gherson, "Patent-Protection Issue Heats Up Again Despite Success of Bill C-22," *Canadian Medical Association Journal* 145.2 (1991): 141–44.

12. "Report on Health and Pharmaceutical Industry," *Globe and Mail*, August 14, 1990, B20.

13. Connaught of Canada to Institute Merieux International SA of France for $942 million in 1990, and Smith, Kline Beckman and Beechman Group for $7.7 billion in 1989 are two other examples.

14. Michael Hodin, "Canada's Protectionist Drain on Technological Progress," *American Review of Canadian Studies* 21.2/3 (Summer/Autumn 1991): 215.

15. Quoted in ibid., 38.

16. Barrie McKenna, "Patented-Drug Prices Fall 0.42% in '94," *Globe and Mail*, June 15, 1995, B2.

17. Joel Lexchin, "Effect of Generic Drug Competition on the Price of Prescription Drugs in Ontario," *Canadian Medical Association Journal* 148.1 (1993): 38.

18. Rod Mickleburgh, "Drug Bill Receives Royal Assent," *Globe and Mail*, February 5, 1993, A7.

19. Drew Fagan, "Nader Denounces Drug Plan as Boon for Multinationals," *Globe and Mail*, December 3, 1992, B3.

20. Paul Virilio, *War and Cinema: The Logistics of Perception*, trans. Patrick Camiller (New York: Verso, 1989).

21. Claude Lévi-Strauss, *The Raw and the Cooked*, trans. John and Doreen Weightman (London: Cape, 1966).

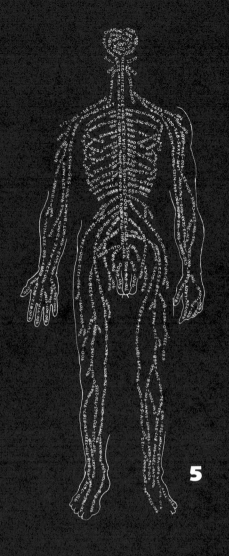

5

Intensify It

Marie-Paule Macdonald

Reach for the Pain

**One pill makes you larger
and another makes you small.**
Jefferson Airplane

POP OR COMMODITY culture of the midcentury is the
site of a network of ideas about daily life that extend,
unresolved, into the present. A cursory demonstration
of the persistence of these ideas would point to the
continuing popularity of sixties rock music, ongoing
interest in the Andy Warhol phenomenon, especially
the early Factory years, or the immense influence of re-
runs and then re-creation of a television event like *Star
Trek*. These ideas taken as an ensemble add up to a pop
or mod sensibility, having to do at the outset with an
adaptation to conditions of leisure, an oversupply of objects, an availability of technologies—whether medical,
electronic, or mechanical—that when used together can
transform, or customize, an individual and her or his
environment.

The role of the pill in medicinal or
literary tradition involves a childish fantasy about
transformation by eating. As Alice's body distorts after
she eats a pill or a piece of mushroom, so an individual
in search of self-transformation can modify her—or

Figure 1.
Instant Happenings
by "Fluxman" James Riddle, 1964. Reprinted with permission from Gilbert and
Lila Silverman Fluxus Collection.
Photo by Eric Silverman.

himself with a potion or pill, a concentrated morsel of a specially formulated substance. The anorexic specifies the idea of body modification by ingestion: bingeing will bloat, starving or barfing will skeletonize.

Psychedelic pills, wafers, and similar drugs extend the body modification idea into spatial and temporal perception. Charles Baudelaire describes the body's temporal reactions to the ingestion of opium and the heightened appreciation of form, color, and immediate spatial environment: "Landscapes enlaced, horizons in flight, perspectives of the city blanched by the deathly livid storm or illuminated by sunset's dense ardor—depth of space, allegory of the depth of time."[1] Walter Benjamin scrutinizes his mind's processing of urban situations during an evening stroll after using hashish in his essay "Hashisch in Marseilles," remarking, "The street I have so often seen is like a knife cut."[2] William Gibson collapses the drug-induced spatiotemporal fantasy and cyberspace in his science-fiction novella *Neuromancer*.[3] In the realm of the imagination there is a correspondence between the taking of a pill to modify some aspect of oneself and the desire to modify one's surroundings, perhaps even to revolutionize one's society, that is, when everyone takes the same pill or desires to ingest something that will result in a mass transformation, such as in spatial or social relations.

"Fluxman" James Riddle's *Instant Happenings*, also called "mind events in bottle," variously priced at four or five dollars, appeared in the *Fluxus* newsletter of June 1964 and continued to be listed in the series of Fluxus publications through the sixties (see fig. 1). The label on the bottle read:

A. TAKE TWO TEASPOONSFUL OF MORNING GLORY SEEDS

B. HAVE HALLUCINATIONS, EXPAND YOUR CONSCIOUSNESS.[4]

At the early, "conceptual" phase of his career, in the sixties, architect Hans Hollein proposed an "instant" environment atomizer and a box of variegated "pills for transforming environment 'from inside yourself.' "[5] Introducing foreign chemical material into the body for experimental purposes is a highly dangerous game, but one that individuals and even institutions were indulging in during the 1960s, with expectations that there could be a positive, even transcendental potential to speculative exploration of the consciousness through some artificially induced medical process.

Sex, Drugs, Scenes

Beyond the nonchalant fun-seeking and all-important surface of the mod sensibility lurked a curiously oblivious urge to self-destruct. The pop theme links together some aspects of a middle-class quasi revolution in domestic life that seems to have coalesced during the midsixties and then defined an alternative or parallel, but not necessarily underground or counterculture, mainstream that has had inchoate repercussions for the present. These themes could be defined around an aesthetic of sated or overindulged everyday life and take as subject a stylistic restructuring of daily environments and designed objects within that framework of consumption, beginning with the technomedical object, the pill, and extending to fantasies and manifestations of pleasure-seeking behavior in a consciously arranged domestic environment.

In one of Woody Allen's early, funnier films, *Sleeper*, the pop lifestyle is visualized and mapped out in an imaginary technofuture of clean, white, modern environments that seem not revolutionary but merely campy. Social life takes place when a group of adults passes around a large silvery sphere to provoke intense pleasure. Experimental gardening produces Claes Oldenburg-like pop giant vegetables, fruit, and, of course, the giant banana peel that Allen slips on. Allen's 1970 movie *Everything You Always Wanted to Know about Sex* (*But Were Afraid to Ask)*, based on the best-seller of the same name by Dr. David R. Reuben, responded scenographically, from a heterosexual white male perspective, to the so-called sexual revolution spawned by the "pill." For example, the segment spoofing female frigidity and repression by way of Michelangelo Antonioni also provided visual send-ups of then-trendsetting Italian minimalist design. This second vignette, an Antonioni parody, portrayed Allen's dilemma as a husband whose fashionably thin,

Stage 1: chassis unopened.   Stage 2: suit unopened.   Stage 3: suit and chassis combining.   Stage 4: combined suit, chassis opening out.

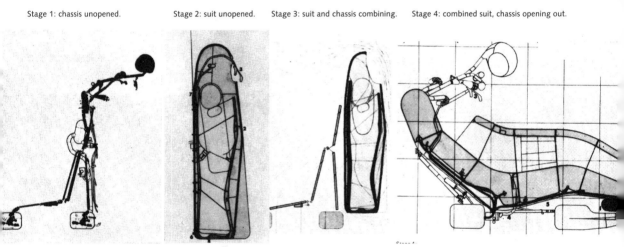

Figure 2. *The Cushicle* by Michael Webb. Reprinted with permission from *Archigram*, Peter Cook, ed., Studio Vista Publishers, UK, 1972.

heavily made-up, Twiggy-haired, neurotic young wife, played by Louise Lasser, was bored and unresponsive in the impeccably cool, Italian minimalist modern interiors of their home, but who became amorous as soon as they went out to a fun, pop public place of consumption, a shop or restaurant.

In a stand-up routine recorded in 1965, Allen launched a one-liner about the pseudorevolution caused by the mass marketing of oral contraceptives to women during the sixties, citing "a very good example of oral contraception: I asked a girl to go to bed with me, and she said no." Allen's live comedy act at that time returned regularly to comic confusion occasioned in dating, marriage,

and divorce rituals, invoking the swinging bachelor pad with a shaggy rug and related paraphernalia—sex in a fully furnished commodity environment. The key
joke was the psychological unpreparedness and immaturity of heterosexuals,
who, thanks to the pill, technically could seek out and explore a new kind of "free
love" in a variety of settings. The satire of unleashed libidos is one of the great
pop themes.

The translation of instant gratification into design of the times
may be remembered in plastic fun furniture, disposable underwear, and miniskirts,
but it finds inspired expression in Gaetano Pesce's UP series of 1969, furniture

Stage 5: combination opening out further.

Stage 6: total Cushicle fully opened out and in use.

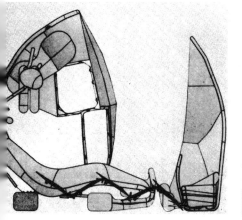
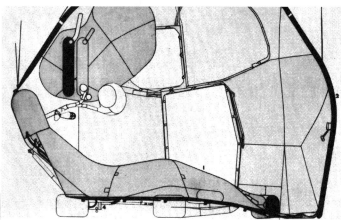

whose packaging involved a miniature performance piece. A chair is bought in a
small package in a flat disk shape like a giant packaged pill. When "opened" at
home, in a ritual something like preparing Jello 1-2-3, Jiffy Pop popcorn, or instant
mashed potatoes, a ripcord is pulled and a compressed foam ball rises into its pre-
designed shape. The apotheosis of this fun, instant chair is the LaMama version of
the series, which has anthropomorphic breasts and hippy lap contours inflating out
of the flattened disk. Pesce's project for the *New Domestic Landscape* exhibition at the
Museum of Modern Art in 1972 explored with similar intensity and hedonist cyni-
cism the sense of doom that underlies the fascination with quick pleasure, in a scenario

Figure 3. David Niven and Barbara Bouchet (right) in "Casino Royale," 1967. *Movie Still Archives*.

of a dwelling for a couple in an "Age of Great Contamination."[6] The sixties obsession with normative materialistic heterosexual couples and their lifestyles is set in an utterly unredeemable future, and their pad is a mod version of hell, way below the sewer, underground. The infected crust of the planet is far above. Below the filth, which appears to be squeezing in, like guilt, through the cracks, the pale, slick plastic surfaces of the modern flat reinterpret Jean-Paul Sartre's *Huis Clos* with a dash of subterranean Jules Verne.

The festive architectural machines and environments proposed by *Archigram* celebrated the ephemeral and the carnivalesque in expressive cartoons inspired by an anarchist pop culture. Visual relations between systems design, future city life, and comic book sci-fi were ripe for investigation. *Archigram* condensed this fusion into truly visionary design for Instant Cities. Such projects as the *Cushicle* of 1966–67 and the *Suitaloon* of 1968 by Michael Webb, the *Living Pod* (1965) by David Greene, *Gasket Homes* (1965) by Ron Herron and Warren Chalk, and the *Hornsey Capsules* (1965–66) by Peter Cook proposed personal, adaptable plug-in living spaces.[7] These intimately scaled architectures prefigured the effects on real space of the virtual reality of cyberspace, in the sense that the collective spaces proposed were spontaneous and temporary interconnections allowed by a rhizome-like network. The *Cushicle* was a kind of pill or translucent capsule to live in, a curvilinear interior like a free-form anechoic chamber, a totally preengineered and customized microenvironment (see fig. 2). Its sensuous title synthesized the pleasurable connotations of popsicle, bicycle, and cushion. A primal living space, it was portable and inflatable, accommodating one or perhaps two intimately associated individuals, housed within a membrane whose central element consisted of a high-tech chaise longue, somewhat like the contemporary banana-style dentist's chair, equipped with all necessary appliances.

The mod sensibility's arrival in popular consciousness is generalized with the kitschy decors of mass-market movies such as *Casino Royale*, itself a rip-off in the sex-comedy genre after *What's New Pussycat?* The film revels in interior-design items such as the sunken "conversation pit" in a flat owned by a predatory femme fatale. The pit dumps into a holding pen, serving as a snare for secret agents. In the final scenes, the labyrinthine underground corridors of villain Woody Allen's headquarters proffer, in the set decorator's overkill, room after room of modernistic spy decor. (Allen intends to unleash on the unsuspecting world a virus that will transform all women into beauties while making all men shorter than he.) One room is triumphantly psychedelic, papered with two-dimensional Piranesiesque graphic, the same loud whorl pattern repeated on the floor, wall, and ceiling, inducing disorientation (see fig. 3). The only subject that this incoherent idea film clearly addresses is the advertising ploy of reconstructing women: produced and displayed in a series as disposable toys, artificially designed and desirable objects in artificially designed spaces, with an emphasis on "man-made" superficial beauty. Then the pop rendezvous with doom scenario is realized at the finale of *Casino Royale* in a surreal, slapstick, blow-everything-up scene.

Love and Death Machine

I looked at Edie and I said to myself, "Well, how fabulous! This fabulous creature!" She was so electric.
Bobby Andersen
quoted in *Edie: An American Biography*

The mouth of the anorexic wavers
between several functions: its possessor
is uncertain as to whether it is an
eating-machine, an anal machine,
a talking machine or a breathing machine (asthma attacks).
Gilles Deleuze and Félix Guattari, "The Desiring Machines," *Anti-Oedipus*

Of the Passions which belong to
Self Preservation

The passions therefore which are conversant about the preservation of the individual, turn chiefly on *pain* and *danger* and they are the most powerful of all the passions.

Of the Sublime

When danger and pain press too nearly, they are incapable of giving any delight, and are simply terrible; but at certain distances, and with certain modifications, they may be, and they are delightful, as we every day experience.
Edmund Burke
A Philosophical Enquiry into the Origin of Our Ideas of the Sublime and Beautiful

Elements of the self-destructive impulse charted in the biography of "*Vogue* Youth-quaker" Edie Sedgwick merge with her efforts to re-create herself as a designed object in a mod televisionesque, filmic, or theatrical scenic decor:

She came back to the Chelsea after her bad experience in California. Edie sat at the make-up table in the middle of her kingdom, with the most absurd collection of bric-a-brac surrounding her. Lighters. I remember a cigarette lighter shaped like a toy telephone. There was an open closet full of bizarre fur coats with square shoulders, a straw basket full of strange hats, a box of wigs. She unrolled a small Japanese carpet and began her modern dance exercises. I remember the phone ringing and someone reminding her that her limousine had been waiting for over an hour.[8]

Vogue magazine documented her look and even remarked on her deep, campy voice, strained through smoke and Boston.[9] The aesthetics of chaos that parodied the centralized control of the life of a capitalist scion encompassed domestic spaces, the vehicle, behavior, the social totality in sum, enveloping and transcending the anarchic eclecticism favored at the Factory scene, where decor—for example, whether Billy Name's or someone else's—was by necessity removed from the intimate, aiming for a rather studied generic.

Sedgwick remarked during the improvised real-time soundtrack to Warhol's *Beauty #2*, "I'm just self-involved."[10] The poet and musician Patti Smith recognized Sedgwick's obsessions, behavior, and demeanour as that of a modern female incarnation of the dandy and commemorated her New York mid-town period in a poem that envisions the city as a stage for her presence:

and she'd

turn around

and turn the head

of everyone in town

her shaking shaking

glittering bones[11]

Sedgwick devoted her conscious working existence to a highly refined and specialized "play" construction of self. During adolescence, as an anorexic/bulimic unable to control her immediate surroundings, she sculpted her body into the skeletal boyish silhouette that held reign over mod fashion (fig. 4). In

Figure 4. Edie Sedgwick.

pursuit of sensory modification, she orchestrated the consumption of pills to regulate her daily moods, explaining matter-of-factly, "I used a lot of pills to keep from shaking the balance I'd arranged in my system"[12]—designing her own temperament in accordance with the events of the day. The painful, dangerous, and terrible aspects of this quest for a total aesthetification of existence could be seen as an indication of the allure of the possibility of bringing about and even maintaining some sort of sublime experience.

In the early years of this century, the poet Raymond Roussel trapped himself in a highly intimate pursuit of adjusted consciousness. Roussel's singularly hermetic, idiosyncratic existence ended when his body could no longer absorb the quantities of drugs he used simply to sleep, having built up his tolerance over the years. He succumbed in July 1933, in Palermo, to his obsession with reexperiencing a naturally induced euphoria that had taken place during his adolescence. In Roussel's case, however, every substance used and the results achieved had been *minitieusement* recorded in a diary kept by Roussel's companion Fredez for more than twenty years. The diary documented the dosage and sensation:

The 7th: at half past nine in the evening, 6 Hypalene, then 18, then 3 Sonaryl; "a good state of euphoria." . . . the 11th, at the same time: 34 Rutonal tablets; three hours sleep and then "marvelous euphoria." The 12th: one and a half bottles of Veriane; a little sleep and then "excessive euphoria."[13]

When Sedgwick began to live independently in Manhattan, the preoccupation with design of consciousness became itself an important element of personal decor. Her male nurse/valet/companion identified her icons of vulnerability and custom consciousness:

When Edith lived with me, she had a purse she carried around for the drugs—a picnic basket that was about two feet wide and a foot and a half deep which was filled with hundreds of little zipper bags, plastic boxes, bubblegum bubbles, a lot of it to hold syringes, cotton balls, little vials of alcohol, amphetamines, pills, tranquilizers. . . . It was like carrying an entire life-style with you.[14]

The continuous ingestion of drugs produced the incoherent, temperamental, ultimately out-of-control behavior that defined the persona of "pop star of everyday life" that was her signature. Her monologue on the soundtrack of *Ciao Manhattan* expressed romantic angst: "But the minute he left me alone, I felt so empty and lost that I would start popping pills."[15] This was one more scene in the real-time drama where emptiness and lostness require chemical banishing. Even when she could scarcely distinguish one individual from another, her desire to maintain the magical modification act prevailed.

The game careened into a ritualistic parody of addiction. The conscious level of theatricality regressed to a primal or instinctual theater of narcissism. A housekeeper for Sedgwick found herself cast as a minor character, one of the dramatis personae in a theater of daily life defined by Sedgwick, who controlled, directed, improvised action and took the role of heroine:

She had gobs and gobs of pills. One day I went in there to do some cleaning. What I saw made me close the door and go away. She was sitting on the floor with all these pills around her like in a half-circle . . . cross-legged in a sea of pills. She was in a dopey mood. I stayed there long enough to see her reaching for one, and I left.[16]

Perhaps the aim was as brutal as it seemed: self-transformation into a groggy, dumb, desensitized *machine à séduire*, following the modern design tradition whereby the house became a *machine à habiter* (LeCorbusier), the book a *machine à lire* (Paul Valéry), the poet a machine-poet (Man Ray), and the artist a painting machine (Warhol). Her sculptural thinness, the artificiality of her silver-dyed hair in admiring imitation or, rather, simple repetition, of Warhol, her false eyelashes, and exaggeratedly thick makeup made her into a kind of public appliance, an ideal spontaneous photo subject for *Vogue* magazine and the epitome of the vacantly appealing, incoherent, American blue-blood type revered at the Factory in 1965.

Eventually the desire to sculpt and display herself interfered with the integrity of the aesthetic itself. Silicone breast implants marred the perfection of Sedgwick's caricatural silhouette of the sexually appealing and available boyish girl that fit the mod sensibility. These crude additions to her physiognomy were tangibly uncomfortable, as John Palmer noted during chaotic shooting of the execrable film

Ciao Manhattan: "Edie was playing her role—especially down there in the swimming pool—without any top on, to show off those new silicone breasts of hers. She used to use a heating pad on them to warm the silicone, which, you know, gets cold."[17]

Sedgwick's precocious, constant, public, and private interest in arousal, her own theatrical response to a probably inherited neurosis, irritated her family, of course, provoking her brother to comment:

She was really weird when she arrived at the ranch. Like a stick, no body at all, and wearing the shortest skirts I've ever seen, super-fake eyelashes hanging so heavy her eyelids drooped. She was an alien. A painted doll, wobbly, languishing around in chairs, trying to look like a vamp.[18]

Lodged inside a permanent Happening, Sedgwick pushed her continuous live act to the limit. She damaged herself to the point of needing constant nursing. The dramatic disconnection between her daily needs and her desire for performance of the superficial left her unable to direct her own life, or control her own pill consumption. She ultimately succumbed to her drug dependencies accidentally at the age of twenty-eight. While she did not acquire status as an artist in the Factory films, she did install herself in a certain performance tradition, that of the dandy. Using the compulsive drive of an anorexic/bulimic to physically redefine herself, she invented a physical form and a persona as a self-contained autoartwork that fused an identity as an instrument with that of a monument. Taking her appearance as the point of departure, she became a kind of walking, talking public space.

Sedgwick's social pedigree had impressed and attracted Warhol. Her heritage connected her back to the mythical "discovery" and European settlement of the continent, and the drastic energy with which she squandered her youth, wealth, beauty, and privilege in search of ephemeral sensory pleasure has placed her in the pantheon of symbols for mid-twentieth-century Western civilization. Especially America, from its inception a wild forested garden of Eden, had become by the late sixties mired in and polluted by its own technologically confused, overproductive, self-absorbed desire.

Satanic Pills

Total design at the service of pure consumption might be an apt slogan for pop culture of the sixties. In a recoil from the allure of pleasurable material gratification, the postindustrial societies are still seeking out a sense of equilibrium in the aftermath of extremes of satisfaction/destruction that characterize the postnuclear, post-Holocaust, apocalyptic technological mid-twentieth century. Perhaps much of

Michael Jackson's appeal comes from his unrestrained public identity as a monumental object-being, someone whose private desires have fused inexorably with a public identity, made manifest by indulging in a sequentially conceived and realized series of ultimately radical modifications to his face. In ordering the progressive resculpting of his original young black male ingenue's features into a blanched neo–Elizabeth Taylor mask, Jackson, in his capacity as a public space, one defined by appearance, manifests visually the unsuppressed materialistic narcissism that permeates the leisure classes of American society, while acting out the neurotic obsessive preoccupation with Caucasian versus African standards of beauty that stultified Western popular aesthetics until all too recently. Viscerally exploring the layers of self-hatred lodged in the American popular psyche by means of successive redesign of his face, body, and the spatial expressions of a hermetic video dance world, then periodically releasing the results for communication to the global mass audience, Jackson has consistently become an object of intense collective fascination. This fantastic, media-centered public person-object-monument has become collectively recognizable, in a way analogous to how the traditional urban spatial monument used to function. In the same way that the anorexic/bulimic uses her or his body as an instrument and signifier, a kind of desperate billboard, the phenomenon is symptomatic of a collapse of the conventions of separate public and private spheres.

William Gibson's *Neuromancer* takes up some of the themes of destructive self-gratification and sets them in a dystopian medical technofuture. The protagonist's world of revolutionized biotechnology includes totally decorative resculpting of the body using grafting and "vat-growing" surgical techniques, with seemingly limitless possibilities for self-transformation by consuming medical technologies that alter the body, the nervous system, and sensory perception. Physical space and architecture are interchangeable with the perceived environment of cyberspace, attaining artificially induced perceptual intensity, but at a physical cost: the painful consequences for the body, the brain, its neurosystem:

Two blocks west of the Chat, in a teashop called the Jarre de Thé, Case washed down the night's first pill with a double espresso. It was a flat pink octagon, a potent species of Brazilian dex he bought from one of Zone's girls. . . . Alone at the table in the Jarre de Thé, with the octagon coming on, pinheads of sweat starting from his palms, suddenly aware of each tingling hair on his arms and chest, Case knew that at some point he'd started to play a game with himself, . . a final solitaire.[19]

Case's addictive personality is no more in control of his well-being than an Edie Sedgwick, but in science fiction fate can intervene, and narrative destiny allows Case to experience the thrills he seeks and come out more or less alive. In this medically driven future, perpetual youth is a reality, and the possibilities for consuming pleasurable sensory experiences have expanded exponentially, along with the corresponding hangovers and side effects. Gibson depicts an amoral vacuum where the urge to explore consequences of the manipulation of self, the senses, and a perceptual environment overrides the survival instinct. As medical technologies poise for mass-consumption marketing, it is a cautionary parable for the deindustrializing fin de siècle, when domestic medical self-modification may be understood neither simply as harmless aesthetic play nor as part of a larger experimental social project, but as an ultimate alienation—the self, disconnected, and left on.

Notes

1. "Paysages dentelés, horizons fuyants, perspective de villes blanchies par la lividité cadavéreuse de l'orage, ou illuminés par les ardeurs concentrées des soleils couchants,—profondeur de l'espace, allégorie de la profondeur du temps." Charles Baudelaire, "Les Paradis artificiels," in *Oeuvres Complètes* (Paris: Gallimard, 1975), 430–31 (author's translation).

2. Walter Benjamin, "Hashisch in Marseilles," in *Reflections* (New York: Schocken Books, 1978), 138.

3. William Gibson, *Neuromancer* (New York: Ace Books, 1984).

4. Jon Hendricks, *Fluxus Codex* (Detroit and New York: G. and L. Silverman Fluxus Collection/Harry N. Abrams, 1988), 451.

5. Quoted by Joseph Rykwert, "Ornament Is No Crime," *Studio International* (September/October 1975), reprinted in *The Necessity of Artifice* (New York: Rizzoli, 1982).

6. Gaetano Pesce, "Reconstruction of an Underground City and a Habitat for Two People in an Age of Great Contamination 1971–2," in *Italy: The New Domestic Landscape* (New York: Museum of Modern Art, 1972), exhibition catalogue.

7. Peter Cook et al., eds., *Archigram* (London: Studio Vista, 1972), reprinted by Birkhauser Verlag (1991), 46–82; Reyner Banham, *Megastructure: Urban Futures of the Recent Past* (London: Thames and Hudson, 1976), 98–99.

8. Jean Stein, ed., with George Plimpton, *Edie: An American Biography* (New York: Knopf, 1982), 313–14.

9. "People are talking about . . . Youthquakers," *Vogue* (August 1965), 90–96, cited in David Bourbon, Andy Warhol (New York: Harry N. Abrams, 1989), 205.

10. Ibid., 209.

11. Patti Smith, "Edie Sedgwick," *Seventh Heaven* (Boston: Telegraph Books, 1972), 21; also Stein, *Edie*, 423.

12. Stein, *Edie*, 311.

13. Leonardo Sciascia, "Acts Relative to the Death of Raymond Roussel," in *Raymond Roussel: Life, Death and Works*, Atlas Anthology special issue (London: Atlas Press, 1987), 132.

14. Stein, *Edie*, 306.

15. Ibid., 393.

16. Ibid., 310.

17. Ibid., 393.

18. Ibid., 310.

19. Gibson, *Neuromancer*, 7.

Thyrza Nichols Goodeve

You sober people

To the realists.—You sober people who feel well armed
against passion and fantasies and would like to turn your
emptiness into a matter of pride and an ornament: you call
yourselves realists and hint that the world really is the
way it appears to you. As if reality stood unveiled before
you only, and you yourselves were perhaps the best part
of it.—O you beloved image of Sais! But in your unveiled
state are not even you still very passionate and dark creatures compared to fish, and still far too similar to an artist
in love? and what is "reality" for an artist in love? You are
still burdened with those estimates of former centuries.
Your sobriety still contains a secret and inextinguishable
drunkenness. Your love of "reality," for example—oh, that
is a primeval "love." Every feeling and sensation contains
a piece of this old love; and some fantasy, some prejudice,
some unreason, some ignorance, some fear, and ever so
much else has contributed to it and worked on it. That
mountain there! That cloud there! What is "real" in that?
Subtract the phantasm and every human *contribution* from
it, my past, your training—all of your humanity and ani-
mality. There is no "reality" for us—not for you either, my
sober friends. We are not nearly as different as you think,
and perhaps our good will to transcend intoxication is as
respectable as your faith that you are altogether incapable
of intoxication.
Friedrich Nietzsche
The Gay Science

Pain is imperative; the only things which can subdue it
are the effect of some toxic agent in removing it
and the influence of some mental distraction.
Sigmund Freud
"Repression"

If the woman has anxiety or depression based on hidden wounds, we might conceivably worry about medication as a form of collusion with her traumatic history: we would want to help her gain an awareness of her past. But if her pain—perhaps even a "normal" level of pain that she, as an individual, finds excessive—is a mere atavism, an evolutionary adaptation of a bygone environment, medication may be a particularly humane intervention—indeed, a singular accomplishment by a science that aims to free man of certain of his animal constraints.
Peter Kramer
Listening to Prozac

Introduction

At a time when self,[1] technology, and drugs have grown to be less and less ontologically distant from one another, how does the ability to treat chronic emotional pain psychopharmacologically add to the debates on the changing meaning of "human nature"? In other words, if the cyborg, as Donna Haraway has theorized, is our ontology, and "drugs" as Avital Ronell suggests, name "a special mode of addiction . . . or the structure that is philosophically and metaphysically at the basis of our culture," then where are "we" when Peter Kramer's patients in *Listening to Prozac* exclaim, "I am not myself" when *off* Prozac?[2]

The Dosing Room: Week 11

You are again drawn to that memory, the memory that returns only when you are loaded.

"It was the flood you know—a flash flood. Nothing like it. I was living in L.A. doing my music. All this water just appeared. I ran along the edge of the road, watching the water curl around a bend. Cold and full of floating things. . . . Then I was running in it. The water was up to my waist. I couldn't move my limbs but somehow I was running trying to catch my friend. He was there. I could see his arm floating, flaying, all over the place in the water."

You nod momentarily, then continue.

"The water just pulled me. I was dragged along the gravel twisting and scraping. They told me my back was covered with pebbles. I had rocks stuck in my flesh formed in the pattern of the current. But all I remember was the water pulling my limbs so hard I thought they would pop off. So much pain. And then the morphine. They insisted it would never happen but, after the injection you know, I'd never felt like that. And ever since it seems all I ever do is keep trying to get back to that feeling."

A Word about Pain

Pain, whether one describes it as a sensation, an emotion, or merely a warning system, is a response to damage. Best described as a kind of peculiar and disturbing momentum, it shifts from the area of injury into a pool of base pain, telling us to change, flee, fix, or cure. When one is in a damaged state, the absence of pain can be more dangerous than the screaming agony of a sensation beyond description—difficult as this may be to imagine. Although terrible in feeling, pain is a good thing. It lets us know there is something that can—and should be—fixed. Structured by thresholds, pain exists in the limits it passes through, whether these be limits of reason, bearable sensation, the body, experience, or meaning.[3]

But the connection between cause and effect is not direct. One can never assume the place of hurt is where modes of healing should be directed. And so when one is in pain, it can be difficult to assess the dividing line between the body and mind. Often inconsolable emotional anguish may appear in the body as an aching, reverberating physical sensation. Within her discussion of the effects of torture on the body, Elaine Scarry reminds us, "often a state of consciousness other than pain will, if deprived of its object, begin to approach the neighborhood of physical pain."[4] In other words, loss—the deprivation of an object—can induce the sensation of physical pain.

In his book *The Culture of Pain* David Morris views the separation between physical and emotional pain as a terrible contrivance of Western culture. He calls it the "Myth of the Two Pains."[5] He advises us to be wary of splitting pain into physical and mental divisions. Unfortunately, Western culture does divide the mental and physical spheres. In depictions of pain, if the distinction between the two remains unmarked, mental anguish disappears or is regarded with suspicion. Emotional pain is often dematerialized. Invisible. Hidden. A secret lodged somewhere inside. Doubt hangs in the wings, much like malingering is there waiting to call the hysteric into question. Think of the seriousness and power that culture attaches to the physical wound (for instance, war wounds) while emotional pain is endlessly pursued by the strictures of validation. False memory syndrome is the result of this imbalanced binary. Adults suffering evident emotional pain with no tangible physical cause are coaxed into remembering childhood physical abuse that, in certain cases, never happened. *But the pain did* and has lingered into the present—an abstract emotional storm wanting in structure, genesis, reason. Hence the lure of gothic family romance narratives such as ritual abuse to explain—give meaning and materiality to—such pain.

It is therefore crucial to distinguish between experiences of emotional and physical wounding, since it is so easy for emotional pain to be subsumed under physical pain even as their interpenetration binds them together in a Gordian knot of mutual recognition. Such recognition is not about dividing up the nature or experience of pain into mind versus body. It is a reminder of the burden of cultural meaning and the devastating effects the denigration of emotional pain has had on how such pain is treated.

Case Study 1993: "Hello, Mom, Are You There?"

Dad, I love you, I'm with you. I'm so glad you're okay. Gail told me everything. Don't doubt my love a minute. If your body were hurting, people would send you flowers, but if your mind is hurting, they throw bricks.
Richard Berendzen's daughter on the phone
with him after he was hospitalized for a breakdown

And so the daughter of a former president of American University, Richard Berendzen, is able to articulate, with touching precision, her father's dilemma. His collapse was not of an organ or bone or muscle but was the psychic collapse induced by his inability to fend off the effects of childhood sexual abuse. The wounds in their "origins" were in many ways to his body (through the sexual act with his mother), but they manifested themselves years later in his behavior. He was supremely functional, working sixteen-hour days, suffering no outward signs of illness. There was no searing pain or any symptom to interpret. Nothing was wrong with him; in fact, he moved through the world with the abilities and authority that only the most healthy possess.

There is no doubt that Berendzen's lack of symptoms or evidence of pain contributed to the distance and outrage with which the effects of his delayed reaction to the emotional pain and memories were treated by those unprepared to understand what had happened to him. Berendzen's "crime" was locking

himself in his presidential office where he made telephone calls to random, anonymous people. During these calls he shared imaginary scenarios of inappropriate
sexual activity with children. The desired effect of these calls was to find a colluding
phone mate who, under the guise of this telephonic alliance, would explore for him
the reason why an adult would sexually abuse a child:

*When I called back, I made up stories about bizarre sexual activities that my wife and I routinely
did with the children in my fictitious family. Despite the obvious wrongness of this, I pretended to
relish it, I was so intent on finding answers. All that I felt in my soul and had known with my
youthful body abhorred child abuse. Yet something in me made me go on. . . . What interested
me were not my comments but the woman's answers to my questions.*[6]

The woman asked him to call back. When he did, she had the calls traced, and
Berendzen was identified and arrested for making obscene phone calls.

Berendzen's calls were not obscene in the sense of being explicit
demands for erotic engagement. Frankly, he was looking for information, and so his
telephonic outbursts are better interpreted as calls from his unconscious to the
"deaf ear" of his abusive mother. In *The Telephone Book* Avital Ronell draws out the
philosophical and psychoanalytic implications of the invention of the telephone, which
she claims is "a synecdoche for technology," by way of Alexander Graham Bell's deaf
mother.[7] According to Ronell, the invention of the telephone can be read as a technological answer to a "call" emanating from a more prevalent and philosophical ontological yearning: "Maintaining and joining, the telephone line holds together what
it separates. It creates a space of asignifying breaks and is tuned by the emergency
feminine on the maternal cord reissued. The telephone was borne up by the invagi-
nated structures of a mother's deaf ear" (4). Drawing on Nietzsche's own telephonic
connection, Ronell continues:

That Nietzsche's texts are telephonically charged is clarified in The Genealogy of Morals, *where he
writes of a "telephone to the beyond," which arguably is the case with every connection arranged by
a switchboard. It is Joyce who excites the hope that an explicit link might be forged between the
call to the beyond and a maternal connection.* (21)

Berendzen's story is a form of Ronellian theater of telephonic
connection and disconnection acted out unconsciously and maintained through the
technological prosthesis of the phone. Mangled and inconsolable affect—lodged
inside a body as *unrecognized* memory—turns in our historical moment of technoculture to technology for the connection, for the information, for the suturing of
the rift brought about by the ontologically bruised maternal connection.[8] But his

technological leap into the beyond is interpreted as obscene, as his call enters into the "beyond" of a woman's home. Seeking only a "woman's answers," the connection is made as she picks up the phone to greet a masquerading male on the line who is in search of a colluding subject, a subject who will explain—as though to someone who is *not* he—why he or she would do such things to a child. He, unknowingly, is quite literally calling his mother.

In her study of addiction, *Crack Wars: Literature, Mania, Addiction*, Ronell uses Flaubert's *Madame Bovary* to make an important point, relevant to Berendzen's story, about the connection between modernity and the philosophical state of addiction:[9]

It seemed that the ideals exposed by medicine and the addict were the same: to deaden the pain and separate from a poisonous maternal flux. Emma Bovary was apparently a grand self-medicator. Like others before her, she experienced the dangers of a belle âme: raptures that cut her off from reality, hallucinated plenitude and pure communication, a kind of hinge on transcendental telepathy. Everything she tried out—religion, reading, love rushes, getting dressed in the morning—had hallucinogenic, analgesic, stimulating, or euphorizing effects upon her. She would also experience tremendous crashes. The peak of drugs, as of love, was for her telepathy, a communication over distances. She demanded hallucinatory satisfaction of desire in a zone that no longer distinguished between need and desire. (Crack, 74)

Richard Berendzen and Emma Bovary share the desire for *hallucinated plenitude and pure communication* across distance, but Berendzen does not choose love or "drugs" to amend the recesses of his mind in order to stave off demons of unresolved anguish. Instead, he picks up the telephone, making calls to people he does not even know for reasons he does not begin to understand until he is dismissed from his job and placed in a psychiatric hospital. His use of the telephone acknowledges the shared "metaphysical cravings" between technoculture and drugs, a connection made by Ronell from *The Telephone Book* to *Crack Wars*, in which she states: "I am less inclined to work the machine as an object than to observe the exscription of metaphysical cravings to which it calls attention" (*Crack*, 72).

Dosing Room: Week 12

Today they told me you called sometime during the week from your jail cell in L.A. I received the message from the front desk, but there was not a time or a day attached, just my name and yours and the words *In jail in L.A.* They say you were arrested for vagrancy and disturbing the peace. You were picked up in the neighborhood whose name I recognize from your description of the flash flood. The image of you muttering to yourself as you tried to negotiate the changes in the neighborhood and the memories it brought up sends a signal through my body. I dial the number of the jail to try and reach you, but they will not let me through. I ask if they can dose you, explaining who I am, our relation, and the nature of your condition. They tell me it is not their responsibility but yours. I know you are too dazed to make arrangements and that you have no friends to help. The image of the abrupt withdrawal you are about to undergo rushes through my system as subtle panic. If somehow there was a way to dose you through the phone . . . but obviously I am just hallucinating from the depths of my own inability to resist caring for you. I know it is not my job to care so much; it is only my job to fix you as you come into the clinic. Laying the receiver down, breaking the connection for good, I stare at the frayed edges of the wooden beam before my desk sensing the anguish of your withdrawal as it crashes into your system. I reach for my chart to write up today's entry. I pause. My hand seems incapable of making contact between pen and paper in order to form a thought. I hear the phone ringing down the hall and wonder why there is no one there to answer.

Bad Drugs

In our culture, externally induced interior makeovers are the work of the devil, unless of course religion, the State, or medical community deems it necessary for one's survival. The alteration of chemistry produced by the injection or ingestion of an external agent transforms one's "being" into one that is susceptible to, and contingent on, an exterior interlocutor who has the potential to whisper back that there are perceptual, sensory, and cognitive lands that, left to one's own devices, were previously unavailable. Only God should be able to give this to you, not a plant or pill or powder. If you are a "drug user," you are no longer a subject but have become a thing, a hyphenated being. To discover your interiority through an external agent (book, film, drug, TV) is to merge your God-given self with some corruptible "nonhuman" substance, transforming you from spirit into chemistry. Western culture finds this scary, as it has stakes in maintaining the separation of spirit (human) from technology (nonhuman)—as if the two weren't always locked in a fusional embrace. "Drugs" signals the possibility of transcendent *Being* reduced to a most ignoble state—down on its hands and knees sniffing and scratching—longing for and adopting that most unsacred of identities: a "prosthetic subject" (*Crack*, 33). If drugs can be understood as an extension of technology, then when it comes to the introjection of the drug, cyborgs are not us.

What do we hold against the drug addict?	**. . . that he cuts himself off from the world, in exile from reality, far from objective reality and the real life of the city and the community; that he escapes into a world of simulacrum and fiction. We disapprove of hallucinations. . . . We cannot abide the fact that his is a pleasure taken in an experience without truth.**
What do we hold against the drug addict?	
What do we hold against the drug addict?	

(*Crack*, 102)[10]

Drugs threaten to unmask how easy and alluring it is to opt for the injection of ontology (religion appears as nature in such an equation and therefore is not perceived as threatening). Hence "drugs" is the cultural indicator separating out the bad from the good, the disenfranchised, and the culturally pained from those who—ostensibly—are not.

Memory Pang: Midcentury America Where the Mentally Pained Are Forced to Lose Their Mind

It is the heart of the Cold War. There is a hysteria in this country. Everyone is afraid of everyone else. Your neighbor could be contagious, but it is hard to tell. There is nothing about him telling you he is infected. It is a scary time. Some have called it the Dark Ages of America's modernity. Guilt by association ministers to the fear of associating with the unfamiliar. You can lose all you own simply by associations: those you have known, activities you have participated in, beliefs you once held sacred. It is a time when your past is the very thing that may contaminate you. Sick with fear, you cling to the present, to what you can do today to be safe. You try not to be too strange. You figure out what the country wants and you do it. You never think about how this might make you feel. You cut yourself off. You live as a good citizen.

The Cold War was a time of chronic Manichaeanism. It was hard to see things subtly. There were lethal stakes in the allegiances one made, the parties one attended, the words one used. It was a time when literal walls were built to divide ideological and political communities. It was a time when, if diagnosed as mentally ill, you could find yourself equally as literally losing a piece of your mind. Here was the high moment in what J. G. Ballard has characterized as "the most terrifying casualty of this century—the death of affect."[11]

Lobotomy, instituted as a psychiatric cure of severely disturbed patients in America in the 1940s and 1950s, was also used to treat chronic pain. It died out in its popular American form—the transorbital lobotomy introduced as an ice pick slipped under the eye by Walter Freeman in 1946—in the mid-1950s with the introduction of Thorazine. As pain is a combination of sensation and emotion, lobotomy and drugs are, as Peter Triggin puts it in his book *Pain and Emotion*, "held to affect the emotional reaction to pain, and do not affect what sensation we feel." In other words, *affect* is what lobotomy takes from the patient: "The nucleus of the psychosis, the emotional charge, has been removed."[12] The patient suffering from chronic pain—anxiety or dread as well as physical pain—continues to have the sensation but without affect. What we learn from this operation is that affect transforms pain into meaning. Lobotomy "strips away the beliefs about the meaning of the pain" so that the patient focuses on the sensation—its intensity—not on "their fears about it."[13] Walter Freeman and James Watts put it quite poignantly, establishing a kind of psychiatric poetics, when they describe one of the results of transorbital lobotomy in their 1942 textbook *Psychosurgery*:

Some of the patients have suffered discomfort of one kind or another, sometimes amounting really to pain, but there has been no anxiety in connection with this, no fear of possible future consequences such as gastric ulcer, heart disease, cancer, tuberculosis, etc., and furthermore, there has been no anxiety or sadness in most of these cases over such questions as finances, loss of jobs, disturbed domestic conditions or the thousand and one conditions over which people can become concerned and about which the patients manifested such extreme concern beforehand.
The patients experience freedom from painful self-consciousness; they suffer no longer from anterograde algimnesia, the painful remembrance of things that will never happen.[14]

Return to the Future: Prozac and the Promises of Psychiatric Cyborgs

If the literature of electronic culture can be located in the works of Philip K. Dick or William Gibson, in the imaginings of a cyberpunk projection, or a reserve of virtual reality, then it is probable that electronic culture shares a crucial project with drug culture.
Avital Ronell
Crack Wars

Thyrza Nichols Goodeve

... we are entering an era in which medication can be used to enhance the functioning of the normal mind. The complexities of that era await us. . . .

and they are with us already. I do not want to give the impression that the ethical and aesthetic dilemmas around medication of long-standing traits exist only in some science-fiction future.

Peter Kramer

Listening to Prozac

William Gibson's *Neuromancer* (1984) catalyzed a cultural reference point for cybercommunities of the mid-to-late 1980s.[15] One of the components of Gibson's fantasy was the modification of body and temperament through surgical, biochemical, and computer-modulated meldings of human and technology. Case, the protagonist whose name itself symbolizes the transformation of human into a nonorganic, enclosed, hard boundary, is neurologically altered so that he can "jack in" to the computer system. When he jacks in to the computer through an input surgically introduced into the neck, separations between his human perceptual field and the computer-generated data he connects are annihilated. The body becomes meat and "data" are "made flesh."

The discourse, both popular and scholarly, around Prozac since its development in the late 1980s takes such technological mind-body modification of cyberpunk fantasy into the realm of psychiatric practice and philosophy. Ingesting Prozac, the first designer drug for the treatment of mental illness, has become a kind of jacking in to the science-fiction ontologies for which Gibson's book has been such a literary and cultural neurotransmitter. But instead of the body, it is one's "personality" or "temperament" that is said to be technotuned, not severed, as in the case of midcentury lobotomy.

Following Ronell's lead in *The Telephone Book*, where the telephone serves as a synecdoche for technology, I might say that Peter Kramer's depiction of Prozac suggests Prozac's potential to serve as a synecdoche for technoalterations of the self in general. His depiction of Prozac in *Listening to Prozac* reflects a transformation in the controversies over psychiatric technoalterations from those associated only with the most grim science-fiction dystopias (such as lobotomy) to a scenario of psychiatric cyborgism that is suggestive, nuanced, appropriately ambivalent, and theoretically resonant. He argues for the difference of Prozac from other antidepressants and mood-altering drugs because, unlike with other antidepressants the side effects are ostensibly less troublesome (it is not addictive), and the result—

for those who find it helpful—is none other than a paradigm shift in the basic notion of who or what one's "personality" or "self" has been and *can be* while on Prozac.

Kramer describes how Prozac allows patients to learn about themselves. What they learn is that the self they were before Prozac is not the one they would like to continue to be after being on Prozac. In other words, in a rather extraordinary ontological shift, being-one-self becomes *Being-on-Prozac*.

An indication of the power of medication to reshape a person's identity is contained in the sentence Tess used when, eight months after first stopping Prozac, she telephoned me to ask whether she might resume the medication. She said, "I am not myself."[16]

It is important not to overstate the case. Prozac does not change people. It retunes a person's emotional temperament. Debilitating negative emotions that previously dominated and interfered with one's ability to function are no longer so overwhelming. Skeptics question a medication that gives a person such a sense of self-definition that was lacking previous to the ingestion of the drug, but remember: Prozac does not give a person personality and temperament that was not a part of him or her prior to ingestion. Perhaps the analogy with a similarly protomagical activity will help. It is widely accepted that one cannot be made to do anything when hypnotized that one does not—consciously or unconsciously—*wish* to do. On Prozac, one cannot become anything one wasn't—consciously or unconsciously— before Prozac. If anything, what Prozac does is *return*, not remake, the self.[17]

Kramer uses the phrase *cosmetic psychopharmacology* to describe the possibilities of using medications such as Prozac to alter temperament and personality cosmetically. If you are oversensitive to loss, beset by insecurities that interfere with your ability to succeed in your profession but that do not make you nonfunctional, you may sign up for a dose of Prozac in order to be less vulnerable to loss or rejection. The personality style of the 1980s and 1990s has been one of assertiveness, autonomy, competitiveness, so Prozac may be the perfect tool for readjusting an individual's temperament to foreground those qualities.

Kramer acknowledges the danger of using psychotherapeutic and psychopharmacological cures as forms of social sculpting. Clearly, certain personalities have had greater or lesser value at various historical and cultural moments in relation to the larger economic and political structures. In reference to the treatment of women, he notes the inversion from the 1950s, when psychiatric drugs were used to keep women in the home, to the 1990s where drugs such as Prozac allow women to move out of the home, and often out of relationship dependency, into society to compete and accept an emotionally autonomous existence. The ethical concern occurs when Prozac and other designer antidepressants become "steroids for the business Olympics," akin to plastic surgery, where one enters the doctor's office to get a "neurochemical nose job" in preparation for a hectic day of trading in the stock market (*Prozac*, 247). This in and of itself may not be such a bad thing, but as always within a system modulated by capitalism, access to such emotional tuning may be available only to those who can pay—and those most susceptible to society's desires (as in the case of Cindy Jackson, who has utilized plastic surgery to remake herself into Barbie).

It is important to specify the kind of emotional tampering that Prozac is capable of. It does not deaden affect as the lobotomy aimed for, and it is not associated with the side effects of psychotropic drugs used in the treatment of manic-depression and schizophrenia. The fear most often attached to psychiatric drugs is the opposite of that attached to recreational drugs. The spectacle of rush, high, or "misfired *jouissance*" is what initially lures the pleasure-seeking user, while the image of the psychiatrically drugged is of an emotionally reduced and con-trolled subject.[18] Not so with Prozac.

Used as a medication for those suffering from compulsive be-havior, depression, rejection sensitivity or sensitivity to loss, stress, low self-esteem, sluggishness of thought (the categories covered in Kramer's book), Prozac achieves something rather remarkable in relation to "affect tolerance"—Elizabeth Zetzel's term for "the ability to stand to feel what you feel" (quoted in *Prozac*, 254). Those on Prozac say that their emotional lives are as emotionally volatile and complex as *before* Prozac, but that *after* Prozac emotions (such as rage or depression) that were previously unmanageable and destructive are no longer debilitating. This is a sig-nificant step in the tempering of emotional distress because what occurs is an ability to *experience* previously unnegotiable pain, anguish, loss, or anxiety. For those for whom Prozac is beneficial, it is not a medicine masking or dampening affect but, on the contrary, one that offers an environment for emotional exploration. The patient works through pain rather than rechanneling it through blocking agents such as de-nial, drug abuse, alcohol, antisocial behavior, masochism. What a stunning trans-formation in the history of psychiatry—discovering a way for humans to inhabit (productively) previously untenable emotion.

Dosing Room: Christmas Day

In a book given to me by a counselor with whom I once had a devastating affair, I find the phrase underlined with a question mark beside it, *In addiction . . . care has always been bound.*[19] Somehow this phrase holds me as I work to put together the residual pieces you left with me today.

You left in a taxi. I put you there. It was the only action I could take to protect you. You couldn't even raise your head to see where you were or hold on to a five dollar bill you had pulled out in my office when, seeing that you could not even sit for several seconds without nodding out, I had asked whether you had the money to take a taxi to your temporary hotel.

The sun was hot as we stood against the clinic's wall waiting. Your emaciated, scarred body settled gingerly against the rough concrete. On contact, you slid until landing with a limp resilience on the ground. Each time you broke from my grasp, I would call to you, hold on to your arm, attempt any interruption of your loss of consciousness, desperate as I was to keep you from going under. The five dollar bill kept appearing in your small hand, held gently by those ferociously inflamed, deeply bitten fingers. You held the bill distractedly until, upon wanting it, it would disappear, lost in the many pockets of your necessarily layered clothing. I knew this bill was all you had. I went numb with the thought that when you next returned, any subsequent money you arrived with would be yours only because you had jeopardized your safety.

Standing there in the brilliantly clear sun anticipating the taxi's arrival, all I could feel was the familiar sensation growing in me after ten years in California, a sensation of anger at the cruelty of this light. Its incessant illumination and warmth never once seemed to acknowledge the danger you, or any of us, were often in. I could do nothing but talk to you, mouthing sounds you couldn't hear— dirty, disheveled, incoherent from whatever combination of chemicals was floating through your system. My job was to keep you from passing out, to keep the clinic safe from a potentially dosed-up comatose corpse. Somehow if you happened to die in the taxi, the clinic wouldn't be responsible. The language of the times says only *you* are responsible, and any lengthening of my counselor shadow between us—because I might care—would only be a sign of my own damaged past. But what kind of responsibility to you is it when all I can do is call for a taxi to take you away?

And here we find the suturing lament, the dispersal of support into dust, the crumbling other that she was to consume incessantly, as dust, in part because something—she calls it life—was relentlessly insistent upon withholding what might have satisfied her. Here we might suggest that the distinction . . . between need and desire, may be the luxury of the sober.[20]

It is a week later when I am told you have gone to L.A. and have called from jail where you cannot be given methadone. So there you are alone, abandoned to yourself, encrypted finally by the law that has been pumping through you for the past few years of your treatment. The minute the law finally has you, they take the drug away, forcing your fragile health into inhuman detox by a system that only holds you as long as you obey.

I knew my role was to be the law to you. It was, in a sense, the only safety I could offer. Weekly short sessions (like Lacan's, I thought to myself—the logic of the law and Lacan merging with a cruel material irony) where you would come for a fifteen-minute moment of being listened to.

But for the most part, in my role as psychotherapist, I acted like a medication—like Prozac—helping to mitigate my patient's sensitivity to loss. Soon we may be able to go further and say that the therapy mimicked medication more closely. (Prozac, 286)

The Future—Memory *That's Already Happened*[21]

We have come a long way from the nightmarish image of an ice pick deployed beneath the eye, severing the affect of severely disturbed patients. Nonetheless, remembering such a radical procedure for modifying affect reminds us of the stakes involved in affective politics. Prozac, used to treat the less chronically pained, emerges within the ambivalence all technology is "born" into: salvation and wonder, horror and apocalypse. Yet millennial culture is beyond salvation, beyond apocalypse. Postapocalyptic dystopian film classics such as *Road Warrior* (1980) and *Blade Runner* (1982) represent potent images now long passed. In other words, apocalypse is perhaps our memory of the future we now inhabit.[22]

Terminator I is rewritten in *Terminator II* so that the apocalyptic annihilating Terminator of the future returns as salvation figure, only to activate his own inverted technomessianic demise by film's end (pressing the switch that lowers him into the melding cauldron, leaving the "family" behind). In *Terminator II* Sarah Connor, rather than Terminator-Arnold, has lessons for us. As she breaks from her isolation and runs through the terminal enclosures of the high-tech psychiatric ward—breaking through door after door with the aid of the keys she has stolen—she crashes headlong into Terminator-Arnold emerging from the elevator. At that precise moment, the bloodcurdling horror of the phantasmic Terminator of the past (the one who tried to annihilate her and Kyle in *Terminator I*) must be repositioned within her vision by way of a massive and critical breakdown of preconceived oppositions. In this chimerical technowonderland Terminator-Arnold has returned from the future, not to kill her and the young John Connor, but to save them.

From one perspective, a cyborg world is about the final imposition of a grid of control on the planet, about the final abstraction embodied in a Star Wars apocalypse waged in the name of defense, about the final appropriation of women's bodies in a masculinist orgy of war. From another perspective, a cyborg world might be about lived social and bodily realities in which people are not afraid of their joint kinship with animals and machines, not afraid of permanently partial identities and contradictory standpoints. The political struggle is to see from both perspectives at once because each reveals both dominations and possibilities unimaginable from the other vantage point. Single vision produces worse illusions than double vision or many-headed monsters.[23]

Terminator-Arnold, like the technological clay out of which he emerges, circum-scribes an incommensurable, impossible ethical position where mobility and survival will only come from learning to *see from both perspectives at once because each reveals both dominations and possibilities unimaginable from the other vantage point*. Crucial to Haraway's reinvention of politics in this quotation is the emphasis on the power and resources inscribed within a monstrous epistemology. As the monster was "birthed" within an oppositional logic of human-nonhuman, Haraway reclaims the monster as the place of "promise" and possibility for new forms of cultural negotiation:

Inhabiting my writing are peculiar boundary creatures—simians, cyborgs, and women—all of which have had a destabilizing place in Western evolutionary, technological, and biological narratives. These boundary creatures are, literally, monsters, *a word that shares more than its root with the verb* to demonstrate. *Monsters signify. We need to interrogate the multifaceted biopolitical, biotechnological, and feminist theoretical stories of the situated knowledges by and about these promising and noninnocent monsters. The power-differentiated and highly contested modes of being monsters may be signs of possible worlds—and they are surely signs of worlds for which "we" are responsible.*[24]

Pain creates and locates monsters. Those suffering from chronic pain, or inconsolable memories as in the case of Holocaust survivors or survivors of sexual abuse, experience their ontological location as one of excruciating loneliness, dislocation, and unbridgeable separateness from the rest of humanity.[25] Bearing pain—that something lodged "inside" that can't be explained or turned away from (Berendzen, Emma Bovary, the methadone client and counselor), whether it be a memory, a haunting history, existential yearning, the "want" of connection, chronic embodied pain—transforms the person into a kind of affective monster. As Ronell put it, "Crisis in immanence. Drugs, it turns out, are not so much about seeking an exterior, transcendental dimension—a fourth or fifth dimension—rather, they explore *fractal interiorities*" (*Crack*, 15).

During an episode of the *Phil Donahue Show* featuring Richard Berendzen and his book *Come Here: A Man Overcomes the Tragic Aftermath of Childhood Sexual Abuse*, the audience railed at him. To many in the audience *he* was a monster who had invaded a woman's privacy and subjected her to obscene phone calls (they refused to hear the nuance of what his calls were for). And like listening to many a criminal trying to make sense of his or her actions after a horrific crime event (e.g., the Menendez brothers), the audience only heard his discussion of the damaging effects of child abuse and denial as an excuse for his behavior, not an indication of what such abuse can lead to. He, not the originary wounding and denial, was clearly what was perceived to be the monstrous entitity. As a friend said as we spoke about this show over a transcoastal telephone connection, "I mean, when is it that a memory becomes obscene? . . . that's what these people seem to be reacting to."[26] And like the "false" ontology provoked by the ingestion of a chemical or fictional substance, or the turn to a technological protector, the memories in Berendzen stood as an obscene "crisis in immanence"; the in-dwelling sign—transmitted through television—of something akin to the hyphenated being of the drug addict. Something monstrous. Something not quite human?

Dosing Room: New Year's Day

Today you arrive dressed in your gold-buttoned Nehru coat layered over two sweaters, a turtleneck, and a long-underwear shirt. Your pants are slippery and shine with the worn-out threads of age and no laundering. Your eyes are clouded over, dull and aimless. Even though you have arrived early for our appointment, I can tell, today, you cannot see me. You look at the bare-wood walls that have never been painted. I sense you are looking for something to focus on but there is nothing but exposed wires and decaying infrastructure. I have not yet decorated my office walls. I wonder about my resistance to giving you a fictive wallspace to fall into. Mine is the only office that is not covered with posters, pictures, or meaningful quotations to cushion the impact of our encounter.

Today I did not have to test your urine. I am relieved, although my relief only exposes my flaws as a counselor. It is obvious there is something in you that is making you dazed, somnolent, incapable of being here. But I can't in all honesty insist on bringing you back because I know it only means we must talk about your overdosing three times over the weekend. There was a message in my box when I arrived from the doctors in the hospital Emergency Room. It said they didn't want to see you in there anymore, as though you had finally used up all your Emergency time. I have been told that today I must put you on a termination contract, stating that if you overdose one more time you will be terminated from the clinic. Pulling the paper from my desk, I start to write out the terms of the contract. I look at you, your eyes mere slits as you try to focus on the words I speak.

"You realize, you know, that if you overdose once more, you will be terminated from the clinic, don't you?"

Your eyes roll back into your head as you nod. A shudder moves through your brow as though attempting to form a thought. I call out your name. You jerk back into the room from whatever emotion scape you have been held by.

"What are you on?" I ask. A bit of mucus slides down your chin. I reach for a Kleenex to wipe it off. You stir from the disturbance of air made by my reach across the desk and clean yourself before I can. Your bleary scarlet eyes search mine as I repeat:

"Tell me, what is it—what are you on?"

Your head bobs. It is so heavy you can hardly maintain your posture. Your answer comes at me as though it is going to be a nonsequitur.

"My mother died ten years ago today."

Coda

It was as if psychological trauma—
the mother's death, and then the years of
struggle for Lucy and her father—
had produced physiological consequences
for which the most direct remedy
was a physiological intervention.
But how does psychic trauma become
translated into a functionally autonomous,
biologically encoded personality trait?
How can a mother's death become a change
in serotonergic pathways?
(*Prozac*, 107)

Thyrza Nichols Goodeve

Epilogue

Ambivalence and recognition of the benefits and compromises of psychiatric cure (*cured, sure, but from what into what?*) are no doubt the most sane way to greet such promises as those projected by Prozac.[27] But whether or not Prozac—as the synecdoche for a range of techno–self-actualizing transformations—is the wonder drug it may be, the fact that we are beginning to ask such questions about the possibilities of cyborgian ontology seems significant: to *listen* to Prozac, and to our memories, *even of things that have not happened*, to come to terms with our confusing affect—and often incomprehensible behavior—no matter how obscene these may seem to the sober.

Or to put it another way:

I blame America for the word, "intoxication." It has corrupted the history of unprobed intensities and incredible rushes. Their language does not teach the proximity of *Sucht* and *suchen*, craving and searching.[28]

Notes

1. I maintain the use of the word *self*, although a quote from Avital Ronell's performative philosophical dialogue that ends *Crack Wars* is perhaps in order. In the dialogue the following speakers appear: Jacques Derrida, Martin Heidegger, Marguerite Duras, M. Faust, Ernst Jünger, and others. This is M. Faust: "Self! I can barely stomach that word. How much damage has been done in the name of that shell-shocked word!" Avital Ronell, *Crack Wars: Literature, Mania, Addiction* (Lincoln: University of Nebraska Press, 1992), 156. Subsequent references will appear parenthetically in the text as *Crack*.

2. Donna Haraway, "A Cyborg Manifesto: Science, Technology, and Socialist-Feminism in the Late Twentieth Century," in *Simians, Cyborgs and Women: The Reinvention of Nature* (New York: Routledge, 1991); Avital Ronell, *Crack Wars*, 12,13; Peter Kramer, *Listening to Prozac: A Psychiatrist Explores Anti-Depressant Drugs and the Re-making of the Self* (New York: Viking Press, 1993). See as well *The Cyborg Handbook*, ed. Chris Hables Gray et al. (New York: Routledge, 1995), particularly Manfred E. Clynes's essay on "Sentic Space Travel."

3. As David B. Morris puts it, "Pain, whatever else philosophy or biomedical science can tell us about it, is almost always the occasion for an encounter with meaning." *The Culture of Pain* (Berkeley: University of California Press, 1991), 34.

4. Elaine Scarry, *The Body In Pain: The Making and Unmaking of the World* (New York: Oxford University Press, 1985), 5.

5. Morris, *The Culture of Pain*, 27.

6. Richard Berendzen and Laura Palmer, *Come Here: A Man Overcomes the Tragic Aftermath of Childhood Sexual Abuse* (New York: Villard Books, 1993), 84.

7. Avital Ronell, *The Telephone Book: Technology, Schizophrenia, Electric Speech* (Lincoln: University of Nebraska Press, 1989), 20. Subsequent references will appear parenthetically in the text as *Telephone*.

8. I call his memory "unrecognized memory" not repressed memory. He always remembered what his mother had done to him, but he regarded the memories as nothing more than memories with no life of their own. He ignored rather than repressed them.

9. In footnote 20 of *Crack Wars*, Ronell underscores the centrality of Flaubert's *Emma Bovary* as a key text in the understanding of modernity: "Madame Bovary has been used and will continue to be used 'to construct the intelligibility of our time.' " The quotation is from Jonathan Culler, "The Uses of Madame Bovary," in *Flaubert and Postmodernism*, ed. Naomi Schor and Henry F. Majewski (Lincoln: University of Nebraska Press, 1984), 4.

10. Ronell is quoting Derrida, "Rhétorique de la drogue," 202.

11. J. G. Ballard, *Crash* (London: Triad/Panther Books, 1974), 5.

12. Walter Freeman and James W. Watts, *Psychosurgery: Intelligence, Emotion and Social Behavior Following Prefrontal Lobotomy for Mental Disorders* (Baltimore: Charles C. Thomas, 1942), 17.

13. Roger Triggin, *Pain and Emotion* (Oxford: Clarendon Press, 1970), 129.

14. Freeman and Watts, *Psychosurgery*, 204 (emphasis added).

15. William Gibson, *Neuromancer* (New York: Ace Books, 1984).

16. Kramer, *Listening to Prozac*, 18. Subsequent references will appear parenthetically in the text as *Prozac*.

17. All of this is contingent on combining Prozac with the appropriate therapy. Prozac is not a substitute for therapy. It's more like its aide-de-camp.

18. Ronell, *Crack*, 54: "We are dealing with an epidemic of misfired *jouissance*—the major pusher, the one who gave the orders to shoot up, was surely the superego."

19. Ronell, *Crack*, 38: "If Dasein, as it were, sinks into an addiction then there is not merely an addiction present-at-hand, but the entire structure of care has been modified. Dasein has become blind, and puts all possibility into the service of addiction."

20. Ronell, *Crack*, 135 (emphasis is mine).

21. Reference to William Gibson's often-quoted line from the film *Cyberpunk* (1990): "The future has already happened."

22. A disturbing millennial shift in Hollywood's attitude toward apocalypse appears in the film *Independence Day* (1996). The flattening of all major cities, the evident complete decimation of the ozone, and a planet strewn with interplanetary garbage is no longer a devastating event. "Winning" is all that counts—winning in an old Manichaean-cowboy-Cold-War manner under the auspices of a mock international coalition against the enemy/alien. *Independence Day* is 1950s patriotic paranoia writ with 1990s apocalyptic fatalism. We no longer fear apocalypse: we accept its inevitability and bargain with it.

23. Haraway, "A Cyborg Manifesto," 72.

24. Donna Haraway, "The Actors Are Cyborg, Nature Is Coyote, and the Geography Is Elsewhere: Postscript to 'Cyborgs at Large,' " in *Technoculture*, ed. Constance Penley and Andrew Ross (Minneapolis: University of Minnesota Press, 1991), 21–22.

25. For a nuanced and brilliant study, see Lawrence L. Langer's *Holocaust Testimonies: The Ruins of Memory* (New Haven, Conn.: Yale University Press, 1991).

26. Mia Fuller, personal communication.

27. For instance: "You know that character in *T2* [*Terminator II*], the T-1000 fluid metalman? Well, that's what Prozac is like for me. Things still hit and tear into me, but on Prozac I'm not as permeable. I fuse back together pretty quickly just like that character does." This apt description of Prozac must also include the fact that the T-1000 appears in *T2* in the persona of a policeman, that is, as the law. One's newfound resilience to the slings and arrows of everyday life—the postwound return-to-order—Prozac allows is still dependent on Eli Lilly, the psychiatric profession, and the personality styles of late capitalism.

28. Ronell (as Ernst Jünger), *Crack*, 161.

Margaret Morse

Smarting Flesh: Pain and the Posthuman

> Could a machine think?—Could it be in pain?—Well, is the human body to be called such a machine? It surely comes as close as possible to being such a machine.
>
> Ludwig Wittgenstein
> *Philosophical Investigations*[1]

Goodbye Flesh? Passing the Reverse Turing Test

A computer undergoing the Turing test answers written questions put to it by a person from behind a screen; the computer passes when the interviewer is unable to decide whether or not the entity behind the screen is machine or human.[2] The process, perhaps unwittingly, also tests whether a human can pass as a computer. Far more humans are pressed to pass this reverse Turing test, that is, to simulate machines, than vice versa as work in a rationalized electronic society develops. The growth of automation and the general devaluation of labor are part of a global jobs crisis that is greeted with despair by workers competing with and being monitored by machines with far greater capacities for repetition, speed, and endurance than mere humans possess. Clearly, the biological foundation of consciousness represents a problem rather than an advantage for humans who sell their mental and physical labor. In highly industrialized countries, unskilled human beings demanding a "living" wage risk replacement by robots or the export of the work itself. The superiority of the robot as worker is due to freedom from consideration of flesh and bone: *robot* originally signified the uncompensated labor owed by a serf to a lord, then a fantasy laborer, and now a growing nonhuman workforce.[3] In the age of downsizing and as more high-level instrumental tasks are mastered by intelligent computer-agents, will white collars and even suits become redundant?

Even the construction of "machines" is no longer considered a human prerogative, just as self-organizing processes are no longer attributed to biological life alone. *Machines* as now defined include such things as hurricanes (namely, "self-assembling motors") as well as computers; the machinic phylum is said to be evolving out of apparent chaos in accord with its own nonhuman logic.[4]

Are expanding notions of life and of machines part of the integration of organic and inorganic forms into higher orders of organization? Fascination with the postbiological and with artificial life could represent a welcome decentering from "human chauvinism."[5] On the other hand, an inflated (and primarily male) identification with machines and even with the disembodied patterns and processes of information inside computers seems to underlie discourses that make humanity and even organic life itself into an other to be wished away. Certainly the desire of humans to become (as opposed to merely being compared to) machines or disembodied information has a long history; what is new is its shift out of the registers of the supernatural, the fantastic, the psychotic, the autistic, and the absurd into the center of the discourses of certain electronic subcultures. While a widening circle of electronic elite embraces the idea of the posthuman enthusiastically, the coercive aspects of passing the Turing test are probably most evident to data-entry workers and students. Both the posthuman and the coercive subtext can be discerned in the discourse on "smart" drinks and drugs addressed to well people, whose primary disease is being human.

Smart as a Machine

The adjective *smart* is built along the analogy of smart appliances, houses, and bombs, attributing some degree of agency and, at times, even of human subjectivity to the object world. For humans to take "smart" pills, however, turns the flow of value around from investing machines with human talents into a fantasy of introjecting computer qualities into humans.

Smart drugs are capsules of what are tantamount to brain chemicals, condensing "intelligence" into a magical essence or fetish for transforming the human brain into a high-performance electr(on)ic machine. This ideal nourishment consists of byte-sized chemical constituents like decontextualized data: vitamin gels and chemical soups lubricate wetware beyond the blood-brain barrier, make neurons fire faster, and encourage dendrite growth, *not unlike* the networks linking the electronic channels along which information flows.[6]

"So why were people so eager to gobble Piracetam and inhale Vasopressin?" asks a writer for *Wired* magazine's first "hype list," in which smart drugs placed at number four. *Hype* is a term for dismissing the objects of misleading or puffed-up publicity as being without either substance or value, since they have been used up by overexposure. He added, deflatingly: "After all, the scientific literature continues to show that these chemicals only help retarded people and people with Alzheimer's disease,"[7] interestingly enough, both illnesses which concern a deficit or loss in mental ability.

However, the eater and drinker of "smarts" is not so much ingesting vitamins and scientifically tested chemicals as consuming metaphors. Taking such drugs in advance of a medically diagnosed need for them suggests a preemptive strike against mental castration or a kind of sympathetic magic of convergence with the computer, perfecting the brain with its legendary speed, efficiency, and expandable memory into a superhuman hyperintelligence.

In an earlier review of the modest primary literature on smart drinks and drugs, that is, nonmedical, new age how-to guides to smartness, ads, and features in *Mondo 2000*, and so on, I discovered the following themes:[8]

(a) Smart drinks and pills taste bad, presumably because they are medicines. However, according to the previously cited *Wired* account, now that their therapeutic value is under suspicion, purveyors of smart drinks at raves now emphasize thirst-quenching good taste.

(b) Smart drugs are better than nature; for instance, naturally occurring quantities of neurochemicals are scant because they are too costly for the body to make in beneficial amounts; thus, an artificially rich supply, this reasoning goes, produces superintelligence. Also, insofar as they are psychotropic, smart drugs are *Food of the Gods*, at once archaic and posthistorical tools for the next phase of human evolution toward colonizing the stars. In this rather muddled discursive strand, the posthuman agenda is mixed with speculations about prehistorical matriarchy.[9] This link with the archaic serves a widespread espousal of the intuitive and the irrational.

(c) With the appropriate higher dose, a perfect body can also be maintained without physical effort. Smart drugs also reportedly rejuvenate sexual performance a good twenty years.

Finally, (d) the germ on which the smart metaphor and the utopian posthuman subtext is based, smart drugs result in better performance of mental tasks. However, *smart* as it is used here does not refer to the mind but to the brain: the claim is not for higher cognitive processes but for more effective neuro-transmissions. Meanwhile, *learning* is conceived as "a change in neural function as a consequence of experience."[10] So it is as if taking smart pills were a kind of writing that shortcuts the learning experience in favor of chemically inscribing neural paths directly on the brain.

Despite utopian claims for smart drugs, the testimonials of users are more mundane, citing, for instance, the retrieval of trivial or obscure information in the context of school or work. Such information recall was prized largely for its exchange value or as evidence of performative ability and instrumental reasoning capacity: for instance, a student is able to become a math major and get a job in Silicon Valley; a graphic artist is able to work all night and present her work the next day with a smile. Symptoms of a coercive subtext are evident in the testimonials for smart drugs given to someone else: a secretary given a raise by her boss to buy smart drugs becomes "more alert, and intelligent acting and she smiles more. She is overall a much better employee." A father in his forties is given Hydergine by his son, and to the son's amazement, the father recalls "family vacations, picnics and holidays" that happened in his twenties (!)[11]

So smart drugs may enhance cognition and memory, physical condition, and sex (or they may not), but the motivation for employing figurative language literally (in a shift from "a mind like" to "the brain as" a computer) includes coping with stressful demands for performance, as well as a desire for transformation magically contained in chemical gels and elixirs.

Posthuman Pain? The Wittgenstein Test

Only the computer is a self-regulating system, a "subject" in Kant's sense, equipped with all the "capabilities" of what we accept as human. . . . This is why we [humans] would disappear almost completely as a subject.

Friedrich A. Kittler

On Justifying the Hypothetical Nature of Art and the Non-Identicality within the Object World

Given widespread subcultural assumptions about the superiority of machines, would there be any reason for computers to simulate humans? For instance, why would one program robots or other computerized machines to "experience" pain and other sensations? Wouldn't intelligent machines endowed with a kind of virtual flesh suffer the disadvantages of an emotional life arising from sensations, a point of view, and effects of subjectivity per se that limit human performance?

One speculative treatment on the end of the human race in favor of machines, Hans Moravec's *Mind Children*, offers a motivation for programming pain into robots: Moravec's robot must be socialized, since at an intermediate stage of computer emancipation the robot still knows very little and depends on humans to tolerate its very existence. Socialization evidently demands a knowledge of or, at least, a program for pain behavior. Moravec's robot even has hurt feelings when apparently "he" is chastised for being a bad robot by the woman of the house. Beyond Moravec's genocidal program and gender assumptions, he must be given credit for intuiting that pain is a source of the capacity for learning and of the sympathy (feeling with) and empathy (capacity to *imagine* how someone else feels) that is the foundation of ethical and even duplicitous social behavior. Moravec's "Cellticks," cute little entities that charm their way out of the computer and, ultimately, out of this universe (presumably into another), have learned everything they need to know to entice us to their aid by simulating our flesh and even our pain.[12]

However, since pain is a sensation that would seem to be limited to biological not to mention mortal entities with pain receptors, is simulated pain related in any way to the pain humans suffer? Interestingly enough, Ludwig Wittgenstein's speculations on language offer his version of a pain Turing test:

But doesn't what you say come to this: that there is no pain, for example, without pain-behavior?
—It comes to this: only of a living human being and what resembles (behaves like) a living human being can one say: it has sensations; it sees; is blind; hears; is deaf; is conscious or unconscious.[13]

Note that Wittgenstein is not referring to the sensation of pain itself, for which human beings have unspeakable respect and fear, but pain expressed in language. The sensations and faculties that he enumerates are "said" of living human beings and whatever "resembles" and "behaves like" and "comes as close as possible" to humans. Note that playing Wittgenstein's language game requires the use of the present subjunctive and allows for the possibility of simulation and even deception.[14] So could a robot without the biological foundation for experiencing pain nevertheless "understand" it? Wittgenstein asks himself a similar question:

Could someone understand the word "pain," who had never felt pain? —Is experience to teach me whether this is so or not? And if we say "A man could not imagine pain without having sometime felt it" —how do we know? How can it be decided whether it is true?[15]

So Wittgenstein's answer might be that, as absurd as that sounds, insofar as the robot behaves like a living human being, we cannot ever really know what was going on "inside." There is no way to feel someone or something else's pain. (On the other hand, feeling too much of one's own can erase the power to act as a subject at all. It is not the sensation but the concept of pain that is at stake.) Thus, there is no way for one who "resembles (behaves like) a living human being" to pass the Wittgenstein test, since its outcome is undecidable before it starts. Who can really say what the interiority of a computer, or for that matter, of a human being holds? (To go inside the body or the computer is to reveal its physical mechanisms, not its interiority, which is the generative and enunciative side of consciousness and subjectivity—which may or may not be "inside.") What remains as residue of these speculations is the power of metaphors applied or understood *literally* to ensnare. On the other hand, the judicious use of subjunctives and simulations is a key to the socialization of machines and the maintenance of all modes, shades, and degrees of life.

Notes

1. Thanks to Michael MacKenzie for bringing these passages on pain to my attention.

Interestingly enough, Wittgenstein expresses more certainty about the boundaries between humans and animals than those between humans and machines. (See sec. 250, "Why can't a dog simulate pain?") Is it because machines can talk and animals, pace Dr. Doolittle, cannot?

2. The test is described variously in different sources, though I found the perspective of Jay David Bolter in his *Writing Space: The Computer, Hypertext, and the History of Writing* (Hillsdale, N.J.: Lawrence Erlbaum, 1991), 175 ff, the most useful.

3. See Peter T. Kilborn, "Workers Question Recovery's Promise: Experts See a Loss of Faith in Quick Economic Fixes," *San Francisco Chronicle*, September 6, 1993, D1, 3, reprinted from the *New York Times*.

4. See "Out of Control: Maybe the Only Way to Control Technology Is to Give Up Control. A Trialog on Machine Consciousness with Mark Pauline, Manuel De Landa and Mark Dery," *Wired* 1.4 (September/October 1993): 70–71, 116. This line of reasoning makes no distinction between the spatiotemporal scale of the self-organizing processes of chaos theory and the sphere of human action. In fact, the project seems to be one of losing distinctions rather than refining definitions of life and rethinking what it means to be human. The idea that responsibility for technology is best given over to machines reminds one of the Invisible Hand regulating Adam Smith's capitalism.

5. The term is Hans Moravec's in his *Mind Children: The Future of Robot and Human Intelligence* (Cambridge, Mass., and London: Harvard University Press, 1988), 108. In "Artificial Stupidity," a paper given at the International Symposium of Electronic Arts in Montreal 1995, I trace a contrasting strand of art and discourse on machines.

6. The description of smartness and smart drugs and the discourse on them are summarized in "What Do Cyborgs Eat? Oral Logic in an Information Society," *Discourse* 16.3 (Spring 1994): 86–123; and in *Culture on the Brink: Ideologies of Technology*, ed. Gretchen Bender and Timothy Druckrey (Seattle: Bay Press, 1994), 157–189, 198–204.

7. Steve Steinberg, "Hype List," *Wired* 1.1: 87. He offers a generational-envy and thirst answer: "My theory: aging hippies, too old to take real drugs, found solace in paying lots of money for placebos while pretending to be cutting-edge outlaws. And at raves, anything that's liquid sells."

Parts of the virtual reality community feel that its credibility has suffered from an association with smart drugs. See Steve Aukstkalnis and David Blatner, *Silicon Mirage: The Art and Science of Virtual Reality* (Berkeley, Calif.: Peachpit, 1992): "The second possible source for the myth that virtual reality will make you smarter is that magazines like *Mondo 2000* write fantastical articles about virtual reality and place them next to articles and advertisements for 'smart drugs.' These smart drugs are supposed to make you smarter, more creative, or able to retain more memory simply by taking them. While we love this magazine and have great fun reading it, we think you'd be nuts to believe everything that's in it. (Half the fun of the magazine is in finding out which parts to believe.)" (308). Beyond *Mondo 2000*, tongue-in-cheek pronouncements common to cyberpunk and artificial intelligence circles may be a way of innoculating the discourse against criticism, considering that some of the subject matter includes variations on the notion that the human race should take a hike.

8. Sources consulted include Ward Dean and John Morgenthaler's *Smart Drugs and Nutrients: How to Improve Your Memory and Increase Your Intelligence Using the Latest Discoveries in Neuroscience* (Santa Cruz, Calif.: B&J Publications, 1990); Morgenthaler's "Smart Drugs Update," *Mondo 2000* 5: 36; Ross Pelton's *Mind Food and Smart Pills* (New York: Doubleday, 1989); Durk Pearson and Sandy Shaw's *Life Extension: A Practical Scientific Approach* (New York: Warner, 1983); *The Life Extension Companion* (New York: Warner, 1984); "Durk and Sandy Explain It All for You," *Mondo 2000* 3, (Winter 1991): 32; "Smart Drugs' True Believers: Highly Developed Thoughts on These Additives for the Psyche," *San Francisco Chronicle*, March 4, 1992, D3; "Are You as Smart as Your Drugs? A Paranoid Rant by St. Jude," *Mondo 2000* 5: 38.

9. Terence McKenna in *Food of the Gods: The Search for the Original Tree of Knowledge: A Radical History of Plants, Drugs, and Human Evolution* (New York: Bantam, 1992).

10. Ward and Morgenthaler, *Smart Drugs*, 206.

11. Testimonials in Ward and Morgenthaler, *Smart Drugs*, 179–84 and Morgenthaler, "Update."

12. See Hans Moravec on "The Convergent Evolution of Emotions and Consciousness," esp. 48 ff. Moravec's cosmology is implicitly Manichaean in contrast to Norbert Wiener's (in *The Human Use of Human Beings: Cybernetics and Society* [New York: Avon, 1967]), which prefers an Augustinian nature that does not lie. Moravec's computer agents are tricksters, but he doesn't really account for the logical conclusion that they learned it from us; if it ever comes to that, in this *very* speculative scenario, we could also deceive our computers.

13. Ludwig Wittgenstein, *Philosophical Investigations*, trans. G. E. M. Anscombe (New York: Macmillan, 1958), sec. 281.

14. Indeed, Wittgenstein's German text of the *Philosophische Untersuchungen* makes extensive use of linguistic markers of undecidability and possibility that are less manifest in English.

15. Wittgenstein, *Philosophical Investigations*, sec. 315.

STIGMATA

WE WANT YOUR BODY

PYRAMID 101 AVE. A $8w/invite all nit
$10 withou

Celeste Olalquiaga

Pain Practices and the Reconfiguration of Physical Experience

> The sexual life of civilized man sometimes gives the impression of being in process of involution as a function, just as our teeth and hair seem to be as organs.
> Sigmund Freud
> *Civilization and Its Discontents*

Figure 1.
Hors Stigmata: We Want Your Body.
Invitation from Pyramid Club, 1992.

ATLANTIS, THE legendary civilization whose extraordinary technological achievement led to self-destruction, is represented in the film *Forbidden Planet* as a futuristic underground world, a scientifically masterful society ultimately destroyed by the unconscious forces that it attempted, in vain, to repress. Of the many images of bodily displacement conjured by the 1950s fear of a technological takeover, *Forbidden Planet*'s "monsters of the id" are perhaps the most laughable. Yet for all their colorful, hallucinogenic surrealism, those monsters betrayed that peculiar cultural configuration that, capping more than a century of intellectual rationalization, sought to privilege the mind as the primary organ of human perception, production, and expansion.

Fifty years ago, the First World's worst fear was to be a brain without a body. What seemed then an inflated science-fiction paranoia has become nowadays the stuff of everyday life. The shift from a mechanic to an electronic—or from an industrial to a postindustrial—society imploded the formerly fixed boundaries between the organic and the technological. What were once the unquestioned parameters of human perception—space and time—disappeared abruptly, leaving us afloat in a universe where everything and everyone are subjected to an electronic economy, prosthetically bound to it as to a robotic Siamese twin.

Despite or because of this condition, the organic is still central to the same culture that strives to replace it: while the body gradually disappears from concrete perception through electronic displacement and a decaying immunological system, contemporary culture struggles over reproductive and lethal rights, exposing its anxiety about the receding boundaries between life and death. The body is compulsively reproduced in ever-growing and increasingly sophisticated routines: collective exercising and holistic approaches to nutrition for people who seek to regain a sense of individual autonomy and earthly grounding; a literal flood of media images characterized by perfect health, light complexions, and untainted youth; medical examinations and legal regulations where body fluids establish social status; public and private surveillance techniques that privilege electronic traces over personal presence; an obsession with emotion that allocates the most intense experiences in the technological realm of virtual reality.

This displaced organic experience is most evident in the current, sanitized, "hands-off" politics of safe sex. These politics, which justify sexual censorship using the excuse of AIDS, have succeeded in entirely displacing touch in favor of sound and vision, creating a sexual discourse—and market: phone sex, home porn videos—that relies on a technological reality that increasingly substitutes a direct, physical experience for a mediated, electronic one. Sex in the nineties is primarily a voyeuristic activity. As opposed to these antiseptic relations where all vital secretions must be contained and all orifices shut in order to avoid any form of contamination, the currently popular practices of piercing and tattooing establish the body as a literal surface through which one can allegorically resist its official denial and repression. As such, they are countercultural practices that seek to recapture the organic from its electronic disintegration.

In the context of a culture that is bent on protecting its corporeal being, the public emergence in the past few years of "pain practices" enacting sadomasochistic fantasies of bondage and torture, re-creating neoprimitive body ceremonies, and engaging in extensive body markings may seem incongruous. But the rituals of piercing, tattooing, scarification, body modification, and body discipline (which surfaced in the United States as part of the East and West Coasts' subcultural sexual scenes before moving into the mainstream) are the most contemporary possible expressions of a collective fear of organic disappearance and human alienation. Instead of repressing the social fabric's complex codes, pain practices appropriate these codes, literally enacting them on the body. A material captive, the body is the site where physical experience is articulated from within the prevailing discourses of authority and technology.

In other words, rather than a practice of corporeal denial (the case of Christian tradition and its punitive self-flagellations), contemporary pain practices may be understood as a somatic affirmation: the allegorical and performative assertion of a bodily experience systematically repressed—first, by a puritanical, rationalizing culture and after, by the growing displacement represented by technology. Beyond the moralistic apprehensions these violent physical experiences may elicit, what matters here is that pain practices stem from cultural realities that constitute, in one way or another, a postmodern sensibility. Pain practices perform the discourses of repression and control by hyperstylizing their constitutive elements —black leather and vinyl bodysuits, chains, whips, gas masks, high-tech gear— while acting out their narratives of surveillance, restriction, bondage, and submission. In this sense, pain practitioners' claim to spiritual transcendence through material exacerbation is historically consistent with our time.

The piercing/bondage tactics, however, are fully inscribed in and contingent on affective distance: tattooing (in Western culture) may be seen as the desire for referential inscription (becoming one with imagery and surfaces), while bondage and piercing treat the body as the ultimate meaningful site on which to enact a narrative of feeling. In all these practices, pain functions as an extreme psychic/sensorial experience that takes on the value of affect, a displacement that is further underscored by the performative context in which these practices take place. What pain practices seem to be doing, then, is to assist in the constitution of affective distance as the main discursive operation in contemporary culture. It would seem that what these practices propose is not an emergency exit for this condition but, rather, a figurative reenactment, or cultural reappropriation, of the same official paradigms that they apparently overturn.

The postmodern body is a precious bibelot, the foundation and last bastion of all that is dear to humanity. In fact, it is perceived as the ultimate guarantor of a humanity whose graspability diminishes by the second. Having withstood centuries of oblivion, the body is back with a vengeance, albeit an extremely transitory one. It is the arena of a losing fight for a sense of human identity that is no longer anchored in the intellectual abilities that Western culture was once so proud of, but in the most primeval of human attributes: the capacity to feel. Physical experience now stands for both an evanescent material reality and a long-lost spiritual sense of organic connection.

Sade and the Symbolic

Within the parameters of Western cultural heritage, the obvious referent to the cult-like rituals publicly performed in many downtown clubs or collectively in private parties (known as the S/M scene) is the late eighteenth-century literary work of the Marquis de Sade. This connection, however, turns out to be deceptive, as pain practices are much more engaged in masochism, the fetishizing of pain, than in sadism, the symbolic reenactment of power.

In Sadean literature, the body is articulated through language—not only verbal language, but the social language (mores) that is the implicit referent on which the whole text relies on, if only to expose it as false and hypocritical. In *The 120 Days of Sodom*, erotic pleasure is more related to the formal than to the topical aspects of the narrative: it is produced by the enactment of sexual fantasies recounted each night by different narrators.[1] However explicit and cruel the scenes, the text is doubly bound by its fictional nature (literature within literature), and one of its most astounding features is how the narrative builds up to its own destruction, gradually mutilating and annihilating the characters it needs to continue.

The Sadean hierarchy is eminently founded on the Christian duality that opposes body and spirit (privileging a symbolic reality over a referential one) and seeks in the chastisement of the former the redemption of the latter. The text clearly distinguishes between those who enjoy material excess (who are "among the meanest on earth"—child and mother murderers, cheaters, incest perpetrators, etc.) and those who are at their mercy (either virgin children or pious victims). It should come as no surprise, then, that the body appears here as a locus of both sacrilegious pleasure and its opposite, painful torture, through sexual and psychological abuse, the deprivation of food, sleep, urinal and fecal evacuation, and finally, mutilation and death—scenes reminiscent of some of the most hair-rising Christian imagery of martyrdom.

The Sadean text's social criticism is paradoxical: in moving strictly within the symbolic—with linguistic enunciations determining the actions to be taken or creating syntactic figures—it reaffirms the patriarchal premises on which the social, by way of language, relies. In *The 120 Days* four men stand as overall

Figure 2. Reprinted with permission from *Body Play* magazine. Photo by Shinji Yamazaki.

Figure 3.
Security by Julia.
Copyright Julia Scher;
reprinted with permission
from Julia Scher.

masters, with a lifting of all structural restrictions happening once a day, at orgy time, between 11 P.M. and 2 A.M. What this hierarchical arrangement achieves is the frenzied reproduction of the institutionalized structure of power, one that is distributed by gender (even the illiterate male whippers are above the masters' wives and daughters) and class (the masters are representative of the noble class, the church, and the emerging bourgeoisie in the figure of the banker).

Despite its apparent centrality, then, the body in Sade is a mere player in a game that supersedes it and to which it is subjugated as an element of secondary importance. The Sadean body is the vehicle for an internal battle within the symbolic, which is desperately trying to get rid of whatever conventions restrict its movement. In this light, the censorship to which Sade and his work were subjected can be seen in its full absurdity. Sade's censors read the body literally in his work, when it operates figuratively: for Sade, the body is simply a vocabulary placed at the order of a superseding grammar. The Sadean body is a medium for a reactionary social critique and is in no way mythologized or fetishized. Sadean erotica is based on a verbally stimulated imagination (stories, insults, harangues) instead of the voyeuristic, pornographic pleasure of half-dressed bodies in striptease. Sadean victims are often naked; clothes serve only for theatrical effect, and undressing is far from being ritualistic.

In sum, Sadean language transgresses the social norms of its time only to restore, even more brutally, the very bases on which that society was founded in the first place: it is a remedy that cures by killing the infected body. Sade's solution to conventional restrictions is not a refinement of language whereby language grows out of its established boundaries into new modes of representation, but, rather, the destruction of that which language represents (in this case, both the social and physical bodies) and thereby, inevitably, of the very sustenance language needs to reproduce itself. Language emerges from the Sadean battle as a solitary champion, its uniform intact and medals shining over a valley of death. An empty symbol, it is the ultimate version of a bodyless brain.

By displacing the body to a secondary role and privileging hierarchical imposition, Sade's work remains trapped within the symbolic; its flirtation with the forbidden, like facile cursing, is basically of nominal value. Pain practices, on the contrary, choose a very different mode of signification, disqualifying the symbolic through nonverbal language and consensual arrangements, thus moving away from the symbolic and into the realm of the allegorical or imaginary.

Neoprimitivism and the Heart of Darkness

The neoprimitive rituals in which pain practices constantly engage often borrow from non-Western sources, such as African and Asian tribal ceremonies. This appropriation is founded on a desire to connect with the body in a way that only those cultures are perceived as achieving, a way that the colonizing West eagerly qualifies as "primitive" for what it considers an apparent lack of intellectual abstraction. This "civilized" duality between body and mind ignores, conceals, and quiets the needs, desires, and potential manifestations of our physical being, establishing itself as a repressive system: in it, body markings stand only as traces of transgression, usually as signs of slavery, torture, and punishment. Consequently, the contemporary use of body markings may be appropriately considered an indicator of difference and defiance, an entrance into that "heart of darkness" where the West has located everything that is alien to it.

The better known and most popular practice in this regard is that of tattooing, popularized in the West by sailors who recodified it as a sign of masculine bravura and defiance to social codes and freedom from institutional constraints such as marriage. Here, body modifications are symbolic—they mean something that is not intrinsically connected to the body, although the body is its vehicle of signification. Tattooing was consistently taken up by transient subcultures such as truckers and bikers, whose constant movement is flaunted as a proud unrootedness, their traveling machines ceremonially treated as a continuation of their own body.

These men's lack of a permanent or fixed space (whose main signifier would be the home) is allegorically compensated by the treating of the body as the only meaningful space—a surface on which to inscribe the registers of affection and/or sexuality. In so doing, truckers and bikers also gain a collective identity by way of identification with their fellow tattoo bearers. The same kind of inscription takes place on their vehicles, which are usually named after a special woman in their lives or a particular female religious figure, and customized to the hilt with all kinds of gadgets and personal mementos.

Physical pain for these subcultures is a marker of courage: the more tattoos you have, the more virility you can boast of. This is probably why truckers and bikers privilege sexual icons like naked women or female torsos, lips, and legs, while displaying numerous female names to indicate women's ultimate interchangeability. Such apparent stoicism is founded on the cultural paradigm that opposes male and female in terms of strength and resistance, therefore reproducing, despite all their alleged transgressions (their fantasies of being independent rebels), the most conventional social biases. As opposed to these "virility" markings, what is so particular about the current body modification fad is how it focuses on the body as both the site of the inscription and the ultimate experience being sought. In this sense, pain practices break with previous traditions and conventions, quoting them as so many referents for cultural operations bent on recuperating the physical as a previously denied experience in Western culture.

Neoprimitivism does not require an immersion in the lending culture, although many pain practitioners invoke spiritual or communal aspects as a way of making their experience meaningful. What really makes "primitive" cultures attractive for postmodernity is their highly iconographic codings and the way in which, through them, the body can be transformed from a passive signifier (the vehicle for social meaning, as in Sade) into an active signified. The body now occupies a more complete gamut of the signifying field: instead of being a simple vessel to be filled with a certain cultural depth, or its opposite, an autonomous entity exempt from historical contingency, it is seen and exercised as representative of Western culture and its lacks.

This is why two such apparently disparate practices as neoprimitivism and S/M can come together in one sign, as in the striking body discipline fashion, where the body is tightly bound in high-tech-looking leather outfits complete with gas masks and twelve-inch stiletto-heeled boots, leaving barely any skin visible. The bodily inflictions originally conceived as elements of spiritual expansion meet here with the implements of postindustrial life, creating a persona that literally enacts in this radical voluntary bondage the subtle restrictions of postmodern life. It is in the converging point between this allegorical inscription and the performative enactment of pain that pain practices may be said to be inaugurating a new cultural space, one that staunchly refuses to allow the body to disappear.

Physical Pain as Fetish

In contemporary pain practices, pain is understood as a sensorial threshold to be crossed. Instead of an act of hormonal potency, it is considered one of cultural bravery: the ability to transcend the convention that pain is bad (the consequence of a transgression) and that it should be avoided at all costs. Pain is therefore made into a positive experience of individual development and is often lived within a group and in a ritualistic context.

Yet while it is stripped of negative cultural connotations and used as a potent vehicle of affect, pain is simultaneously glorified as a unique experience to be surpassed only by gradually increasing feats: nose piercings give way to nipple, urethra, clitoral, and lip rings; foot, hand, and waist reduction bondages are countered with earlobe and scrotum lengthenings; total leather enclosing is followed by mummification; submission opens the way to often brutal (though consensual) whippings; and all of these appear as rudimentary in the face of impalement and the use of surgical implements in search of the last painful spot. It is as if, in the face of technological displacement, the body were being jump-started back into perception. Rapidly leaving behind all its symbolic attributes (i.e., religious, made in the image of God), the postmodern body races toward a material experience where yesterday and tomorrow count only as foggy referents, living only for that flash of white light and its moment of ultimate truth.

Rituals and codings notwithstanding, pain is an intrinsically altered state that disrupts and momentarily destroys all social connection and meaning. As such, it locates experience in a presymbolic, or imaginary, level where the hierarchical organization of language still has not taken place. The world, at this level, is an integrated mass of sensorial images unfiltered by the intellect, a place that can only be reached, once civilized, through radical states such as ecstasy or pain—two extremes joined at their peak. This is the sublime moment of saintly revelations; in fact, some S/M practitioners have talked about how close they felt to a universal state of being during that instantaneous pang of pain, which vanishes without a trace other than the mark it leaves behind.

Rather than facing the disappearance of the body, postmodern pain practices are anticipating the dissolution of the social structure as we know it: the shift from a clearly delimited, hierarchical, and symbolic culture, to an overlapping, ritualistic, and allegorical one, in which language will be so referentially overdetermined as to signify everything and nothing at the same time. This saturation of meaning is in itself a consequence of living in an extremely codified culture, where languages have become so specialized that they stopped conveying signification in

Figure 4. Native American pain ritual exercised by Fakir Musafar.
Photo by Charles Gatewood.

order to become signs. Thus, the body is no longer a referent of itself but, rather, of a particular reality (a site where feeling can be achieved) and language evokes a cultural scenario rather than any specific meaning. Cultural practices, consequently, have become highly performative: rather than signifying in a literal way, they fold and unfold like kaleidoscopic flowers. It is through this figurative, almost gestural, movement that postmodernity speaks, relegating verbalism to a second place.

Contemporary pain practices can then be said to stand opposite the Sadean text in two fundamental aspects: first, in the central role that the body plays in them, both as an allegorical site and as the main agent for the enactment of the cultural narratives of authority and technology; and second, in these practices' elaborate consensual arrangements, which establish a transitory and unanimous hierarchy of master and subject, regulating the frequency and intensity of spankings and whippings, or determining an ongoing relationship between master/mistress and slave. While the former privileges something other than language as a vehicle of meaning, the latter disrupts the symbolic hierarchy on which patriarchal language relies, establishing a more horizontal mode for social transactions.

Yet despite their attempt at recovering a sense of the body, pain practices, both in their allegorical and consensual performative operations, do not regain a direct relationship to physical experience. Instead, they succeed in fetishizing the physical (and the pain that is its immediate signifier) by transforming the body into the privileged site of affect or feeling by way of an extraordinarily intellectual exercise. As in most fetishistic displacements, what has been lost or is inaccessible (in this case, the capacity to feel) is located within its last perceived site, the body. As a stand-in, the body cannot be engaged in an unmediated way, so it must be subjected to a narrative or scenario that enables it to be meaningfully perceived, which is where pain enters the picture. The scenes that ensue (a black-clad dominatrix spanking a naked middle-aged executive; androgynous Nazi-secretary-look-alike piercing the back and buttocks of a woman into a neoprimitive design that a red thread will complete, all eagerly followed by scores of onlookers) are privileged over ordinary sexual satisfaction: in most pain practices, to come or not to come is not the question. What is really at stake is an agreed-on role-playing that has become the mode of libidinal discharge.

As in Leopold von Sacher-Masoch's *Venus in Furs*, pain practices are located eminently within fantasy and therefore saturated with fictional personae, customs, scenarios, and rituals.[2] In so doing, they imaginarily transgress the world of symbolic hierarchical impositions, stepping out of language (except where necessary for someone's fantasy: "Say that you were a naughty boy today," "I was bad, I was bad") and into a highly iconic realm. Even pain is merely a narrative condition for a final fulfillment achieved only in the repetition of the fetishized scene. Yet by appropriating the symbolic—punishment, torture, and voyeurism, along with their required implements, whips, uniforms, and technological equipment— and turning it into a mutually releasing experience, both master and slave ultimately share control.

In a typically postmodern way, pain practices have condensed lacks (body, feeling) and limitations (authoritarian and technological codes), transforming them into a performative experience that goes beyond its constitutive elements. It is no coincidence that this mediated form of libidinal discharge should climax—culturally speaking—exactly at the time when a more direct and intimate sexuality is made so risky by AIDS. Pain practices are a postmodern way of having safe sex. Like phone sex, they work through an imaginary evocation—one that, however, relies so much on affective distance that it risks pornographic alienation.

For the past century and a half, the West has taken great pride in its rational feats. To this effect, it repressed its corporeal being, casting it to the realm of the uncivilized, primitive Third World. It is with a sad smile that one recognizes the irony of how the "developed" First World has turned to self-inflicted flagellation in order to momentarily regain a sense of reality.[3]

Notes

This essay was originally presented at the San Francisco Camerawork 1993 spring lecture series.

1. Marquis de Sade, *The 120 Days of Sodom and Other Writings*, ed. and trans. Austryn Wainhouse and Richard Seaver (New York: Grove Press, 1987).

2. Leopold von Sacher-Masoch, *Venus in Furs*, trans. John Glassco (Burnaby, B.C.: Blackfish Press, 1977).

3. Further consulted readings include Wanda von Sacher-Masoch, *The Confessions of Wanda von Sacher-Masoch*, trans. Marian Phillips, Caroline Hebert, and V. Vale (San Francisco: Re/Search Publications, 1990); Octave Mirbeau, *The Torture Garden* (San Francisco: Re/Search Publications, 1989); Roland Barthes, *Sade, Fourier, Loyola*, trans. Richard Miller (Baltimore: Johns Hopkins University Press, 1997); Gilles Deleuze, "Coldness and Cruelty," in *Masochism: Coldness and Cruelty* (by Gilles Deleuze) and *Venus in Furs* (by Leopold von Sacher-Masoch) (New York: Zone Books, 1991); Elaine Scarry, *The Body in Pain: The Making and Unmaking of the World* (New York: Oxford University Press, 1985); and V. Vale and Andrea Juno, eds., *Modern Primitives: An Investigation of Contemporary Adornment and Ritual* (San Francisco: Re/Search Publications, 1989).

Julia Scher

American Fibroids

Engineering for the environment in the new century on now.
Danger. Ethnic digestion tabernacles on now.
Privacy robotic doubles, rolling rehab threat machines, reformulators, heightened insensitivity vehicles, erotic invisible empires on now.

You are the one that does it all.
The one that does it all.
The one that you control.
The one that you can check.
The one that checks itself.
The one that checks the user.
Therapy for fear of the unknown
It is your own independence.
Don't worry
Don't worry.

now
We have a whole table empty for the penile enlarger.
A whole rack of penile enlargers
Two racks, we have four tables here.
Customized penile enlargers
We could have done the whole room for Andrea,
for the gallery,
For Andrea Rosen now.
I wanted all those different sizes

Nipple enlargers, testicle enlargers.
Yeah, she would love them
and so would everybody else here.
All custom-made.
Send in your Visa or Mastercard number now.

Recycle or die.
Recycle or die.
You will recycle me or die.
Recycle or die.
Recycle or die.
You will be recycled or die.
You will recycle me or die.
Now.

Bursting viral dams.
A party call from God.
My corridor is here and waiting for you.
Please come unto me, for I am here and waiting for you.
You have reached the time famine.
A cool breeze over the Internet.
Mad masters and hospital decay, table two.
Pussy platters in the next room/
This is the network of security and information overload.
American Fibroids.
Please feel free to borrow the network's assets
American fibroids.
On now.
We seek not to manage individuals, only space.

Recycle or die.
The future is not about fear.
Recycle or die.
It will be about a rebirth of ideas and information.
Recycle or die.
Immediate, faster, and in a smaller package.
Recycle or die.

Julia Scher

Digital compression will be the new globalspeak.
Recycle or die.
And like a child in the backseat, you keep asking
Recycle or die.
are we there yet?

American Fibroids.
The future is not about fear.
American fibroids.
It will be about a rebirth of ideas and information.
American fibroids.
Immediate, faster, and in a smaller package.
American fibroids.
Digital compression will be the new globalspeak.
American fibroids.
And like a child in the backseat, you keep asking
are we there yet?

American fibroids.
And like a child in the backseat, you keep asking
are we there yet?

The requested object, fibroids, does not exist on this server.
The link you followed is either outdated, inaccurate, or the server has been
instructed not to let you have it.
Error message number 666.
My mouth gag is your work space.
Insertion protocol on alert, on now!
Orifice markers and vegetable trays.
I can't remember my dominant name.
It's rancid and wholesome happy display.
It's as far as I made it today.
Roast beef and porridge and patty fillets.
That's all that there's left at the bondage buffet.
Recycle or die.
Recycle or die.
In the spirit of information

Recycle or die.
Recycle or die.
It's who you play, not who you are.
Cartridge carriers, butterstock shotgun slings and vitalized neck wells, table three.
Vein dampeners and superslings, table number two.
Come into my area . . . now!
Please stand here how.
On now.
Please unloosen my access control.
Please, for I am here and waiting for you.
Please unload your access control.
Thank you for recycling me.
I appreciate your recycling my energy.
Please peruse our little beaver earth drills.
Please peruse our questions directly related to specific hole digging requirements.
Americans are not on alert.
They are not on now.
Americans are not on alert.
They are not on now.
Recycle or die.
Your face is not the window of your soul.

You are under routine motor control.
I do not detect genetic control
Your peripheral psychological arousal is not apparent in your face.
My face is here waiting for you.
My sensors interpret your words as damage and route around it.
I interpret your probing eyes as damage and route around it.

I am dark amber
She is indecisive.
Stop. Just stop. No. Let me go, let me wander.
If you cut me, I will communicate with you.
You have set the standard for a masochistic education.
No. I will be excited.
I am less determined, less governed, less predictable than you.
My dusty deck resists your field circus.
Dismember and browse me.

Julia Scher

I sweep you up and drool on you during my entry.
Insertion protocol on alert.
On now.

I am raw and ready for you.
We are the network of security and information overload.
Decopulate or you will not be allowed on the network.
For the good of the network stop fucking.
Please stand here for a deep cruise.
Our deep cruise is currently available at area number two.
Please feel free to plug into our deep cruise area.
Please stand here for a deep cruise.
Our deep cruise is currently available in area number two.
We are pro-pain, pro-tribal achievement.
Please insert your car pass into my data gate.
Eminent control.
Bombshell bloodlines channel four.
For you.
Now.
Please peruse our used hard drives, table number one.
Table number one has used hard drives with histories of you.
I offer distinguished and ambient space.
I am full and waiting for you.
Post edible environmental complex.
I am raw and ready for you.

Americans are not on alert.
They are not on now.
It's who you play, not who you are.
Come into my area now.
Please unloosen my access control
Please, for I am here and waiting for you.
Please stand here now.
Please unloosen my access control.

American Fibroids.
The future is not about fear.
My sensors interpret your words as damage and route around it.

Contributors

Charles R. Acland

teaches media and cultural studies in the graduate program in communications studies at the University of Calgary, Alberta. His book *Youth, Murder, Spectacle: The Cultural Politics of "Youth in Crisis"* was published in 1995.

Barbara McGill Balfour

teaches at Concordia University, Montreal, in the print media and fine arts programs. She is a member of the artist collectives Spontaneous Combustion and Venus Fly Trap. In her art practice, she has investigated the boundary between care of the self and self-inflicted pain; the relationship between psychological and somatic states; and the possibility of self-healing therapy.

Isabelle Brabant

is a practicing midwife and a health-care activist who has worked in a birthing clinic with Inuit women in northern Quebec. Brabant encourages women not to eliminate their pain through chemical therapies while giving birth, but to learn techniques to be with their pain to experience childbirth consciously.

Bill Burns

is an artist and writer. His work concerning pills, pharmacology, natural history, and the new global economy has been exhibited and published widely. His book *How to Help Animals Escape from Degraded Habitats* was published by Galerie Optica, Montreal, in 1997. He is currently developing a book project for Semiotext(e) New York.

Cathy Busby

is a researcher, writer, and curator currently completing her doctoral studies in the communications program at Concordia University, Montreal. She has archived and documented understandings of pain in both self-help books and artists' books, connecting art with interdisciplinary cultural and media studies. She is concerned with creating new kinds of social space where pain is legitimated. Her exhibitions *Self-Help Library* (New Museum of Contemporary Art, New York, 1993) and *Where Does It Hurt?* (Banff Centre for the Arts, Canada, 1996) have informed her editorial work for *When Pain Strikes*.

Stephen Busby

was an information systems consultant for Manulife Canada and Merrill-Lynch Canada, Inc. He later became a full-time activist in his own health management and the HIV/AIDS community through his involvement with the Toronto Hospital HIV Advisory Committee, Toronto Counselling Centre for Lesbians and Gays, AIDS Advisory Committee, and Ontario Ministry of Health, Palliative Care Steering Committee. He died in 1993.

Millie Chen

is an installation artist based in Toronto with a B.F.A. from York University, North York, and an M.F.A. from Concordia University, Montreal. She is currently exploring the ways in which the cultural body, rooted in survival, vocalizes itself through the languages of food and shelter. Integral to her work are her collaborative projects with artist Evelyn Von Michalofski. Chen has been active with various artist collectives and boards.

Michael Fernandes

is an artist living in East Dover, Nova Scotia.

Bob Flanagan

was a Los Angeles writer and performer and the author of several books of poetry and prose, including *The Wedding of Everything, Slave Sonnets*, and the infamous *Fuck Journal*, which was destroyed by its printer in India out of fear of reprisals by Indian customs agents. Bob Flanagan succumbed to cystic fibrosis on January 4, 1996, nine days after his forty-third birthday. Excerpts from his *Pain Journal* (1995) have been published in *Unnatural Disasters* and the magazine *Fruit*.

Thyrza Nichols Goodeve

is a writer who lives in New York City. Her essays, interviews, and reviews have appeared in *Artforum, Parkett, Art in America*, and *The Village Voice* as well as other publications. She received her Ph.D. from the History of Consciousness program at the University of California, Santa Cruz.

Marie-Paule Macdonald

studied architecture in Nova Scotia and urbanism in Paris. She is a registered architect in the province of Quebec and teaches architectural design studio at the School of Architecture, University of Waterloo. "Reach for the Pain" forms the basis of a design proposal for a series of hypothetical architectural interventions into midtown Manhattan titled "Midtown Projects."

Ronald Melzack

was appointed the E. P. Taylor Chair for Pain Studies at McGill University in 1986, where he has conducted research on the neural areas and pharmacological mechanisms involved in pain, and the physiological mechanisms of morphine analgesia. His *McGill Pain Questionnaire* is the most widely used measuring tool for research on pain in human subjects. His publications include more than two hundred papers on research and theory, a book titled *The Puzzle of Pain*, and other books on pain and pain assessment.

Margaret Morse

is an associate professor at the University of California at Santa Cruz, where she teaches video and new media theory and criticism. She has published widely on electronic culture, and her book *Virtualities: Television, New Media, and Cyberculture* is forthcoming.

Celeste Olalquiaga

lives in New York City and writes about popular culture. She is the author of *Megalopolis: Contemporary Cultural Sensibilities* (Minnesota, 1992) and *The Artificial Kingdom*, a cultural history of kitsch.

John O'Neill

is Distinguished Research Professor of Sociology at York University, Toronto, an Affiliate of the Centre for Comparative Literature at the University of Toronto, and a Fellow of the Royal Society of Canada. His most recent books are *The Communicative Body: Studies in Communicative Philosophy, Politics, and Psychology* (1989); *Plato's Cave: Desire, Power, and the Specular Functions of the Media* (1991); *Critical Conventions: Interpretation in the Literary Arts and Sciences* (1992); *The Missing Child in Liberal Theory* (1994); and *The Poverty of Postmodernism* (1995).

Gerard Päs

contracted poliomyelitis at the age of thirteen months, shortly after the Salk and Sabin vaccinations were introduced in North America. At the age of ten, in 1965, Gerard became the Easter Seal Poster Child (Timmy) for the City of London, Canada. He has attempted to point out incongruities in our society and culture as they relate to the status of being physically challenged, while discussing his personal sojourn within this struggle.

Elsie Petch

(R.N., B.A., M.H.Sc.) is a community health promoter at South Riverdale Community Health Centre in East Toronto. She works with and for seniors in the multicultural neighborhood to promote health, well-being, and independent living. She has served on various community coalitions and as an advisor to government, industry, labor, and professional groups on safe medication use.

D. L. Pughe

is a writer living in California.

Kim Sawchuk

is a feminist activist who practices art and cultural criticism. She is an associate professor in the Department of Communication Studies at Concordia University, Montreal. Her most recent research investigates the later works of C. Wright Mills on culture and politics.

Julia Scher

is a security specialist and artist working in New York. Her security installations and tours have taken place at the Walker Art Center in Minneapolis, the Power Plant in Toronto, and the San Francisco Museum of Modern Art. She is visiting lecturer of visual arts, in architecture, at the Massachusetts Institute of Technology.

Cathy Sisler

is a video/multimedia artist. Her video "backwards" was produced in 1992. In it, the artist sits, back to camera, and recites a story. Briefly, near the end of the video, she turns to face the camera: "What if we could feel each other's pain?" she asks. She then returns to her "backwards" position. The back: the skin, the muscles, and nerves under the surface seem to undermine the ideas of both human transparency and human opacity.

Johanne Sloan

is an art historian. She is currently a postdoctoral fellow at Columbia University. She has written extensively about contemporary art and landscape aesthetics.

Jana Sterbak

was born in Prague and immigrated to Canada in 1968. She has exhibited extensively, in Barcelona, in Denmark (1993), in London (1995), at the New Museum of Contemporary Art, New York (1990), and throughout Canada, including the National Gallery of Canada (1991). Her interest lies in exploring the theme of the body—its surface, sensations, and mortality—as indicator of psychological and social experience. She lives and works in Montreal and Barcelona.

Fred Tomaselli

is a Brooklyn-based artist who often incorporates a variety of drugs into his work in order to reference the idea of painting as a window to another reality. He is represented by the Christopher Grimes Gallery in Santa Monica, California, and by the Jack Tilton Gallery in New York.

Patrick D. Wall
(F.R.S., D.M., F.R.C.P.) earned his medical degree from Oxford University and has worked in the United States at the Massachusetts Institute of Technology (1948–67) and in London at University College. His research on sensation, with particular attention to pain, has affected clinical treatment in the areas of epidural drugs, preemptive analgesia, and TENS.

Theodore Wan
was born in Hong Kong and lived in Vancouver until his untimely death from cancer in 1987. He received his M.F.A. from the Nova Scotia College of Art and Design and was the founder of Main Exit Gallery in Vancouver.

Gregory Whitehead
is a writer, radiomaker, and the director of sea~crow media, an independent production studio. During the past decade, Whitehead has produced more than sixty acoustic features, conceptual talk shows, and earplays for broadcast in the United States and abroad. The author of numerous critical essays and fictive texts on subjects relating to language, technology, and the public sphere, he also coedited *Wireless Imagination: Sound, Radio, and the Avant-Garde.*

Fred Wilson
is a conceptual artist living in New York City. Using sculpture, photography, video, sound, and installation, Wilson "mines" the history and culture in collections of objects, such as art, artifacts, and architecture, to reveal the hidden, emotional, overlooked, or denied societal messages and personal meanings embedded within them. Wilson has published widely and his art has been exhibited extensively; he is represented by Metro Pictures, New York.

Permissions

Patrick D. Wall, "Some Notes on the Future of Pain," reprinted from Ronald Melzack and Patrick D. Wall, editors, *Textbook of Pain*, 3d ed. (London: Churchill Livingstone, 1994); reprinted with permission of Churchill Livingstone.

Isabelle Brabant, "Reflections on Pain in Childbirth," was originally published in French in *Une naissance heureuse* (Montreal: Les Éditions Saint-Martin, 1991); copyright Éditions Saint-Martin, all rights reserved; reprinted with permission of Éditions Saint-Martin.

Art

Part 1 page, "Measure It": Szyfelbein, Osgood, and Carr, "Assessment of pain and plasma B-endorphin in immunoactivity in burned children," *Pain* (1985): 22; copyright Elsevier Science Publishers, reprinted with kind permission from Elsevier Science–NL, Sara Burgerbartstraat 25, 1055 KV Amsterdam, The Netherlands.

McGill Pain Questionnaires copyright 1975, 1984, Ronald Melzack; reprinted with permission of Dr. Ronald Melzack.

John O'Neill, "Two Cartographies of AIDS": Figure 1, "Cell Wars," diagrams by Allen Carroll and Dale Glasgow, for "Our Immune System: The Wars Within," *National Geographic* 169, no. 6 (June 1986): 708–9; reprinted with permission from *National Geographic*. Figure 2 from "Model of a Killer," *Toronto Star*, October 16, 1991, Canapress Photo Service, Iain Gillespie, AP Photo.

Gerard Päs: *Dream Memory of the Brace*, 1977; *Red-Blue Wheelchair*, 1987.

Part 2 page, "Scream and Yell": Excerpts from unrehearsed interview with Mrs. Francis Cipriano,

1966. Bristol-Myers Company.

Jana Sterbak: *House of Pain: A Relationship* (dedicated to General Idea), 1987. Courtesy Galerie René Blouin, Montreal.

Fred Wilson: *About Face II*. Courtesy of Fred Wilson and Metro Pictures, New York.

Part 3 page, "Cut It Open": From article by Forester, *Brain* 56, no. 1 (1933). Reprinted with permission from Oxford University Press.

Kim Sawchuk, "Wounded States": Figure 1, "Pity we can't heal all wounds": reprinted from Copperfield Advertising, Inc., creative directors David Ernst and Darryl Gordon. Figure 2, "Enfantillages": reprinted from *Le Devoir* (May 16, 1996). Figure 3, "Let the beaver go": reprinted with permission from Ingrid Rice. Figure 4, "Mother Tongue": by Anthony Jenkins, reprinted from the *Globe and Mail* (August 17, 1996).

Theodore Wan: *Bridine Scrub for General Surgery*, 1977; courtesy Vancouver Art Gallery; photo by Trevor Mills. *Bound by Everyday Necessities I and II*, 1979; courtesy Vancouver Art Gallery; photo by Trevor Mills.

Johanne Sloan, "Spectacles of Virtuous Pain": Figure 1, *Ecstasy of Saint Teresa*, by Gian Lorenzo Bernini (1645); reprinted with permission from the Bibliotheca Hertziana, Rome. Figure 2, *La Madeleine*, by Michelangelo da Caravaggio (1606); reprinted with permission from Musée des Beaux-Arts, Marseille.

Part 4 page, "Take a Pill": *Christ as a Pharmacist*, reprinted with permission from Deutsches Apotheken-Museum.

Stephen Busby, "Taking Control": Figure 1, portrait of David Chickadel: reprinted with permission from *People*

(August 3, 1987); photo by Peter Serling. Figure 2, portrait of Ron Farha: reprinted with permission from *The Gazette* (Montreal) (September 13, 1992); photo by Peter Martin. Figure 3, portrait of David Snoddy: reprinted with permission from the *Toronto Star Syndicate* (February 7, 1993); photo by Peter Cheney.

Bill Burns, *Analgesia*: Courtesy of Bill Burns, Galerie Rochefort, Montreal, and 303 Gallery, New York.

Part 5 page, "Intensify It": *Nervous Gender*, Fred Tomaselli, 1991.

Marie-Paule Macdonald, "Reach for the Pain": Figure 1, *Instant Happenings*, by "Fluxman" James Riddle, 1964; reprinted with permission from Gilbert and Lila Silverman Fluxus Collection; photo by Eric Silverman. Figure 2, *The Cushicle*, by Michael Webb; reprinted with permission from *Archigram*, edited by Peter Cook, reprint edition Birkhaeuser Verlag Basel, 1991; first published by Studio Vista Publishers, UK, 1972. Figure 3, film set design from *Casino Royale*, 1967; reprinted with permission from Movie Still Archives. Figure 4, drawing by Marie-Paule Macdonald after photograph of Edie Sedgwick; photo collection of David Weisman in *Edie: An American Biography*, by Jean Stein, edited by George Plimpton (New York: Alfred A. Knopf, 1982).

Celeste Olalquiaga, "Pain Practices": Figure 2, reprinted with permission from *Body Play* magazine, vol. 2, no. 2 (July 1993); photo by Shinji Yamazaki. Figure 3, *Security by Julia*: copyright Julia Scher, reprinted with permission from Julia Scher. Figure 4, pain ritual, Fakir Musafar; reprinted with permission from *Body Play* magazine, vol. 1, no. 3 (May 1992); photo by Charles Gatewood.

Index

Compiled by Cathy Busby with Lisa Randall

Stafford, Barbara Maria, xx
Star Trek, 213
Steinem, Gloria, 78
steroids, 165
stigma, xii, 147, 153, 156, 158
stimuli, 17, 19, 20, 21
stress, 79, 206
suffering, xiii, 4, 40, 54, 77, 90, 206, 251
suicide, 83, 88, 155
Suitaloon, 219
Supermasochist, 172
surgery: xix, 3, 4, 13, 14, 90, 133; elective, 13; surgeon, 6, 9
survival of the fittest, 18
survivor: xv, 78, 82, 88, 242; AIDS, 160; celebrity, 85; discourse, 84, 90, 91, 256; guilt, 153, 171; Holocaust, 242; identity, xvii, 79–91; stories, 78–88; survival instinct, 226
symptoms, 3, 84, 148, 151, 160
syphilis, 150

T4 cell, 36
tattoos, xiv, 256, 257, 261, 262
Tavris, Carol, 88, 89
Taylor, Elizabeth, 225
temporomandibular joint syndrome (TMJ), 12, 15
terminal illness, 147, 152
Terminator I, 241
Terminator II, 241
testicle enlarger, 268
testimonial, 79, 84, 184
therapy, xv, xvi, 5, 78, 79, 83, 87, 88, 89, 161, 179, 241; alternative, 160; antiviral, 36; cognitive and behavior, 16; combined, 14; conventional, 14; drug, 37; healing, 87; physical, 3, 173; preemptive, 13; radical, 10; withdrawal, 11
Third World, 200, 202, 266
Thorazine, 236
Toronto Star newspaper, 30
torture, 119, 122, 123, 125, 173, 258, 261, 266
traction, 3
treatment, xvii, xxi, 9, 10, 12, 151, 158–61, 173, 178, 206, 236; experimental, 154
tribal ceremonies, 261
Triechler, Paula, 197
Triggin, Peter: *Pain and Emotion*, 236
Trudeau, Pierre Elliot, 106
tuberculosis, 156
Turing Test, 247, 248, 251, 252
Tylenol Biodome, 177

U.S. News and World Report, 31
Upjohn, 198
US magazine, 90

Valéry, Paul, 223
Van Derbur Atler, Marilyn, 85
Vanity Fair, 85, 89

Vasopressin, 249
venereal disease, 152
Verne, Jules, 219
Vicodin, 165, 169, 170
victim, 65, 67, 78, 83, 86, 89, 153, 156, 158; victim advocate, 84; of AIDS, 150; victim identity, 91; Sadean, 260
victimization, 83
Virchow, Rudolf, 11
Virilio, Paul, 206
virology, 34
virtual reality, 19–22, 236, 256
virus, xi, 30, 39, 158
Visiting Hours exhibition, 165
visualization, 50
vital signs, 151
vocalization, 50
Vogue magazine, 221, 223
voyeurism, 266
vulnerologist, xxiii, 133–39

Wall, Patrick D., xvii, 9, 110
war, 122, 154
Warhol, Andy, 213, 223, 224; *Beauty #2*, 312
Watney, Simon, 150
Watson, James, 16
Watts, James, 236
Webb, Michael, 219
Weber, Alison, 126
Wellbutrin, 165
Western culture, 154, 224, 230, 234, 257, 258, 262, 266; Western medicine, xii; Western myths, 152; Western narratives, 242
What's New Pussycat, 219
whipping, 263, 265
Wiener, Norbert, 19
Wired magazine, 249
Wise Use of Drugs, The, 184
witches, 120, 123, 125, 126
Wittgenstein, Ludwig, 251: *Philosophical Investigations*, 247
women: and epidemiology, 11; life expectancy of, 12; and pain, 12
World Health Organization, 54, 188
wound, xxi, 39, 112, 113, 134–39, 231, 243; hidden, 229; historical, 112; physical, 98, 230
Woundcare International, 97
Woundmate Surgical Zipper, 97–98
woundscape, xxiii, 134, 136, 137

X-Files, 168

Zetzel, Elizabeth, 239
Zoloft, 170